The Writer's Quotebook

"

The Writer's

500 Authors on Creativity, Craft, and the Writing Life

Compiled, arranged, and edited by

Jim Fisher

Quotebook

Rutgers University Press
New Brunswick, New Jersey, and London

Library of Congress Cataloging-in-Publication Data

The writer's quotebook : 500 authors on creativity, craft, and the writing life / compiled, arranged,
and edited by Jim Fisher.
    p. cm.
  Includes bibliographical references and index.
  ISBN-13: 978–0–8135–3882–2 (hardcover : alk. paper)
1. Authorship—Quotations, maxims, etc. I. Fisher, Jim, 1939–
  PN6084.A86W75 2006
  808'.02—dc22

                                  2005035516

A British Cataloging-in-Publication record for this book is available from the British Library.

Manufactured in the United States of America

I have a half dozen quotations written on index cards taped to the wall beside my writing desk. I read them when I want to know why I'm doing what I think I'm doing.

JOHN DUFRESNE

Contents

Acknowledgments

Thanks to Veronica Fisher, who spent weeks working with the source material, a difficult task performed with skill and accuracy.

Thanks also to William S. Cox, who encouraged me from the beginning and made helpful suggestions along the way. I'd also like to thank my wife, Sue, who helped me whenever I ran into a computer problem.

Introduction

Like most writers, my principal connection with the literary world has been through books and magazines. I've probably read a thousand books about writing, publishing, and the writing life by well-known writers, how-to authors, editors, literary agents, critics, journalists, and writing teachers. Besides literary biographies and autobiographies, as well as the published letters and journals of literary figures, I enjoy reading memoir/how-to books by celebrated writers. Examples of this genre include *The Spooky Art* by Norman Mailer, *On Writing* by Stephen King, *On Writing* by George V. Higgins, *The Summing Up* by W. Somerset Maugham, *On Becoming a Novelist* by John Gardner, *None but a Blockhead* by Larry L. King, and *Chandler Speaking* by Raymond Chandler. My library is also stocked with collections of author interviews, such as the *Writers at Work* series featuring the *Paris Review* interviews conducted by George Plimpton and his colleagues. Interviewees in this eight-book series, which ran from 1958 to 1981, include Ernest Hemingway, Irwin Shaw, John O'Hara, John Cheever, and James Jones. I also like to read so-called "conversation with" books, collections of interviews featuring a single writer such as Mary McCarthy, Norman Mailer, Truman Capote, Gore Vidal, Graham Greene, Tom Wolfe, and Eudora Welty.

In his book *Shoptalk*, Donald M. Murray points out how one can learn to write from books in this genre:

> These are some of the books on my shelves that have made me feel that I am a part of a community of writers. . . . I have emphasized collections of interviews with writers since this is the resource least used in the academy. . . . The serious student of writing and the teacher of writing should know that the existence of the extensive testimony of writers has largely been ignored by composition researchers. What writers know about their craft has been dismissed as the "lore of the practitioner."[1]

Fiction writing professor Stephen Koch, in his book *Writer's Workshop*, makes a similar point:

---

1. Murray, *Shoptalk*, xiv.

Most writers love to talk, and one of the things they love to talk about is writing. In interviews and letters, in table talk and memoirs and manifestos, writers have always held forth in surprisingly full detail about how they do what they do. It adds up to a vast, largely untapped literature on technique.[2]

In her book *How to Get Happily Published*, Judith Appelbaum notes how published writers' journals and collections of author interviews have trained and inspired people who want to write for publication:

> [T]o further advance their educations, many authors turn to behind-the-scenes books like Virginia Woolf's *A Writer's Diary* and the diaries left by Chekhov, Hawthorne and Thoreau, which deal directly with how a writer creates and organizes material, how private reading feeds constantly into present and future projects and how to deal with writer's block, self-doubt and other psychological hazards of the trade. Similar subject matter characterizes anthologies like the *Paris Review Interviews*, in which writers not only talk about their craft but also reveal whether they wrote reclining nude on a sofa or standing up in an A & P parking lot.[3]

In her introduction to *Writer's Roundtable*, Margaret Culkin Banning acknowledges the importance to her of what certain authors have written about writing:

> Writers have helped me when members of my family could not. Some writers have been closer than dear friends, even though I never have seen them in the flesh. For example, when I have read some of the Prefaces of Somerset Maugham, and his *The Summing Up*, the lucidity of his view of the writing profession illuminated dusky corners of my mind. When he tells of his successes and his thwartings, of the appraisal of his writing as "competent," it meant to me that, with more or less importance or notice, many writers go down the same paths of experience and feelings. . . . I have been helped by other writers.[4]

What follows is a collection of quotations by novelists, short story writers, nonfiction authors, critics, teachers, and editors on the creative process, craft, and the writing life.

---

2. Koch, *Writer's Workshop*, xv.
3. Appelbaum, *How to Get Happily Published*, 12.
4. In Hull and Drury, eds., *Writer's Roundtable*, 3.

One

Where do writers get their ideas? Why are some people creative and others are not? Are writers born or made? What is talent? Is there such a thing as a writer's personality? Writers' responses to questions like these are fascinating, complex, and diverse. For some, the creative process is a mystery best left unexplored, while others find nothing mysterious about why some people write and write well when others who want to write can't.

The Creative Process

1

Creativity

Many writers are reluctant to talk about the creative process—that is, how and where they get their talent, ideas, and inspiration to write. Many deny that talent is an inborn phenomenon, while others ridicule the notion that writers have to be inspired to create. Perhaps creativity is less a mystery than lack of creativity is. When a reader tells a writer that he can't image how one can produce a book, some writers may wonder how one cannot.

Creativity is as natural to human beings as having blood and bone.

JULIA CAMERON

I believe that the creative impulse is natural in all human beings, and that it is particularly powerful in children unless it is suppressed.

JOYCE CAROL OATES

A would-be writer is supposed to have either a rich inner life or a rich outer one. I had neither. Still, I had to get material from someplace, and so I stole it, piecemeal, from my family.

ELIZABETH McCRACKEN

In going where you have to go, and doing what you have to do, and seeing what you have to see, you dull and blunt the instrument you write with. But I would rather have it bent and dull and know I had to put it on the grindstone again and hammer it into shape and put a whetstone to it, and know that I had something to write about, than to have it bright and shining and nothing to say, or smooth and well-oiled in the closet, but unused.

ERNEST HEMINGWAY

Those of us who aspire to art—writers, painters, sculptors, designers— like to think of ourselves as creative individuals. The truth is, we are creative only because we create.

REBECCA McCLANAHAN

3

INSPIRATION

Many people assume that the artist receives, at the outset of his career, the mysterious sealed orders known as "inspiration," and has only to let that sovereign impulse carry him where it will. Inspiration does indeed come at the outset to every creator, but it comes most often as an infant, helpless, stumbling, inarticulate, to be taught and guided; and the beginner, during this time of training his gift, is as likely to misuse it as a young parent to make mistakes in teaching his first child.

EDITH WHARTON

For the vast majority, the inspiration to write emerges from three formative stages in life: early childhood, early adolescence, and the first few years of young adulthood when a person leaves home, explores the world, or immerses oneself in education.

MARK ROBERT WALDMAN

The idea of "inspiration," as it is commonly understood, does a great deal of damage to writers. For one thing, it devalues *craft*, which I think is the most important part of writing. It also . . . reinforces the notion that the writer himself or herself is somehow not enough. That some special talent or knowledge or divine gift—something outside of the writer—is necessary.

DENNIS PALUMBO

Only writers in movies wait for inspiration. Real writers work on schedules, different ones for different writers, but always structured. Ask any writer you know.

ED McBAIN

A lot of young writers wait for inspiration. The inspiration only hits you at the desk.

ROBERT ANDERSON

I find that what I write when I force myself is generally just as good as what I write when I'm feeling inspired.

TOM WOLFE

We must be on our guard against that feverish state called inspiration, which is often a matter of nerves rather than muscle. Everything should be done coldly, with poise.

TRUMAN CAPOTE

I don't know anything about inspiration, because I don't know what inspiration is—I've heard about it, but I never saw it.

WILLIAM FAULKNER

Many undergrads hang on tenaciously to the conviction that literature is produced spontaneously, through inspiration alone.

MARTIN RUSS

IDEAS

Oh, it is interesting, the creative process. Where was this story before I wrote it down? I don't know. It certainly wasn't in my head.

GORE VIDAL

An idea isn't a plot, and a plot isn't a story. An idea is a spark that ignites the individual creative imagination.

WILLIAM G. TAPPLY

Whenever there's something wrong with your writing, suspect that there's something wrong with your thinking. Perhaps your writing is unclear because your ideas are unclear. Think, read, learn some more. When your egg is ready to hatch, it'll hatch. In the meantime, sit on it a bit longer.

PATRICIA T. O'CONNER

Ask a professional writer about ideas. . . . In all likelihood, he'll ask, "Which ideas?" because he's got a million of them, and his biggest problem is choosing one.

RICHARD CURTIS

[I]deas are everywhere. There are ideas enough in any daily newspaper to keep a man writing for years. Ideas are all about us, in the people we meet, the way we live, the way we travel, and how we think about things.

LOUIS L'AMOUR

For me, ideas pop into my head from several sources. The first is from character. Sometimes I decide that I want to write *about* a particular sort of character caught up in a particular sort of situation, and from that grows the expanded idea of the novel which grows the plot. . . . I also [get ideas] from intriguing newspaper stories, from a beguiling turn of

phrase . . . from some topic I find interesting and wish to pursue . . .
from something I've heard and never forgotten.

ELIZABETH GEORGE

Many times, I just sit for three hours with no ideas coming to me. But
I know one thing: if an idea does come between nine and twelve, I am
there ready for it.

FLANNERY O'CONNOR

One of the most common faults I have seen over the years is the attempt
by the novice author to seek out an idea "that has never been done before."

MARTIN P. LEVIN

I have a big folder of ideas and when it comes time for me to write a
new book, I'll pull it out and go over everything that's in there.

JAMES PATTERSON

People say to me, "Where do you get all these sick ideas of yours?" And
I say, "Well, all you have to do is read your morning newspaper."

THOMAS TRYON

Ideas, concepts, patterns—they can come from anywhere like flashes of
lightening—and can vanish as swiftly unless they are put down on paper
for future reference.

DEE BROWN

If you're a doctor, you get sick people; if you're a lawyer, you get cases;
if you're a writer, the Almighty sends you stories, sometimes too many.

ISAAC BASHEVIS SINGER

Writers who say, "It just came to me," are lying sacks of shit.

DOROTHY ALLISON

I have rarely attempted any book without having considered it for at least
ten years, and in two cases I have notebooks and photographs that prove
that a subject on which I had done much preliminary work did not come
to fruition until forty years later.

JAMES A. MICHENER

Novelists—most of them—have a lot of ideas that are brief and minor, that cannot or should not be made into books. They may make good or spectacularly good short stories.

PATRICIA HIGHSMITH

I have never claimed to create anything out of nothing; I have always needed an incident or a character as a starting point, but I have exercised imagination, invention, and a sense of the dramatic to make it something of my own.

W. SOMERSET MAUGHAM

I never begin a story with an idea. . . . I have to be smitten by a subject—and then it's total immersion or nothing. Writing, at least for me, is a delightfully mysterious business. I poke around and wait for something to explode in my head.

ELEANOR CLARK

In the author's mind there bubbles up every now and then the material for a story. For me it invariably begins with mental pictures. This ferment leads to nothing unless it is accompanied with the longing for a form: verse or prose, short story, novel, play or whatnot. When these two things click you have the author's impulse complete.

C. S. LEWIS

To me, the creativity begins not when I sit down to write, but back when I'm envisioning the book and what kinds of situations I can insinuate myself into.

TED CONOVER

There is, I am sure, a direct connection between passionate love and the firing of the creative power of the mind. . . . The mind of the restrained or sexually discontented man wanders off into shallows.

V. S. PRITCHETT

In the writing process, the more a story cooks, the better. The brain works for you even when you are at rest. I find dreams particularly useful. I myself think a great deal before I go to sleep, and the details unfold in the dream.

DORIS LESSING

[A] writer is working from the instant the alarm clock goes off to the moment when he goes to bed. For that matter, the [creative] process does not stop when I'm asleep. The old subconscious mind takes over then and sifts things around and sets the stage for the next day's work.

LAWRENCE BLOCK

I never mention my work till it's finished: I find the moment you've talked about a thing you're rather dissatisfied with it.

AGATHA CHRISTIE

I like to discuss my work in progress with people. I've never worried that my inspiration would evaporate from exposure; it's more likely to dry up under my withering self-scrutiny.

GAIL GODWIN

A certain ruthlessness and a sense of alienation from society is as essential to creative thinking as it is to armed robbery.

NELSON ALGREN

I think melancholy is useful. In its aspect of pensive reflection or contemplation, it's the source of many books.

SUSANNA KAYSEN

Freud wrote somewhere that he worked best in a condition of moderate misery. I find that to be true. A slight malaise—physical, mental, or emotional—is helpful; for writing is essentially a curative process, I believe, but there must be something to cure.

PEG BRACKEN

I write best when I am happy, because I then have that saving sense of objectivity which is humor and artistic perspective. When I am sad, it becomes a one-dimensional diary. So a full, rich life is essential.

SYLVIA PLATH

When I'm writing, I'm living in the world of the novel, not "ordinary reality," and there's always that sense of shock when I come back to the world at the end, when the job is finished.

AYN RAND

[A] person's best writing is often all mixed up together with his worst. It all feels lousy to him as he's writing, but if he will let himself write it and come back later he will find some parts of it are excellent. It is as though one's best words come wrapped in one's worst.

PETER ELBOW

[W]hile you're in the midst of a story, so many things in your daily life seem to apply to it—you see something on the bus and think how you can use it. The story's like a magnet and without it, you'd never notice all these things.

PHILIP ROTH

The terrible thing about public schools is they take young children who are natural poets and story writers and have them read literature and then step away from it and talk "about" it.

NATALIE GOLDBERG

How does the creative impulse die in us? The English teacher who wrote fiercely on the margin of your theme in blue pencil: "Trite, rewrite," helped kill it. Critics kill it, your family. Families are great murderers of the creative impulse, particularly husbands. Older brothers sneer at younger brothers and kill it. There is that American pastime known as "kidding"—with the result than everyone is ashamed and hang-dog about showing the slightest enthusiasm or passion or sincere feeling about anything.

BRENDA UELAND

Harsh criticism can harm our creative process, but so can a reliance upon praise. Praise is nice, of course. It feels good to get a positive response to our work. That ego stroking shouldn't be why you write, though. If you become dependent on praise, your creative flow gets displaced. You become removed from your own source.

GAYLE BRANDEIS

Reverie is the groundwork of creative imagination; it is the privilege of the artist that with him it is not as with other men an escape from reality, but the means by which he accedes to it. His reverie is purposeful. It affords him a delight in comparison with which the pleasures of sense are pale and it affords him the assurance of his freedom.

W. SOMERSET MAUGHAM

The one thing that other aspiring artists have over writers is that many of them can view their mentors at work. A painter can sit at the back of a studio and watch her mentor paint, a ballet dancer can watch his mentor rehearse and perform. But you can't really observe the creative process of a fiction writer.

ROBERT OLEN BUTLER

I don't think getting older is good for the creative process. Writing is so hard. It's the only time in your life when you have to think.

ELIZABETH HARDWICK

[D]eadlines do much more than just get products finished. They serve as creative midwives, as enthusiastic shepherds adept at plucking the timid inspirations that lurk in the wings of our imaginations and flinging them bodily into the bright light of day. The bigger the artistic project, the more it needs a deadline to keep marshaling those shy ideas out onto the world's stage. Nowhere is this more true than in novel writing.

CHRIS BATY

Are crop circles supernatural imprints, or the work of human hoaxers? . . . In England, at least, folks have confessed to sneaking into fields to effect these transformations, but I was happier when they remained a mystery. I think *writing* is like swinging a scythe in the dark and finding in the morning, if you're lucky and looking from the right angle, a mysterious, well-formed pattern has emerged.

AMY HEMPEL

2

Talent

What is literary talent? Is it something one can acquire? If so, how? How much talent does a writer need to become successfully published? Is raw talent, by itself, enough? If not, what else is needed? The following quotations contain answers to these and other questions about what it takes, in terms of ability, personality, and talent, to be a successful writer.

Writing is like breathing. I believe that. I believe we all come into life as writers. We are born with a gift for language and it comes to us within months as we begin to name our world.

JULIA CAMERON

Everyone has talent. What is rare is the courage to follow that talent to the dark place where it leads.

ERICA JONG

I believe that talent is more common that we think, that it is all over the place, and that almost everyone has some degree of it—something worth developing.

WALLACE STEGNER

Everybody is talented because everybody who is human has something to express.

BRENDA UELAND

I never felt any sort of egocentricity about my writing. I think I felt that it was a dispassionate gift that some force had given me. And I still think that.

PAULA FOX

Writers may not be special—sensitive or talented in any usual sense. They are simply engaged in sustained use of a language skill we all have.

Their "creations" come about through confident reliance on stray impulses that will, with trust, find occasional patterns that are satisfying.

WILLIAM STAFFORD

One of the most interesting things about the writing talent is that it contains some magical power of synthesis—I don't know where it comes from. But you can take disparate elements—a theme, a character—and set them in motion and somehow, if you're a good writer, you tap some unconscious level of the mind that enables it to come together.

WILLIAM BOYD

Everybody has [talent], some more than others, perhaps; but that hardly matters, since no one can hope to use up more than a very small portion of his or her native gift.

JOHN GARDNER

I just think God hits some people with the talent stick harder than He hits others. And it kills a lot of people. It's like dynamite: they blow up.

STEPHEN KING

Be it modest or magnificent, you've got to have some talent. It may be latent; it may be undeveloped; it may be neglected. But it must be there.

STEPHEN KOCH

Talent is like murder—it will out.

LORETTA BURROUGH

A writing gift doesn't have to manifest itself in childhood or adolescence in order to exist. For some people it may well be the blessing of their later years.

DEENA METZGER

Would I like more talent? Yes. But you cannot get more talent.

JERZY KOSINSKI

I believe that each human being has within himself or herself at least one poem or short story, or perhaps a full-length book.

DEE BROWN

I've been increasingly drawn to the belief that talent is much as I believe intuition to be, something accessible to everyone who takes the trouble to gain access to it.

LAWRENCE BLOCK

Writers like to think that talent is 95 percent genius . . . and 5 percent material. I think the proportions are more like 35–65.

TOM WOLFE

[An] indicator of the novelist's talent is intelligence—a certain kind of intelligence, not the mathematician's or the philosopher's but the story-teller's—an intelligence no less subtle than the mathematician's or the philosopher's but not so easily recognized.

JOHN GARDNER

Really, talent is vocation: there is such a thing as having a natural apti-tude for a way of life; not everybody can become a monk.

CHRISTOPHER ISHERWOOD

The one talent that is indispensable to a writer is persistence. You must write the book, else there is no book. It will not finish itself.

TOM CLANCY

The consensus . . . seems to be that drive is surprisingly more important than talent in producing creative work.

DR. ALICE W. FLAHERTY

Talent cannot be taught, although it can be nurtured. Matters of craft, however, *can* be taught, and learning them will not damage a writer's native ability.

ROBERT DeMARIA

Writing is at the very least a knack, like drawing or being facile on the piano. Because everybody can speak and form letters, we mistakenly suppose that good, plain, writing is within everybody's power. Would we say this of good, straightforward, accurate drawing? Would we say it of melodic sense and correct, fluent harmonizing at the keyboard? Surely not. We say these are "gifts." Well, so is writing, even if the writing is of a bread-and-butter note.

JACQUES BARZUN

Talent is not only overrated but all too often used as an excuse not to try. "I have no inborn talent, alas, so why bother?"

MARC McCUTCHEON

All you need is a perfect ear, absolute pitch, the devotion to your work that a priest of God has for his, the guts of a burglar, no conscience except to writing, and you're in. It's easy.

ERNEST HEMINGWAY

Personally, I think it's [the talent to write] a disease, and the fact it produces books that people buy doesn't make it any more healthy.

JAMES M. CAIN

Most people who have strong talent also have impedimenta. There is something wrong with their character one way or another. It's not accident that so many talented writers are heavy drinkers and all that.

NORMAN MAILER

What are the hallmarks of a competent writer of fiction? The first, it seems to me, is that he should be immensely interested in human beings, and have an eye sharp enough to see into them, and a hand clever enough to draw them as they are.

H. L. MENCKEN

Fiction, first of all, involves the invention of a world. Here the writer needs, not the gift of writing, but the ability to create scenes, particulars and persons—to make imaginary lives and objects.

WILLIAM H. GASS

If you write something for which someone sent you a check, if you cashed the check and it didn't bounce, and if you paid the light bill with the money, I consider you talented.

STEPHEN KING

The Difficulty of Writing

Just plain writing, for most people, is easy. Writing well, writing creatively, writing for publication, is not so easy. But then nothing done well is easy; excellence comes at a price, and the price is hard work. To make the task of top-notch writing manageable—indeed, possible—most writers inch up to excellence by writing several drafts. It's a lot like painting a house: first you slap on the undercoat without regard to perfection; then come the final, more careful applications.

Elizabeth Berg, in her book *Escaping into the Open,* suspects that many writers purposely overstate the difficulty of writing: "I am fully aware that many people find writing to be hard work. I am also aware that a lot of writers deny the inherent joy in working hard at something they love, and feel they must instead affect a certain artsy anguish in order to earn satisfaction, whether that is from themselves, their peers, or their audience."[1]

If you have difficulty with writing, do not conclude that there is something wrong with you. Writing should never be a test of self-esteem. If things are not going as you want, do not see it as proof of an unknowable flaw in your subconscious.

AYN RAND

I do find writing a very painful process—I never understand writers who say it's enjoyable. I think it's the hardest work in the world.

TOM WOLFE

[T]here's always pain in good writing; if you're not hurting, you're not stretching. But the pain is supposed to buy, at the end, the deep satisfaction that flows from a creative work well done. The sorrowful thing is that so many writers know so much suffering and so little satisfaction.

WILLIAM E. BLUNDELL

---

1. Berg, *Escaping into the Open,* 151.

Oh God! how I have to beat myself over the head to get started every morning.

KATHERINE ANNE PORTER

In addition to the usual problems of talent, craft and imagination, what makes the profession of writing so difficult is that it requires constancy. You have to do it every day, with consistency and will, just like any other occupation. . . . Anybody can be a writer for one day.

DENNIS PALUMBO

I have never thought writing novels was hard work. . . . Novels have more to do with desire—translating desire into prose—and a temperament that accepts concentration over the long haul, meaning the ability to sit alone in one place day by day.

WARD JUST

[T]he assumption . . . is that writing a novel is so easy anyone can do it if only there weren't the pressures of an important busy schedule, which apparently you, dear writer, do not have. . . . In fact, a good story often reads so easily that civilians [nonwriters] seem to think that the darn things write themselves. Whenever I leave the house, I make sure that one of my novels is hard at work. I expect five pages by the time I get back.

DAVID MORRELL

There is nothing more difficult than writing a story, simply because the writer begins with nothing. He has a blank sheet of paper, a typewriter, and an idea. Nothing is started; there is no format, no procedure. He must bring it all forth from a vacuum.

LEONARD S. BERNSTEIN

Line by line, writing's not so hard. You put in a comma, then you move it somewhere. You do a little sentence and then another little sentence. It's when you allow yourself to think of the totality of what you have to do, of the task which faces you with each book, that you feel it's hard, even terrifying. In my daily work, minimizing the terror is my object.

HILARY MANTEL

I have never been one of those "writing is fun" people. Writing has never been a pleasure for me.

REYNOLDS PRICE

[B]eing a true novelist, even if one's work is not worth the price of a cherry to public or publisher, takes all that one has to give and still something more.

ELLEN GLASGOW

I'm in my old agony again trying to write a novel. I've got some ideas that excite me and a few scenes and characters, but the rest is coming like my first pair of long pants—slow as hell. Never mind, I'll get it out, it just takes time to do *anything* worthwhile.

RALPH ELLISON

To learn to write and write decently is simply a much longer and harder thing than is generally admitted.

JAMES GOULD COZZENS

The aesthetic gift is a process that begins with conception, often exciting, goes through gestation, usually exhausting, and ends with birth, which is invariably laborious, protracted, and painful.

JAMES M. CAIN

In case no one's noticed, a novel is long. The prospect of writing four hundred pages about something yet undiscovered is daunting at best. The first page is as far as many writers get, frozen as they are into a solid block of ice.

SHELDON RUSSELL

Writing should be a snap. We've been telling stories all our lives; we know all of these words; we've got a pen and some paper and a million ideas. We fiddle. We put on some music. We scribble. We stare out the window. We remember we have that wedding to go to next August. Better buy a gift soon. We smooth out the paper. We consider how none of our errands are getting done while we sit. We get up. And now we know what writers already know: that writing is difficult, that it is a disorderly and unnerving enterprise, and because it is, we all have, it seems, developed an unnatural resistance to the blank page.

JOHN DUFRESNE

Large numbers of people apparently want to write, or think they do. They speak as if they are going out to catch a bus or whip up a batch of fudge: "One of these days I'm gonna sit down and write a book," or "I got an uncle Carl, he's real funny; if he'd just come spend a long weekend then me and him could write a book."

LARRY L. KING

[M]ost people secretly believe they . . . have a book in them, which they would write if they could find the time. And there's some truth to this notion. A lot of people do have a book in them—that is, they have had an experience that other people might want to read about. But this is not the same as "being a writer." Or, to put it in a more sinister way: everyone can dig a hole in a cemetery, but not everyone is a grave-digger. The latter takes a good deal more stamina and persistence.

MARGARET ATWOOD

Some kinds of writing are more debilitating than others, and it took me years to learn which, for me, is which. Instructional writing—the pure how-to article—is the worst.

JOHN JEROME

The most enjoyable time is when I suddenly get the idea for my work. But when I start writing it is very, very painful. . . . To write or to commit suicide. Which will it be?

ABE KOBO

While working on the book, I had every stress-related illness that can be listed in a medical textbook. Along the way, I thought I had a heart attack, liver cancer, and phlebitis. My back was so bad at one time that I had to work lying down.

RICHARD BEN CRAMER

The difficulty of writing lies in turning from our reasonable, pragmatic selves long enough to idle our way into the imagination. Once there, however, the creative engine runs smoothly and time flies past.

MARVIN BELL

I get a fine warm feeling when I'm doing well, but that pleasure is pretty much negated by the pain of getting started each day. Let's face it, writing is hell.

WILLIAM STYRON

[W]hat you ultimately remember about anything you've written is how difficult it was to write it.

ERNEST HEMINGWAY

Writing is hard work. Only those more bothered by shirking it than doing it can ever succeed at it.

GEORGE V. HIGGINS

There are much easier, more pleasant ways to pass the time [than writing], though few so rewarding intellectually and spiritually. But it's no sin to be honest and admit it if you'd rather garden, fish, or socialize with friends than go it alone as a writer, with no guarantee of success. If you aren't sure you're up to all that writing demands of a person, go no further.

JOHN JAKES

Writing is a nerve-flaying job. . . . [C]lichés come to mind much more readily than anything fresh or exact. To hack one's way past them requires a huge, bleeding effort.

JOAN ACOCELLA

Writing a book is an endurance contest and a war fought against yourself, because writing is beastly hard work which one would just as soon not do. It's also a job, however, and if you want to get paid, you have to work. Life is cruel that way.

TOM CLANCY

The anxiety involved [in writing] is intolerable. And . . . the financial rewards just don't make up for the expenditure of energy, the damage to health caused by stimulants and narcotics, the fear that one's work isn't good enough. I think, if I had enough money, I'd give up writing tomorrow.

ANTHONY BURGESS

Every book I write is harder than the last book. You would think that it would get easier in time, but it doesn't because the challenges are bigger, and your own ego pushes you to do better. . . . You want your writing to be cleaner, and I don't want to repeat myself—and that gets hard after so many books—but you don't want the same plot line, and the same characters, you want to keep it fresh. That's one of the hardest things, but it's just absolutely necessary.

NORA ROBERTS

Why Writers Write

If writing is so difficult, so unrewarding, so *painful*, why do people do it? Where does the desire to write, the compulsion, come from? Why are so many people afflicted with this need? Is it some kind of sickness, some kind of mental or emotional abnormality? If so, can it be cured?

[A] blank sheet of paper holds the greatest excitement there is for me — more promising than a silver cloud, prettier than a little red wagon. It holds all the hope there is, all fears. I can remember, really quite distinctly, looking a sheet of paper square in the eyes when I was seven or eight years old and thinking, "This is where I belong, this is it."

E. B. WHITE

[Elementary, middle school, and high school] teachers seem to play a big role in making it harder for people to write. Yet they can't quite stamp out the desire.

PETER ELBOW

[T]here are many ways for people to obtain public recognition. For some of us — especially the bookish, unathletic, socially uneasy among us — writing novels is a natural path to this type of self-esteem. Writing lets us stay at home. It carries us away from what is unpleasant in everyday life, while at the same time instantly conferring upon us the mystical status of "novelist." Even if you have not published, your friends are sure to be impressed when you tell them you are working on a novel.

DONALD MAASS

There are writers who write for fame. And there are writers who write because we need to make sense of the world we live in; writing is a way to clarify, to interpret, to reinvent. We may want our work to be recognized, but that is not the reason we write. We do not write because we must; we always have choice. We write because language is the way we keep a hold on life.

BELL HOOKS

Some of us want fame and critical recognition. Some of us want to make a lot of money. Some of us want to write in such a way as to influence people. Some of us are more interested in using writing to get in touch with our inner selves, and some employ it to gain entrance to the world of imagination.

LAWRENCE BLOCK

[I write because] I want to impose my personality upon the world. Or, you could say that I want people to know that I have lived.

JAMES JONES

Many of us have been writers since we were ten because we've been hams in one way or another. We want our times dramatized. We don't want to be erased by time, and I think that's what it's all about.

BARRY HANNAH

Many people become writers because of their love of reading.

WILLIAM MAXWELL

I write because I am driven to do so.

ISAAC ASIMOV

I do it for love, because of compulsive need, out of a requirement that I cannot shake: That I justify my time on the earth by telling stories. That's what I do. I have to do it.

FREDERICK BUSCH

I write because it's the only thing that I'm really good at in the whole world. And I've got to stay busy to stay out of trouble, to keep from going crazy, dying of depression.

S. D. WILLIAMS

I write because I was meant to write, I was called to write, I was told to write. I write because that's who I am.

ELIZABETH GEORGE

There is only one reason to write a novel and that is because writing fiction is absolutely essential to one's well-being. It is to mine and it always has been. In other words, it is the work that really counts, the sense of creation that is the important thing to me.

BARBARA TAYLOR BRADFORD

I think the urge [to write] has to come from a deep root, and not just an idea that you want to write a book or be famous. It has to come from a deeper place.

NATALIE GOLDBERG

I write basically because it's so much fun.

JAMES THURBER

I suppose I write because I want to reach people and by reaching them, influence the history of my time a little bit.

NORMAN MAILER

It is easy to lose sight of the fact that writers do not write to *impart* knowledge to others; rather, they write to *inform* themselves.

JUDITH GUEST

It's a nervous habit I contracted about age 15 and 60 years on, I can no more kick it than I can kick tobacco and booze.

JAMES GOULD COZZENS

My interest is in solving the problems presented by writing a book. That's what stops my brain spinning like a car wheel in the snow, obsessing about nothing. Some people do crossword puzzles to satisfy their need to keep their mind engaged. For me, the absolutely demanding mental test is the desire to get the work right. The crude cliché is that the writer is solving the problem of his life in his books. Not at all. What he's doing is taking something that interests him in life and then solving the problem of the book—which is, how do you write about this?

PHILIP ROTH

I write to please myself, for the most part. I try to write a book that I can't find on the shelf to read.

MOLLY GLOSS

The fact that I can just put sentences down and bring something to life lets me feel a lot more constructive and useful than anything else I do.

BEN MARCUS

What I want to do is reproduce the primacy of the reading art that was so precious to me when I was younger, when I was discovering my own excitement about books.

JONATHAN LETHEM

I write, as I believe all artists perform their art, to exorcise internal conflicts and supplant reality with something more shapely and gratifying.

IRA LEVIN

Reading usually precedes writing. And the impulse to write is almost always fired by reading. Reading, the love of reading, is what makes you dream of becoming a writer.

SUSAN SONTAG

Neurologists have found that changes in a specific area of the brain can produce hypergraphia—the medical term for an overpowering desire to write.

DR. ALICE W. FLAHERTY

Why I write, sheer egoism. It is humbug to pretend that this is not a motive, and a strong one. Writers share this characteristic with scientists, artists, politicians, lawyers, soldiers, successful businessmen—in short, with the whole top crust of humanity.

GEORGE ORWELL

I am a compulsive writer. I not only love to write; I *must* write. If a day passes when I have written nothing, I am depressed. . . . But several hours of writing leaves me in a state of euphoria. It may be lousy stuff. But it is *there*, and I can make it better tomorrow. I have done something worthwhile with my day.

RICHARD MARIUS

[B]efore you have advanced far enough in the profession to earn a living, you write because you have found it is writing which makes you feel alive.

MARGARET CULKIN BANNING

I write to keep myself educated and when I don't write, I feel myself—
and my intelligence—rapidly fading into oblivion, where I'm perfectly
content to be the ne'er-do-well my parents were once so concerned I
would become.

BOB SHACOCHIS

The first question for the young writer to ask himself is: "Have I things
in my head which I need to set forth, or do I merely want to be a writer?"
Another way of putting it is, "Do I want to write—or *to have written?*"

JACQUES BARZUN

Nothing ever seems to me quite real at the moment it happens. It's part
of the reason for writing, since the experience never seems quite real
until I evoke it again. That's all one tries to do in writing, really, to hold
something—the past, the present.

GORE VIDAL

Anyone who has ever written knows that the desire to create can be, at
times, delicate and shy and easily scared off. It can also be a powerful
impulse, impossible to ignore.

MITCHELL IVERS

My preoccupation with portraying my dreamlike inner life has relegated
everything else to a secondary position; other interests have shrunk in a
most dreadful fashion, and never cease to shrink. Nothing else can ever
make me happy.

FRANZ KAFKA

A true writer's imagination is always bigger than he is, it outreaches his
personality. Sometimes this can be felt palpably and thrillingly in the
very act of writing, and perhaps it is for this infrequent but soaring sen-
sation that writers, truly, write.

GRAHAM SWIFT

Writing is thinking. It is more than living, for it is being conscious of living.

ANNE MORROW LINDBERGH

I don't feel, you know, God dictated that I should write. . . . No bony
finger comes down from the cloud and says, "You, you write. You're

anointed." I never felt that. I suppose it's a part compulsion, part a channel for what your brain is churning up.

ROD SERLING

[W]riting is the only thing that makes me feel that I'm not wasting my time sticking around.

ERNEST HEMINGWAY

It isn't the money that makes people write; it is the *hope of publication.* The exhibition of the ego in public places means more to us writers than money. Those lonely, timid, fine souls who write and never show it to any human being at all, show it to God; they are the supreme egotists. They think nobody else would appreciate it.

DON MARQUIS

[T]here are dozens of reasons not to write: We are too old or too young. We don't have enough education, experience, or talent. We have no ideas. Our spelling is atrocious. If only we didn't have jobs, if we didn't have children, if we weren't so tired, if we lived on the beach or in the mountains. . . . It will do no good to decide we're going to write if we don't first ask ourselves why we haven't been doing it all along.

REBECCA McCLANAHAN

5

Writer's Block

In an article in the *New Yorker* called "Blocked," Joan Acocella defines the term *writer's block* this way:

> Sometimes, "blocked" means complete shutdown: the writer stops producing anything that seems to him worth publishing. In other cases, he simply stops writing what he wants to write. He may manage other kinds of writing, but not the kind he sees as his vocation. . . . Writer's block is a modern notion. Writers have probably suffered over their work ever since they first started signing it, but it was not until the early nineteenth century that creative inhibition became an actual issue in literature, something people took into account when they talked about the art.[1]

According to Acocella, the term was coined in the 1940s by psychoanalyst Edmund Bergler, a Viennese émigré. She also notes that it is principally an American phenomenon and that some writers become blocked simply because the concept—the term—exists.

I can't understand the American literary block—as in [Ralph] Ellison or [J. D.] Salinger—unless it means that the blocked man isn't forced economically to write (as the English writer, lacking campuses and grants, usually is) and hence can afford the luxury of fearing the critics' pounce on a new work not as good as the last (or the first).

ANTHONY BURGESS

I know I am not alone in my recurring twinges of panic that I won't be able to write something when I need to, I won't be able to produce

---

1. Joan Acocella, "Blocked: Why Do Writers Stop Writing?" *New Yorker* (14 and 21 June 2004): 110.

coherent speech or thought. And that lingering doubt is a great hindrance to writing. It's not a constant fog or static that clouds the mind. I never got out of its clutches till I discovered that it was possible to write something—not something great or pleasing but at least something usable, workable—when my mind is out of commission.

PETER ELBOW

I think that most writers suffer from writer's block because they're trying too hard to make it perfect out of the gate when in fact, they should be writing it for themselves, as if no one is ever going to read it at all.

TERRY McMILLAN

What is one to do on a day when thoughts cease to flow and proper words won't come? One cannot help trembling at this possibility.

SIGMUND FREUD

There are few experiences as depressing as that anxious barren state known as writer's block, where you sit staring at your blank page like a cadaver, feeling your mind congeal, feeling your talent run down your leg and into your sock.

ANNE LAMOTT

When I can't write, I feel so empty.

JOHN STEINBECK

[P]ublishers always begin to harass me when I show signs of lagging, and, no matter what psychologists might be able to make of this, pressure of that sort simply throws me into a catatonic state, paralyzes my will, muddles my mind, and hurts my feelings.

KATHERINE ANNE PORTER

When we try too hard to keep the fans and the bean counters and the critics happy, we lose our nerve. We become afraid to take risks, to go off in some fanciful new direction. . . . We become so fearful of writing badly. . . . We begin to dread writing anything at all.

TESS GERRITSEN

Some people, especially people new to writing, simply tense up or go blank whenever they begin writing something or even think about writing something. This general fear of writing often comes from having had small-minded and sharp-tongued English teachers.

SCOTT EDELSTEIN

I get stuck on stories, and spend days on end lying in bed, looking at the ceiling, and at times it seems impossible for me to go to the typewriter, or do anything except pound my problem and wonder if I am headed for the booby hatch.

JAMES M. CAIN

For me, writer's block is a state of mind of not knowing what to do, not knowing what comes next. Although it may seem like a block, it's sort of a testing internally. Then a solution may come and I can move ahead.

OLIVER SACKS

After depression, anxiety is probably the second-clearest link between writer's block and a psychiatric illness.

DR. ALICE W. FLAHERTY

The extraordinarily prolific writer whose output flows unchecked is often an object of awe for the blocked writer who, envying him in the same way that an overweight person envies the anorexic, fails to see that this deluge of words often conceals an inverted case of writer's block.

VICTORIA NELSON

Regardless of the issues a writer struggles with—creative blocks, procrastination, fear of failure, etc.—the very act of writing tends to stoke the energy, continue the flow, direct the current of further writing. Writing begets writing.

DENNIS PALUMBO

The trail of literary history is littered with those who fell along the way because the anxiety of trying to write paralyzed their hand. Many non-writing writers are gifted. The best writers I know teach school and sell real estate. Some still plan to write "someday." Others have given up altogether. Their block lies not with their ability or skill but with their nerve.

RALPH KEYES

When you are stuck in a book; when you are well into writing it, and know what comes next, and yet cannot go on; when every morning for a week or a month you enter its room and turn your back on it; then the trouble is either of two things. Either the structure has forked, so the narrative, or the logic, has developed a hairline fracture that will shortly split it up the middle—or you are approaching a fatal mistake. What you had planned will not do. If you pursue your present course, the book will explode or collapse, and you do not know about it yet, quite.

ANNIE DILLARD

I have always felt that in writing first drafts it is obligatory to maintain forward movement, to keep the sequence of ideas firmly established but to follow various tangential inspirations to their logical conclusions. To flounder about in what is popularly known as "writer's block," so often seen in the motion pictures about writers or other creative people, is to indulge in self-pity, and when I see the tortured novelist angrily tear up his manuscript, or the painter slash his canvas with black paint, or the composer crash his hands on the piano with frustration, I often wonder how you depict a sculptor expressing his disgust with a block of stone.

JAMES A. MICHENER

No writer has ever lived who did not at some time or other get stuck. . . . And for every writer in working trim there may be a dozen persons of great ability who are somehow self-silenced. At long intervals they turn out remarkable fragments—half essays or embryo stories; but they cannot seem to pull themselves together and finish anything, much less begin at will.

JACQUES BARZUN

[Writer's block is] one of my greatest fears. . . . [T]he one thing I cannot comprehend or come to terms with is just drying up as a writer.

STEPHEN KING

Blocked writers are now being treated with antidepressants such as Prozac, though some report that the drugs tend to eliminate their desire to write together with their regret over not doing so. Others are being given Ritalin and other stimulants, on the theory that their problems may be due to the now fashionable condition of attention deficit disorder.

JOAN ACOCELLA

My cure for writer's block is to have some low-paying project that demands a certain number of words. Write five thousand words for game design or technical writing—and the mind will decide to cooperate to avoid boredom.

DON WEBB

Sometimes the [writer's] block will pass by itself, mysteriously slouching off as silently as it came, and you will never know why it appeared . . . or why it slogged away.

SOPHY BURNHAM

The best way of all for dealing with writer's block is never to get it. Some writers never do. Theoretically there's no reason one should get it, if one understands that writing, after all, is only writing, neither something one ought to feel deeply guilty about nor something one ought to be inordinately proud of. . . . The very qualities that make one a writer in the first place contribute to block: hypersensitivity, stubbornness, insatiability, and so on. Given the general oddity of writers, no wonder there are no sure cures.

JOHN GARDNER

6

The Writer's Personality

Is there such a thing as a writer's personality or type? Are there behavioral quirks, personality traits, and emotional temperaments common to writers? Do writers fit some kind of psychological profile? Are writers, as some people think, emotionally disturbed egomaniacs? (In the acknowledgments to *Wild Mind: Living the Writer's Life,* Natalie Goldberg thanked her typist, her agent, her editor, her acupuncturist, and her therapist.)

Some writers openly reveal in memoirs, journals, and letters that they consider themselves, at least in some respects, psychologically strange and abnormal. Such revelations are quite often the most interesting aspects of their life stories. Take, for instance, mystery writer Dorothy L. Sayers, who, in a letter to a friend, writes:

> I thoroughly dislike *all* retrospect. . . . I should like to know the meaning of this particular mania. . . . I want to forget anything I can . . . with a completeness which entirely prevents the possibility of resurrecting it. I can abolish names and places and even states of mind beyond all recall. I could not reconstruct a past state of things—supposing, for example, I wanted to do so in a novel—so as to carry conviction to anybody. The most flattering explanation of the phenomenon is that I have a violent kind of forward looking vitality. Another—a more likely one, I am afraid—is that my present vanity despises and dislikes my former self. I think this is probably correct, because it hangs together with my general dislike of children and everything immature and unfinished. I don't think I have ever met anybody else with this extraordinary and undiscriminating impatience of the past.[1]

In addition to being odd, many writers have outsized egos and are pathologically competitive. George Bernard Shaw, for example, said this

---

1. Reynolds, ed., *Letters of Dorothy L. Sayers,* 291.

of himself: "With the exception of Homer, there is no eminent writer, not even Sir Walter Scott, whom I can despise so entirely as I despise Shakespeare when I measure my mind against his."[2] Writers have also shown themselves to be compulsive, whiny, petty, and cruel. When Truman Capote died, his rival Gore Vidal was supposed to have referred to his passing as "a good career move."

[Writers are] a bad lot on the whole—petty, nasty, bilious, suffused with envy and riddled with fear.

ROGER ROSENBLATT

There are lots of very smart people and there are lots of very trusting people. But it's very hard to get both of them together in one body. That's why there are so few great artists and so few great books. You either get a sweet trusting book or you get a smart cold book.

ALLAN GURGANUS

Do you have a new idea almost every day for a writing project? Do you either start them all and don't see them to fruition or think about starting but never actually get going? . . . Do you begin sentences in your head while walking to work or picking up the dry cleaning? Do you blab about your project to loved ones, coworkers or strangers before the idea is fully formed, let alone partially executed? Have you ever been diagnosed with any combination of bipolar disorder, alcoholism, or skin diseases such as eczema or psoriasis? Do you snap at people who ask how your writing is going? *What is it to them?* Do you fear that you will someday wonder where the years went? How is it that some no-talent you went to high school with is being published everywhere you look? . . . If you can relate to the above, you certainly have the obsessive qualities—along with the self-aggrandizement and concurrent feelings of worthlessness— that are part of the writer's makeup.

BETSEY LERNER

I like routine and rituals and I hate leaving home; I have a sense of digging my heels in. I refuse to drive on freeways. I dread our annual vacation.

ANNE TYLER

---

2. Cited in John Mason Brown, "George Bernard Shaw, Headmaster to the Universe," in Editors of the *Saturday Review*, eds., *Saturday Review Gallery*, 416.

I have a growing obsession with order, I organize my closet, my papers, create an unburdened atmosphere, no useless objects, everything ready to be found, lived with. Reduction. Papers classified, medicines in order, as if ready for a trip, clothes in order. To make living smoother, faster. Order gives me serenity.

ANAÏS NIN

The studio where I write contains a medley of tidily arranged shelves, bookcases, and surfaces, jars neatly bristling with writing implements, and notebooks arranged by size, category, and date, all within arm's reach. I'm pathologically tidy.

PETER SELGIN

Writers mainly fall into two groups; either they are forest clearers or explorers. Some like to tidy the world and reduce it to a clear and understandable diagram. Others prefer to wander in the wilderness, rejoicing in it for its own sake. I like the wilderness. I have tried to put down a few human ambiguities without attempting to tidy them away.

BRIAN W. ALDISS

Most writers I know have a combination of self-loathing and great narcissism.

ANNE LAMOTT

A surprising proportion of writers are manic-depressive.

DR. ALICE W. FLAHERTY

Apparently, it's in fashion again—the notion that the creative impulse, with its accompanying emotional difficulties, is merely the product of a psychological disorder. The current favorite diagnosis for artists, particularly writers, is bipolar disorder—a condition that used to be called manic depression.

DENNIS PALUMBO

One has to be an egomaniac to be a writer, but you've got to hide it.

JAMES JONES

Writers are such private, solitary people. They may become things other than that, but the writing almost without exception gets done because of an inwardness, a sense of privacy that you retain, even though you know that the piece you write may go public.

ANN BEATTIE

Unsurprisingly, a psychological survey of the Iowa Workshop showed that 80% of writers in the program reported evidence of manic depression, alcoholism, or other lonely addictions in themselves or their immediate families. We're writers. Who ever claimed we were a tightly wrapped bunch?

TOM GRIMES

Writers as a class I have found to be oversensitive and spiritually under-nourished.

RAYMOND CHANDLER

[T]o reach the highest levels of the craft, above all you'll need *confidence*. Unshakable confidence to leap forcefully into the realm of creation.

NOAH LUKEMAN

Writing is a great comfort to people like me, who are unsure of themselves and have trouble expressing themselves properly.

AGATHA CHRISTIE

[Sigmund Freud] said that writers and artists are people who discovered as youngsters that they lost out in the hurly-burly of the playground. They discovered, however, that they had the power to fantasize about such things, about the fruits of power, such as money, glory and beautiful lovers.

TOM WOLFE

You might want to become a nonfiction writer, and yet at every turn you distort things, exaggerate and embellish them, and even introduce characters, places and events that had nothing to do with the original material. In that case, you are a born fiction writer, which is much nicer than saying you are a born liar.

JOSIP NOVAKOVICH

The most essential gift for a good writer is a built-in, shock-proof shit detector. This is the writer's radar and all great writers have had it.

ERNEST HEMINGWAY

Most great writers have a streak of the charlatan in them. Some acquire it in early years as a defense against their surroundings, others in later years as a means of disposing of their otherwise unsalable wares.

FRANK O'CONNOR

I don't think people become writers, for the most part, unless they have experienced a peculiar distancing, which generally occurs in childhood or youth and makes the direct satisfactions of living unsatisfactory, so that one has to seek one's basic satisfactions indirectly through what we can loosely call art. What makes the verbal artist is some kind of shock or crippling or injury which puts the world at one remove from him, so that he writes about it to take possession of it. . . . We start out thinking we're writing about other people and end up realizing we're writing about ourselves.

ROSS MacDONALD

I have the wrong personality for a writer. I am too loquacious, live too much in talk. "Real" writers do not talk about work in progress (and also do not, in the popular stance, know what it "means"). Whereas when I dislike what I have on the page, feedback reassures me that it has potential.

JANET BURROWAY

[T]he [writer] . . . possesses a reality of a different order from that of the ordinary man. His ego is entirely identified with his creative processes which for him constitutes the entire meaning and purpose of his life. . . . He is known to be emotionally unstable, neurotic, and often appears mentally unbalanced or even psychotic. Genius and madness have from time immemorial been associated, and the lives of the creative artists and geniuses in all fields do reveal an overwhelming preponderance for erratic conduct, emotional stress and irrational reactions with definite psychic disturbances manifested in conflict, struggle and mental disorder.

DR. BEATRICE HINKLE

It is no accident that the popularity of literary biography has increased most notably in the past century and a half, a period which has also been masked by a growing sense that the artist as a person is detached from society, indeed is a special kind of being quite apart from the common run of men.

RICHARD D. ALTICK

Arguably the biggest group of amateur writers comprises those who are suffering from something: bereavement, illness, exile, "narcissistic injury" to self-esteem, adolescence. Suffering triggers limbic system and temporal lobe activity through their roles in emotion . . . and increases the desire to write and communicate.

DR. ALICE W. FLAHERTY

To be a good novelist one must be shameless.

CZESLAW MILOSZ

Novelists are oxymorons. They are sensitive and insensitive. Full of heart and heartless. You have to be full of heart to feel what other people are feeling. On the other hand, if you start thinking of all the damage you are going to do, you can't write the book—not if you're reasonably decent.

NORMAN MAILER

Writers' minds, I think, are active or disturbed enough to need the soothing aura of a cat in the house. A writer is not alone with a cat, yet is enough alone to work.

PATRICIA HIGHSMITH

Any person who sets out to be a writer obviously suffers from an acute form of megalomania. He has convinced himself that what he has to say is important enough to be put into print or be spoken before large audiences; in addition, he demands that he be paid for it.

MERLE MILLER

There are very few writers who are not cranks is some way. I think most people would find just the process of writing odd—I think they would say, "Why do you spend so much time doing it?"

PAUL THEROUX

I cannot get drunk and feel a great love for my fellow men. Convivial amusement has always somewhat bored me. When people sitting in an ale house or drifting down the river in a boat start singing I am silent. I have never even sung a hymn. I do not much like being touched and I have always to make a slight effort when someone links his arm in mine. I can never forget myself. The hysteria of the world repels me and I never feel more aloof than when I am in the midst of a throng surrendered to a violent feeling of mirth or sorrow.

W. SOMERSET MAUGHAM

I'm a loner. I don't like groups, schools, literary circles. . . . I don't have any writer friends, because I just want to have—distance.

HARUKI MURAKAMI

Stupid people do not write good fiction. Arrogant, smart people write good fiction. Their arrogance is what impels them to demand center stage as the teller of the stories. Their intelligence is what enables them to conceal that arrogance. If you are a good writer, you are a sneak.

GEORGE V. HIGGINS

My findings show consistently . . . that members of the artistic professions [including] . . . all forms of writing—suffer from more types of mental difficulties, and do so for longer periods of their lives than members of other professions. . . . Poets show a high prevalence of both mania and psychosis. Poets, actors and fiction writers, and musical entertainers are more likely to attempt suicide.

ARNOLD LUDWIG

[T]he manic-depressive has a better chance of winning the title of genius than someone of equal talent and training who does not have the disorder. Consequently, manic-depressives will constitute the majority of geniuses. It is conceivable that a few individuals may possess talents so extraordinary that they can successfully compete for recognition as geniuses without the assets provided by manic-depression. For this reason, we believe that manic-depression is almost, but not absolutely, essential in genius; however, it is not the only important element.

DR. JABLOW HERSHMAN

The fiery aspects of thought and feeling that initially compel the artistic voyage—fierce energy, high mood, and quick intelligence; a sense of visionary and the grand; a restless and feverish temperament—commonly carry with them the capacity for vastly darker moods, grimmer energies, and, occasionally, bouts of "madness."

KAY REDFIELD JAMISON

My greatest fault, at least to me, is my lack of ability for relaxation. I do not remember ever having been relaxed in my whole life. Even in sleep I am tight and restless and I awaken so quickly at any change or sound. It would be fine to relax.

JOHN STEINBECK

Psychologist Anthony Storr has found that people drawn to writing tend toward complexity, incompleteness, individuality, impulsiveness and expansiveness. There are other studies that claim writers are more prone to mental illness than are other groups of people because we, as a group, have a lesser capacity to filter our environment and are therefore easily overwhelmed or confused by it.

BONNI GOLDBERG

Writers should have a psychiatrist on retainer. Only a psychiatrist can understand the dreadful insecurities and self-deceptions—those devilish tricks the ego plays—that govern the personality caught in the fever grip of creativity.

LEONARD S. BERNSTEIN

Two

In his 1942 book, *Characters Make Your Story,* Elwood Maren makes a strong point regarding the importance of craft in writing for publication:

> There is a strange fallacy abroad among laymen, as well as among writers who have yet not become commercially successful, to the effect that writing is an art, pure and simple, that it is in no way dependent upon or subservient to mechanics. By mechanics I mean specific procedures, methods, and acquired skills. Nothing could be further from the truth. Worthwhile writing is produced by an almost equal blend of mechanics and art.[1]

Stuart Dybek, in *Novel Voices,* an anthology of writers' essays on writing, adds this to the idea that craft is integral to the creative process: "Craft makes us better than we are, smarter, wiser, sharpens observation into vision, quickens reflexes, allowing an intellectual activity to be more blessedly instinctive."[2]

---

1. Maren, *Characters Make Your Story,* 6.
2. Stuart Dybek in Levasseur and Rabalais, eds., *Novel Voices,* 70.

Craft

In what has become a how-to classic, Dorothea Brande, in her 1934 book, *Becoming a Writer,* says this about craft: "During the period of my own apprenticeship—and, I confess, long after that apprenticeship should have been over—I read every book on the technique of fiction, the constructing of plots, the handling of characters, that I could lay my hands on."[3]

In a *Saturday Review* article entitled "One Way to Write Novels," Ellen Glasgow, a Pulitzer Prize–winning novelist of the 1930s, offered this advice to the beginning novelist:

> Study the principles of construction, the value of continuity, the arrangement of masses, the consistent point of view, the revealing episode, the careful handling of detail, and the fatal pitfalls of dialogue. Then, having mastered, if possible, every rule of thumb, dismiss it into the labyrinth of the memory. Leave it there to make its own signals and flash its own warnings.[4]

Successful writers, mindful of the importance of craft in what they do, do not treat the techniques of craft as trade secrets. Donald M. Murray agrees:

> Writer's secrets are *not* secret. There is an enormous quantity of writer testimony available. Writers have written about their craft in books about writing, in essays, in journals and notebooks, in their autobiographies, in letters, in commentary on their work and the work of other writers. They have been interviewed on radio and TV, for journals and magazines, newspapers and books.[5]

---

3. Brande, *Becoming a Writer*, 20.
4. Ellen Glasgow, "One Way to Write Novels," in Haverstick, ed., *Saturday Review Treasury*, 45.
5. Murray, *Shoptalk*, xv.

Outlining

Among fiction writers, there seem to be three schools of thought about outlining the plot before starting a novel or story. Some do not outline at all, others do a little outlining, and some spend a lot of time outlining before they begin the actual writing. Fantasy writer Terry Brooks, while acknowledging that many successful writers do not outline, argues strongly for outlining as a key step in the production of a novel:

> If you outline your book in advance, you will force yourself to think your story through. To some degree, depending on how thorough you choose to be, you will have to juggle plot, characters, settings, points of view, and thematic structure in order to assemble your story. You will have to build a story arc—a beginning, middle, and end—that comprises the gist of your book. You will have to consider all the possible choices you can imagine in crucial situations and select the ones that seem best. You won't do this for every twist and turn the book takes, but you will do it for the big ones. You will take this information and you will write it down in some recognizable fashion so that you can refer to it later.[1]

By writing an outline you really *are* writing in a way, because you're creating the structure of what you're going to do. Once I really know what I'm going to write, I don't find the actual writing takes all that long.

TOM WOLFE

The danger of outlining is that, from the standpoint of writing, once you've outlined a lot of the fun is over.

MICHAEL CONNELLY

---

1. Brooks, *Sometimes the Magic Works*, 83.

There are two kinds of writers in the world: the organized ones and the organic ones. When you're organized, you do an outline, you do character studies, you do all of this and all of that *before* you write. The other approach is the organic one. You know where you're going and you kind of just let it take you there. The outline I'm working from now happens to be my first draft.

JEAN AUEL

Being forced to write a synopsis before you've written the book is necessary for some of us and is eating away the artistic souls of others. Figure out which one you are.

SUSAN ELIZABETH PHILLIPS

There's nothing deadlier than an outline; I've tried it. You wind up forcing a bunch of people to do what the outline says, rather than letting them do what comes naturally.

DONALD HAMILTON

Another of my oddities (and this one I believe in absolutely) is that you never quite know where your story is until you have written the first draft of it.

RAYMOND CHANDLER

I almost know how a book's going to end before I start. In some cases, I have a good last paragraph before I start on page one.

WILLIAM BOYD

I don't plot. I don't sit down and plot a book. It sort of unreels as I write.

NORA ROBERTS

The liability of plot outlines is that they're time-consuming to produce and tedious to read. . . . Reduced to essentials, the majority of plot summaries will put you to sleep. To be interesting, plots require dramatization, but for many beginning writers, the completion of the outline has been so major a goal that it's hard to muster the energy to approach the far more daunting objective of starting the book. . . . Moreover, it's difficult to overcome the insecurity that an outline can create. By now, you're so familiar with the story you begin to wonder whether it's as interesting as you first thought.

DAVID MORRELL

Sometimes, in a book, I may try to get a little scribble outline of one or two pages to get some sense that, yes, this will all come together. But rarely that, even.

LAWRENCE BLOCK

I think with the mystery novel you have to know where you're going, but not in any great detailed sense.

SUE GRAFTON

I sit down with a very rough concept of the story, and then over the next eight months, I do a very elaborate outline. That's my full-time job: doing the outline six or seven days a week, eight to ten hours a day.

JEFFERY DEAVER

The plot outline doesn't forbid the inspiration of the moment, but it does prevent a wild hare, something out of character that drags the story off in a wrong area.

ELIZABETH GEORGE

Why not an outline? Well, for my taste, outlines are useless, fettering, imbecile. Sometimes, when you get into a state of anarchy, or find yourself writing in circles, it may help to jot down a sketchy outline of the topics (or in a story, of the phases) so far covered. You outline, in short, something that already exists in written form, and this may help to show where you started backstitching.

JACQUES BARZUN

If you are writing longer pieces than Poe tended to do, and you haven't outlined, you'll be marching boldly forward into the dark.

IAN JACKMAN

You can either do the hard work up front or do it at the end. By outlining, you are doing the hard work in the beginning—the thinking, the organization, the weighing and considering, and the making of choices. By doing it early, you can save yourself a lot of time and effort at the end. Put it off, and you pay the price later.

TERRY BROOKS

I learned that it is better to know the ending early on rather than to be unsure—then you know what you're aiming for and can arc the story toward that end.

TRACY CHEVALIER

I have these grid things for every book. It's just a way of reminding my-self what has to happen in each chapter to advance the plot. And then you have all your subplots. It's just a way of keeping track of what is going on.

J. K. ROWLING

I haven't the slightest idea what my future books will be like, even ones immediately to follow. My charts and plans are the slenderest sort of guides: I scrap them at will.

HENRY MILLER

I rarely have a very clear idea of where I'm going when I start. Just peo-ple and a situation. Then I fool around—writing and rewriting until the stuff gels.

JAMES THURBER

I always plan before I write, which means I always know the end in advance. I do not blithely set off on some big literary adventure, ever hopeful that my characters are going to elucidate matters for me as we travel on toward who-knows-where.

ELIZABETH GEORGE

Structure is often mistaken for plot. Plot . . . is simultaneous develop-ment of many elements, while structure is more strictly speaking the sequential organization of narrative events; it is the skeleton of form. You can easily outline structure; it's difficult to outline plot.

DAVID MADDEN

[T]he most important thing in making a big book . . . is the outline, see-ing where you're going. . . . A nonfiction book, especially if it's on a com-plicated subject, must have a dramatic structure. If you're writing a novel, the author has the advantage over the reader because the reader doesn't know whether this figure's going to be a hero or a villain, so you can do what you want with him. But if you're writing a nonfiction work about famous and important people and about major events in history, people know how it turned out. . . . So the writer has to create what I would call a willing suspension of knowledge and make a drama of the facts of the past.

DANIEL BOORSTIN

8

Plots and Plotting

In true crime, biography, and other types of nonfiction, I prefer the narrative form. In other words, I like nonfiction that reads like a well-plotted novel. In my opinion, writers who have succeeded in this form include Tom Wolfe, Truman Capote, and Joseph Wambaugh. In fiction, I like crime writers who know how to plot and tell a good story. In this group I include Jim Thompson, Donald Westlake, Evan Hunter, and Thomas H. Cook. There are, however, highly regarded writers, even in the mystery genre, who are weak plotters. In this group I include Dashiell Hammett and Raymond Chandler. People read out of curiosity and the desire to be told a good story. While perhaps critically acclaimed, nonfiction writers and novelists who disdain drama and a good story are not widely read.

If you read interviews with many prominent authors . . . you will notice how many of them seem to turn up their noses at the mention of plot. "I never begin with plot," they'll say. "Characters (or situation or setting or thought) is where I begin my novels." What's the implication? Only *bad* authors begin with plot. Some of these writers don't just imply it, they say it: A well-plotted book just isn't really "artistic." Books like that are for the great mass of dunderheads who read trash, not for us sophisticates who appreciate literature.

J. MADISON DAVIS

I define story as a narrative of events (external or psychological) which moves through time or implies the passage of time, and which involves change. I define plot as a form of story which uses action as its mode, usually in the form of conflict, and which closely and intricately connects one act to another, usually through a causal chain, ending in a climax.

URSULA K. LE GUIN

Plots are nothing devious. I have heard some literary or dramatic critics talk of plot in ways that indicated they had no grasp of the idea at all. A

45

plot is nothing but a normal human situation that keeps arising again and again . . . normal human emotions—envy, ambition, rivalry, love, hate, greed, and so on.

LOUIS L'AMOUR

Most successful fiction today is based on the structure that uses a series of *scenes* that interconnect in a very clear way to form a long narrative with linear development from the posing of a story question at the outset to the answering of that question at the climax.

JACK M. BICKHAM

Plot is the things characters do, feel, think or say, that make a difference to what comes afterward. . . . No thought, in and of itself, is plot. No action, however dramatic, is plot if the story would have been the same if it hadn't happened at all. Any action, however seemingly trivial, can be vital and memorable if it has significant consequences and changes the story's outcome.

ANSEN DIBELL

When I plot a story, I let things and images drop into my mind until a shadowy story forms. This is a lovely easy dreaming period that makes me keep postponing the real work, i.e., getting an outline on paper.

DOROTHY EDEN

Most writers think up a plot with an intriguing situation and then proceed to fit characters into it. With me a plot, if you could call it that, is an organic thing. It grows and often it overgrows. I am continually finding myself with scenes that I won't discard and that don't want to fit in. So that my plot problem invariably ends up as a desperate attempt to justify a lot of material that, for me at least, has come alive and insists on staying alive. It's probably a silly way to write, but I seem to know no other way. The mere idea of being committed in advance to a certain pattern appalls me.

RAYMOND CHANDLER

You can begin the story just before the beginning; you can begin it right at the beginning; or you can begin it after the beginning. . . . No matter how you choose to begin your novel, you have to think about creating an opening that either *possesses* or *promises* excitement, intrigue, or high interest for the reader.

ELIZABETH GEORGE

Plot-driven commercial fiction needs to have large stakes, something that's a threat to the lead character from the outside.

JAMES SCOTT BELL

MFA's [masters of fine arts] write lovely stuff. Rarely, though, have I read a novel by an MFA that had a terrific plot. MFA's do not generally make their living writing novels; mostly they teach, and perhaps there is a connection.

DONALD MAASS

If you look at any number of famous and popular books, the plot is often surprisingly simple or even, at first glance, banal.

IAN JACKMAN

A woman never remembers the pain of childbirth and a writer never remembers his plots.

JAMES M. CAIN

Starting in the late 1960s and continuing on through to the 1980s, plot became a dirty word in literary circles. Fiction lost its way. A great novel comes when there is beauty of language, illumination of character and a great plot.

DENNIS LEHANE

Many writers spend the majority of their time devising their plot. What they don't seem to understand is that if their execution—if their *prose*— isn't up to par, their plot will never be considered.

NOAH LUKEMAN

I think plots are made up of strings of events, elaborated by description and dialogue.

STUART WOODS

A plot isn't merely a string of occurrences; it is a carefully orchestrated telling of events that might include breaking up their temporal order, taking out certain pieces or emphasizing other pieces. It is that manipulation that a simple story becomes a plot.

ROBERT KERNEN

An idea is not a story. A first draft is not a story. A moral is not a story. A character is not a story. A theme is not a story. A plot—now, that's a story! So where do I get me one? You might ask. At your writing desk.

Because plots don't exist. They can't be shopped for or ordered on-line. They are coaxed into being. They develop. They grow in the course of the writing.

JOHN DUFRESNE

Since a novel is a recreation of reality, its theme has to be dramatized, i.e., presented in terms of action. . . . A story in which nothing happens is not a story. A story whose events are haphazard and accidental is either an inept conglomeration or, at best, a chronicle, a memoir, a reportorial recording, *not* a novel. . . . It is *realism* that demands a plot structure in a novel.

AYN RAND

[T]heme is not the same as plot, although the two are often confused. The theme is the basic idea, the concept, if you like, from which your story springs; the point you are making. In simpler terms, what the whole story is about. It will usually be something abstract, such as jealousy, ambition, rebellion against injustice, vengeance, love, obsession, the futility of war, the self-fulfilling prophecy, the agonies of divided loyalty, self-sacrifice, idealism or martyrdom. The theme is likely to be timeless, while the actual plot, i.e. the scenes and moves through which it is played out, must be firmly keyed to the period.

RHONA MARTIN

I distrust plot for two reasons: first, because our *lives* are largely plotless, even when you add in all of our reasonable precautions and careful planning; and second, because I believe plotting and the spontaneity of real creation aren't compatible.

STEPHEN KING

Know the story—as much of the story as you can possibly know, if not the whole story—before you commit yourself to the first paragraph. . . . If you don't know the story before you begin the story, what kind of a storyteller are you?

JOHN IRVING

Probably more than any other type of story, a mystery must have a tight plot. . . . It is not enough to get your protagonist in deep trouble and out again. When the problem is finally solved, it must be done in a satisfying way. This means the solution comes about *in a logical manner*, not through coincidence or happy accident. The solution must also come about *through the actions of the protagonist.*

STEPHANIE KAY BENDEL

Never raise expectations you don't plan to meet. You might forget a casual teaser, but readers won't. And what you see as an insignificant aside (*He knew he had to fix that step one of these days*) might seem a portent to your readers. Don't leave them hanging.

PATRICIA T. O'CONNER

A reader can buy one coincidence, but when you start throwing in coincidence after coincidence, then it becomes very difficult [for the reader].

MICHAEL C. EBERHARDT

[D]on't distract a mystery reader with a romantic subplot.

FLORENCE KING

[O]nce you have one good idea you should wait until you have a second one because it's much better if there are two plots going on. It seems to take up the slack.

JAY BRANDON

As far as I'm concerned, in the abstract there's only *one* plot, and it goes like this: A person or group or entity (an animal or an alien, whatever) *wants* something. . . . Another person or group or entity (nature, for example, or a destructive inner self) throws up every barrier imaginable to stop that goal from being achieved.

DAVID MORRELL

[S]how me a villain and I'll show you conflict. Show me conflict and I'll show you a struggle. Show me a struggle, and I'll show you drama. Show me drama, and I'll show you readers paying attention.

WILLIAM NOBLE

I'm incapable of long-distance plotting. I plot as I go along. . . . When I'm writing a novel I begin with a character who has a particular occupation, an unusual occupation, and then I find out about the character, through the disparate episodes in which the character is involved. One discovers what one wants to say by saying it, as other people have pointed out.

STANLEY ELKIN

The best plot twists rise not from the plot's needs but from your characters' lives.

DAVID KING

A good ending must satisfactorily resolve the conflicts dramatized in the story. These conflicts must be resolved tragically, comically or even indeterminately, but they must be resolved.

DAVID MICHAEL KAPLAN

Contemporary popular fiction steers away from flashback as a storytelling device; the reasons for it don't speak well of how readers approach books these days. Readers today complain that they don't have time to read and may be away from a book for a day or two between chapters; therefore, they want things short enough to gulp and simple enough so that when they begin reading again, they don't have to reread a few pages to get back up to speed.

MICHAEL SEIDMAN

Flashbacks come in handy when you need to infuse a clue or two into a mystery story or when some character trait needs to be enhanced or explained. . . . Flashbacks are quick. Back stories, because they drag in the baggage of a character or situation, are longer.

RON ROZELLE

Flashbacks [in dramatic nonfiction] operate best when they are vividly portrayed. When the reader grasps the story development easily. Clarity is important because we want the reader to understand what the flashback offers and how it impacts on the story.

WILLIAM NOBLE

If you feel a need to have a flashback on the first or second page of your story, that's a clear sign that your story should simply begin with the events being told in the flashback. In that case, don't flashback—tell the events in the order in which they happened.

ORSON SCOTT CARD

[A]ny gain made through flashback must be paid for. *Any* use of this method distances readers from the action; flashbacks shatter the illusion that readers are witnessing events as they happen, *right now*. The flashback, by definition, is already over.

NANCY KRESS

Beginning a story and then almost immediately going into a flashback, particularly one that lasts longer than the paragraph or two that opens the story, is almost always suspect. First, it usually stalls the main story. And if it's a long flashback, by the time we get back to the main story, we've often forgotten it.

DAVID MICHAEL KAPLAN

A work of fiction is in serious trouble when its flashbacks are more interesting than its main action.

THOMAS MALLON

Setting

In his narrative nonfiction classic, *In Cold Blood*, Truman Capote begins the story by taking the reader to the site of the 1959 mass murder of the Clutter family:

> The village of Holcomb, Kansas, stands on the high wheat plains of western Kansas, a lonesome area that other Kansans call "out there." Some seventy miles east of the Colorado border, the countryside, with its hard blue skies and desert-clear air, has an atmosphere that is rather more Far West than Middle West. The local accent is barbed with a prairie twang, a ranch-hand nasalness, and the men, many of them, wear narrow frontier trousers, Stetsons, and high-heeled boots with pointed toes. The land is flat, and the views are awesomely extensive; horses, clusters of grain elevators rising as gracefully as Greek temples are visible long before a traveler reaches them.[1]

When you read this passage, you know that Capote's account is going to be more than just a murder story; it is also going to tell us how the crime affected the people who live in this particular culture and place. *In Cold Blood*, like all good true-crime stories, is strong on setting.

One of the first things I learned about the difference between good and bad writing is that good writing is not entirely dependent upon the setting. And bad writing sometimes is. . . . Even though good writing is not entirely dependent upon the setting, a writer of fiction would be paving the way to miserable failure if he did not first create, using every tool at his disposal, the most clearly depicted time and place he could come up with. Because a story will not get very far—more specifically, your reader will not *go* very far—without a setting that has been meticulously crafted.

RON ROZELLE

---

1. Capote, *In Cold Blood*, 3.

The setting of a story is an integral part of it. No matter how fundamental the story line is, *where* it happens will make a difference.

STEPHANIE KAY BENDEL

Ideas can come from setting if the writer gets herself out to explore the place she wishes to use in her novel. Likewise, setting can be yet another tool that illuminates everything from character to theme. . . . Setting not only promotes the reader's understanding of what kind of novel he's reading, it also establishes a feeling that the reader takes into the experience. Setting triggers mood as well.

ELIZABETH GEORGE

To avoid confusion that leads to disinterest, you must let your reader know immediately where and when the story is taking place. You can go back in time or leap to the future, but remember to take your reader with you.

LOU W. STANEK

Stories must happen somewhere, but apart from this the most obvious and general function of setting is to increase the credibility of character and action. This is well known by anyone who has attempted to convince a listener of the actuality of some strange event. It is for this reason that stories of the supernatural or of the bizarre frequently posit a very real background.

JARVIS S. THURSTON

When readers read a piece of fiction, they expect it to feel real, even if it's a life they don't and will never know. They want to enter into it, to live there, with the characters. Setting—which refers simply to time and place—grounds the reader in the story in the most physical sense.

CAREN GUSSOFF

When you choose setting, you had better choose it wisely and well, because the very choice defines—and circumscribes—your story's possibilities.

JACK M. BICKHAM

If the setting is very significant, you should know it well and weave details carefully into the fabric of events. If the setting is not very significant, do not burden your reader with unnecessary details. Too much description can get in the way of the story.

ROBERT DeMARIA

[M]any writing teachers use the technique of the SINGLE BIG DETAIL when they ask writing students to sketch a set scene. It could be a single room or a parking lot or a group of runners or even a covey of animals. The point is to train the writer's eye so the most important detail in the scene is highlighted. The hope is that the detail highlighted will convey strong enough mood and atmosphere to carry the story along.

WILLIAM NOBLE

I have always tried to keep the settings of my books as far as possible within the confines of my own experience.

NGAIO MARSH

A real location must be accurately portrayed, if you name it, but within its boundaries you can take all the fictional liberties you wish. Sometimes, of course, it's fascinating to invent a whole city or town.

PHYLLIS A. WHITNEY

Environment includes surroundings, conditions, and forces within that environment. Setting is the more immediate surroundings of a story or a character and may be anything from a town to a telephone booth.

ELWOOD MAREN

Many writers make use of their hometown or the various places in which they have lived. And why not? These are the places one knows best.

ROBERT DeMARIA

Generally, in a novel, the convergence of a single figure or group of figures in a bare unpopulated landscape foreshadows a grim outcome.

MARY McCARTHY

Many of the traditional themes of fiction—the corrupting powers of ambition, the nature of one's responsibility to self and to others, the tragedy of loneliness, the paradoxes and ambiguities of compromise—all seem congenial to the city's qualities—its crowded loneliness, its veneration for the new, its bustling immorality, its commercialism, its sense of busy pointlessness. The city is available as a symbol of opportunity and freedom and success, and of the empty underside of these qualities.

RUST HILLS

Natural settings have a generalized relationship to character (rainy weather, rain in the heart), and their variety (if not their power) seems rather limited. Man-made settings (parks, gardens, cities, villages, rooms) are more varied, and offer the writer a more complex range of possible relations to character: economic, social, cultural, psychological, etc. The interiors of our houses openly or subtly reveal our character, for they are a projection of what we are and desire.

JARVIS S. THURSTON

For most novelists the art of writing might be defined as the use to which we put our homesickness. So powerful is the instinct to memorialize in prose—one's region, one's family, one's past—that many writers, shorn of such subjects, would be rendered paralyzed and mute.

JOYCE CAROL OATES

The great novelists of the past and the breakout novelists of today employ many approaches to setting, but all have one element in common: detail. A setting cannot live unless it is observed in its pieces and particulars.

DONALD MAASS

Almost anything drawn from "real life"—house, town, room, park, landscape—will almost certainly be found to require *some* distortion for the purpose of plot. . . . Wholly invented scenes are as unsatisfactory (thin) as wholly invented physiques or characters.

ELIZABETH BOWEN

Setting is as important as character. Go to the bookstore, open up a bunch of books and read the first line. You'll find the majority of opening sentences have something to do with setting and evoking an emotion with the reader.

BOB MAYER

A good novel avoids monotony by changes of pace and of mood—and of setting. Move around a little—give your characters a glimpse of color on a rainy day, a breath of fresh air when they've been in the house too long. Contrast in setting not only sharpens your main focus, but also adds interest similar to that of conflicting emotions within a character.

HELEN HAUKENESS

If I had to write a university novel, I wouldn't give a damn which one it was. They're all alike.

ROBERT PENN WARREN

In scenes, events are seen as they happen rather than described after the fact. Scenes usually have settings as well, specific locations that the readers can picture. In Victorian novels these settings were often described in exhaustive (and exhausting) detail. Nowadays literature is leaner and meaner, and it's a good idea to give your readers only enough detail to help them picture your setting for themselves.

RENNI BROWNE

[I enjoy] creating a model-train layout. I know where everything is in that town. My son once made a map of it so that I wouldn't get confused about the location of various businesses in relation to the river that goes through it. As a Midwesterner I don't have the advantage, or the disadvantage, of calling upon areas that everybody knows about, such as New York, San Francisco, Los Angeles—instantly recognizable places with certain rules that lots of people know.

CHARLES BAXTER

Point of View

Sol Stein, in *Stein on Writing,* notes that without a solid understanding of point of view—meaning the character whose eyes are observing the action, the perspective from which a story is told—the writer cannot fully exploit his talent. Stein has this advice for the beginning novelist:

> [Do not] mix points of view within the same scene, chapter, or even the same novel. It is unsettling to the reader. If you mix points of view, the author's authority seems to dissolve. The writer seems arbitrary rather than controlled. Sticking to a point of view intensifies the experience of a story. A wavering or uncertain point of view will diminish the experience for the reader.[1]

Perhaps the single most important decision a writer makes when he begins a story is who the narrator is and where he's going to stand. The decision casts itself in the first sentence and is more complex than it seems on first sight. In making it, the writer answers a surprising number of questions, and those answers lay down the ground rules for the story he is writing. They will forecast the shape his story is going to take, and they will inform his style.

KIT REED

[M]y friend Richard Ford changed the point of view in one of his novels. He worked on it for two years, and he felt it wasn't right, so he spent another year changing the entire point of view. That's dedication. And real seriousness in what you're doing.

RAYMOND CARVER

When a novelist writes, "It was raining that morning," and there is clearly no other narrator to ascribe the statement to, then the novelist himself

---

1. Stein, *Stein on Writing,* 129.

is using omniscient powers to convey information to the reader about weather. These are called omniscient powers because the novelist is playing God.

ROBERT C. MEREDITH AND JOHN D. FITZGERALD

I like the feeling of a *told* story, where you hear a voice but you can't identify it, and you think it's your own voice. It's a comfortable voice, and it's a guiding voice, and it's alarmed by the same things that the reader is alarmed by, and it doesn't know what's going to happen next either. So you have this sort of guide. But that guide can't have a personality; it can only have a sound, and you have to feel comfortable with this voice, and then this voice can easily abandon itself and reveal the interior dialogue of a character.

TONI MORRISON

For me narrative is always secondary to *voice* in the conception of a given work—and so "point of view" comes as a natural extension of the voice I discover. I look for a character who wants to tell a tale—whether it's in the first person . . . or the third.

JONATHAN LETHEM

FIRST PERSON

It is always dangerous to write from the point of "I." The reader is unconsciously taught to feel that the writer is glorifying himself, and rebels against the self-praise. Or otherwise the "I" is pretentiously humble, and offends from exactly the other point of view.

ANTHONY TROLLOPE

I beg the reader not to be deceived by the fact that a good many of my stories are told in the first person into thinking that they are experiences of my own. This is merely a device to gain verisimilitude. It is one that has its defects, for it may strike the reader that the narrator could not know all the events he sets forth; and when he tells a story in the first person at one remove, when he reports, I mean, a story that someone tells him, it may well seem that the speaker, a police officer, for example, or a sea-captain, could never have expressed himself with such facility and with such elaboration. Every convention has its disadvantages.

W. SOMERSET MAUGHAM

First-person narratives often appeal to beginners because writing one feels like being an actor and slipping into disguise. Actually, a novel could be made up of more than one character addressing the reader in the first person, but to attempt such things you require a good ear for voices because each of them must be instantly recognizable.

LESLEY GRANT-ADAMSON

[I]f a story centers on the narrator's ability to survive life-threatening dangers, some suspense will be lost in the first person because the character will have to survive to finish the story!

SOL STEIN

The first-person device, by permitting the reader to identify himself with one character from beginning to end, not only serves to juxtapose one force with another and gives both meaning, but makes for easier reading. In writing for popular magazines I have found the first-person—as-told-to or ghostwritten—story has a far wider audience than the third-person narrative; it gives the reader a feeling of being part of things rather than an observer. That this type of writing is not for the "intellectual" is doubtless true, although it should not offend them.

JIM THOMPSON

Even in the touchstone masterpieces of first-person narration, the teller of the tale is not necessarily the protagonist.

STEPHEN KOCH

A useful variant of first-person narrative is *second-person address*—which is entirely different from *second-person narrative*. In second-person address, the reader is an important character, but not as a protagonist—as the *audience* of the story, being talked to by the first-person narrator. This isn't the same as making the reader a character in the story; as a matter of fact, when you think about it, the reader-as-listener really isn't much of a lie at all.

JOEL ROSENBERG

When I write in first person, I tend to be too wordy. My first-person narrators tend to tell everything.

ANDRE DUBUS

The appeal of first-person narrative to any writer of historical fiction is obvious enough: the intimacy and immediacy of the speaking subject seems like a way to jump the temporal chasm. And yet, just as a lawyer knows to keep certain defendants off the stand, there are reasons for novelists to avoid allowing certain protagonists to testify on their own behalf.

THOMAS MALLON

Quite a few beginning writers employ [the first-person] viewpoint because superficially it appears to be the easiest. . . . When a writer uses this, she stays with the narrator throughout the novel. She's in that character's head and no one else's, and that is the character who tells the reader the story. Doing this, she gives the reader a fine opportunity to identify strongly with the character. . . . However, this viewpoint has its disadvantages, the most notable of which is the difficulty that can arise with plotting. A first-person narrator is on the stage at all times. . . . The reader can only see, hear and know what the narrator sees, hears and knows. . . . Unless you're writing an autobiography, the first-person narrator's voice is *not* your voice. How could it be unless you're a character in your own novel?

ELIZABETH GEORGE

A first-person character is under the disadvantage that he must be a better man to the reader than he is to himself. Too many first-person characters give off an offensively cocky impression. That's bad. To avoid that you must not always give him the punch line or the exit line. Not even often. Let the other characters have the toppers. Leave him without a gag.

RAYMOND CHANDLER

Just write your novel in the first person, and you won't be tempted to let the viewpoint wander. If your hero or heroine is "I" instead of "he" or "she," you'll never find yourself slipping into any other viewpoint accidentally, just because it makes the plot work out more easily. You're locked into one character for good or ill.

DONALD HAMILTON

THIRD PERSON

Third-person singular, past tense, is most natural and inevitable. . . . But you'd best beware of the monotone in it and the temptations toward false wisdom, cleverness. First person is where you can be more interesting as a fool, and I find this often leads to the more delightful expedition. . . . I'm also wary of the glibness that third person invites.

BARRY HANNAH

A story told in the third person will differ radically—in style, content, even structure—from the same story told in the first person.

DAVID MADDEN

Whether I write in third or first person, emotion can be more readily felt by the reader when I stay in the single viewpoint.

PHYLLIS A. WHITNEY

Point of view and voice are such an important part of fiction writing, but in journalism, the point of view is generally that of an objective bystander.

MARY KAY ANDREWS

Omniscient point of view means that the author shows us the story through the eyes of many characters. Multiple point of view does this, too, but usually in orderly fashion, limiting each point of view to one scene or one chapter.

NANCY KRESS

If the author uses he, she, it or they and tells the reader everything in every character's head and heart, then the novel is written in unlimited point of view, which has also been called third-person point of view or the omniscient point of view, since the author has been likened to an all-knowing creator God in the Judeo-Christian tradition. The author reveals every character's thoughts, feelings, motivations and actions. This is the only point of view not limited in some fashion, hence its name.

SHERRI SZEMAN

Switching Point of View

If you have a scene involving several characters, and you describe it first through one person's eyes, then through other's eyes, then through another's and so on, the whole structure of the scene becomes muddled and loses in intensity.

GRAHAM GREENE

A particularly strong dramatic effect with point of view is to shift it around, first one point of view—then another—then another, changing scenes and changing points of view. . . . A novel may offer several points of view, each one providing a different perspective on the unfolding story.

WILLIAM NOBLE

When a writer switches point of view for no good reason, readers become disoriented. A case in point: *As Leo gazed lovingly into her blue-gray eyes, Molly realized he was standing on her foot.*

PATRICIA T. O'CONNER

I don't like to see a switch of point of view in a love scene. You might want to write more than one love scene, or break it up. Have one of the characters take a nap, then write from the other's perspective.

CHRISTOPHER KEESLAR

Beginning writers . . . often think that describing different characters is changing point of view; so if one paragraph is about Charles, the next about Emma and the third about Rodolphe, they believe that the author has changed point of view. If the author has written about Charles, Emma and Rodolphe in unlimited [omniscient, written in third person] point of view, however, and not varied from that, then the author has not changed point of view. He has changed his focus from one character to another but not how he has written about them.

SHERRI SZEMAN

The twentieth-century development in fiction of a thoroughly limited point of view has been overemphasized, I think, especially in the light of more radical recent developments. One could argue that the use of limited point of view is positively old-fashioned.

ANNIE DILLARD

If it's crucial to withhold some information from the reader, then you can't choose as a point of view character someone who knows that information. When readers are inside a POV character's head, they're entitled to know everything the character does. Anything less will make them feel cheated. This is one reason murder mysteries usually use the detective as the POV. In the beginning, he knows just as little as the reader. We get to learn information at the same rate he does.

NANCY KRESS

Most nonfiction writing does not trouble itself with point of view. Mostly, these works are written in the voices of their authors or in unlimited point of view, where the author provides all the information her readers may need.

SHERRI SZEMAN

11

Characterization

When discussing characters and characterization, principally in the context of fiction, writers speak of round versus flat characters, changing versus static characters, dull versus interesting characters, and characters drawn from real life versus characters entirely imagined. Writers who have developed the skill to create compelling characters have also mastered the crafts of dialogue and description. It seems that the relative focus on characterization, vis-à-vis plot, is one of the elements that distinguishes genre from serious fiction.

The first step in the creation of any character is research. Since most writing is a personal exploration into new territory, it demands some research to make sure that the character and context make sense and ring true.

LINDA SEGER

My stories write themselves, and the characters do and say whatever they please without reference to me at all. I am not responsible for them, and their views are not necessarily mine.

ISAAC ASIMOV

My characters write my stories for me. They tell me what they want, and I tell them to get it, and I follow as they run, working at my typing as they rush to their destiny.

RAY BRADBURY

Whenever characters get out of control, it's a sign that the work has not arisen from genuine inspiration. One doesn't go on then.

ALBERTO MORAVIA

Fictional characters are made of words, not flesh; they do not have free will, they do not exercise volition. They are easily born, and as easily

63

killed off. They have their flickering lives, and die on cue, for us, giving up their little paragraph.

JOHN BANVILLE

The notion that, once set in motion, [characters] live a demanding life of their own is a literary conceit invented by writers who are not quite sure of what they are doing. A writer should be in control of his material. If he's not, he should wait until he is in control before he takes pen in hand, or he should look for gainful employment in some other field.

JEROME WEIDMAN

I try to get the right people assembled, give them right-sounding names, and then I'm off and running.

ELMORE LEONARD

[A]void wishy-washy names that don't say much about the character, such as Joe Smith or Jane Jones. And avoid giving all of your characters similar names, like Mike, Mark, Mick, and Mary, as that only serves to confuse the reader. Instead, look for ways to reveal something about your characters through their names.

BRANDI REISSENWEBER

The writer, like a good actor, is able to get under the skin of the character and play the part.

JACK HIGGINS

You are a minor god breathing life into your characters. If a character does something that is politically incorrect, then you have to let them.

SUSAN ISAACS

It's hard to be a gentleman and a writer. . . . Any real character is always your portrait of someone you have seen and you cannot play tricks with—any change you make will be a false note, and that the identifying details are by definition the details that matter.

JAMES GOULD COZZENS

Some [characters] come from real life. . . . If I explained how that is sometimes done, it would be a handbook for libel lawyers.

ERNEST HEMINGWAY

I should say that the practice of drawing characters from actual models is not only universal but necessary. I do not see why any writer should be ashamed to acknowledge it.

W. SOMERSET MAUGHAM

In practice I prefer to draw a character from someone I hardly know.

NORMAN MAILER

When we speak of "traits," we mean the general attitudes of your character, such as patience, arrogance, humility, selfishness. Traits define the basic personality of your character, just as we use traits to define people in real life. When we speak of "mannerisms," we mean specific movements of a character: the way he holds his head, the way she walks or talks, his facial expressions, and so on.

BRANDILYN COLLINS

If you can't create characters that are vivid in the reader's imagination, you can't create a damn good novel. Characters are to a novelist what lumber is to a carpenter and what bricks are to a bricklayer. Characters are the *stuff* out of which a novel is constructed.

JAMES N. FREY

If you were to examine the surviving novels of this century, you would find that a majority of the most memorable characters in fiction are to some degree eccentric. Eccentricity has frequently been at the heart of strong characterization for good reason. Ordinariness . . . is what readers have enough of in life.

SOL STEIN

Let your characters look like real people. Let them have bad tastes in their mouths and big moles on their arms and cellulite and dark circles under their eyes and real, beating hearts. Let them be beautiful, if the story calls for it, but let their beauty be unique, not carbon copy beauty. Writing is more vivid when it includes the rough patches of skin, not just satin fantasy flesh.

GAYLE BRANDEIS

[T]he most difficult hurdle any writer must get over in attempting to create character is that of the dull and ordinary man and woman. No matter how dull or ordinary they may be, they must not bore the reader.

Characterization ■ **65**

Characterization of them, therefore, poses the question of how to give them their true characteristics of dullness and ordinariness and yet interest the reader in what happens to them, in their fate, as it were. I have often thought that the capacity to do this is one of the best measures of a good writer.

CHRISTOPHER LaFARGE

The schlemiel story is a genre I always thought I'd avoid if I were an editor, for it has seemed to me that stories about losers, twerps, dullards, and schnooks would be of interest only to an audience of losers, twerps, dullards, and schnooks, at best, and no such people would be reading anything I edited.

ROBERT SILVERBERG

Your characters must be memorable, or each time you bring them back into the action a large portion of your audience will have forgotten who they are. And that's bad. Any character who can't be remembered from scene to scene is almost useless to the writer.

ORSON SCOTT CARD

Avoid the strange, the extremely unusual, the bizarre character. The character that most people like to read about is the known type, but he is also an individual within the type.

ELWOOD MAREN

Ruling sympathy out, a novel must contain at least one *magnetic* character. At least one character capable of keying the reader up, as though he [the reader] were in the presence of someone he is in love with. This is not a rule of salesmanship but a pre-essential of *interest*.

ELIZABETH BOWEN

I like to write comic dialogue; it's fun. But if my characters were all comic it would be boring. Those comic characters are a kind of stabilizer to my mind; a sense of humor is a very stable thing. You have to be cool to be humorous. When you're serious, you could be unstable; that's the problem with seriousness. But when you're humorous, you're stable. But you can't fight the war smiling.

HARUKI MURAKAMI

Any story has major and minor characters. And for me, whether they're major or minor has little to do with how much they are on stage. It has to do with whether they develop and change over the course of the story.

CHRISTOPHER TILGHMAN

Characters take on life by luck, but I suspect it is when you can write most entirely out of yourself, inside the skin, heart, mind, and soul of a person who is not yourself, that a character becomes in his own right another human being on the page.

EUDORA WELTY

You often have characters who are put upon, who have troubles, but the writer has not transformed that into a dynamic yearning in the character and that's what I find missing. If you do not build your fiction around human yearning, there's no way it's going to be successful.

ROBERT OLEN BUTLER

For characters to be read, they must be in conflict. That is where the action comes in. The novelist creates conflict from every premise.

SONIA LEVITIN

Your protagonist will almost certainly need a worthy opponent. If your main character is smarter, nicer, richer, *and* harder working than the other characters, your reader's interest may falter, because it's likely that the protagonist will eventually prosper.

LAURIE HENRY

Too often, in the effort to make a character believable, an unskilled writer will go into elaborate detail about things that don't matter at all. Endless explorations of thought to discover motives about things that don't matter are the hallmark of bad literary fiction.

ORSON SCOTT CARD

Every character must have a past, a present, and a future. And in terms of these three dimensions, each one must talk, move, act, and grow. Characters who represent only the present, without any past and future, are straw men.

LAJOS EGRI

On page 3 the character is mourning his dead wife and on page 4 he's happily shopping for a pair of jeans, and there is no emotional journey between the two experiences. This leads the reader, of course, to not believing the story's emotional authenticity. Characters have to work to move from grief to happiness.

ANN HOOD

One great difference between the persons of real life and the persons of fiction is that the persons of real life are creatures of impulse. . . . I think what has chiefly struck me in human beings is their lack of consistency.

W. SOMERSET MAUGHAM

One of the most frequent faults I find in submissions, particularly from mid-career novelists in crisis, is that their main characters are unsympathetic.

DONALD MAASS

I once had to kill off a character that my editor, quite rightly, said was too whiny to be likable. That was a difficult thing to do—to wipe some-one off the page entirely, like wiping her off the face of the earth. How-ever, once I'd done it, the novel improved almost instantly.

CARRIE BROWN

I have never had any idea about character. It is one reason I don't think I could teach literature. I only seem to see what people do.

ROBERT CRICHTON

You'll have to find out how your [historical] characters moved and car-ried themselves; what they were like at various ages; what they thought about; what they read, studied and wrote; even how well they spelled.

JAMES ALEXANDER THOM

My female characters tend to dominate the male. I see man as a kind of artifice, and woman as a kind of reality.

JOHN FOWLES

I'm not a good narrative writer. I put all my energies into my characters and let the characters carry it.

ELMORE LEONARD

It's a mistake to think that an author deliberately decides that a character will be constructed in such or such a way and will have this or that preference. The creation of a character takes place largely in the subconscious.

GEORGES SIMENON

If, after you have created your character, you still do not see them in your mind's eye walking, talking, breathing, perspiring, you might try a little psychoanalysis. Put them on the couch and start asking them questions.

JAMES N. FREY

To even begin to accurately bring a character to life on the page you must do your homework, quiz yourself fastidiously about every last detail of your character's inner and outer life. . . . Once you really know your character, your knowledge will flow unmistakably through the text; like an undercurrent, it will authenticate every word, gesture, and action.

NOAH LUKEMAN

Most people, though not all, are fairly honest with themselves when they are thinking. That is why thoughts are helpful to the writer in characterizing an actor.

ELWOOD MAREN

A stream of complaints may develop insight into the character, may even add to the story background, but it is not what a reader will find enticing in long doses. . . . For the most part, a stream of complaints pushes the reader back from the developing story because they leave a bad taste. No one . . . finds that appealing, and the result dampens drama and punctures interest.

WILLIAM NOBLE

In society the novelist finds his models, but he loses there the leisure and also often the right to represent those models truthfully. The best solution, perhaps, that of Proust: having known society, to escape from it through illness or withdrawal. Solitude is a difficult prescription in the life of any artist.

ANDRÉ MAUROIS

In the course of fashioning a character, you invariably reach a point where you recognize that you don't know enough about the person you are trying to create.

NORMAN MAILER

Since almost every profession or trade can supply its own rack of cos-
tumes and container of character traits, it is possible to create any number of *type characters*: the stooped, nearsighted, absentminded professor,
wearing a frayed tweed jacket and the suede patches at the elbows. . . .
Type characters are used because they establish an immediate sense of
familiarity and predictability, so that character development is accom-
plished in one stroke.

HARRY FENSON

Change in fortune usually occurs in stories that move primarily along
plot lines, rather than psychological development. Changes in the protagonist's attitude are usually the result of a psychological process in
which the character is his or her own antagonist. In early drafts, writers
are not always certain where they want the emphasis—on change in attitude or fortune. The reader who says, "A fairly interesting story, but so
what, what's the point?" probably feels that no growth or change has
occurred for the protagonist.

DAVID MADDEN

The over-thirty characters in my undergrad stories are pompous, insensitive, vulgar, unimaginative, crossly materialistic, hypocritical, self-
deluding, stupid, and often totally wrongheaded about everything.

MARTIN RUSS

I find characters who are at cross-purposes with society, or opposed to
society in some way, interesting because they are by definition the under-
dogs. They have to be clever, cunning, imaginative, dogged and wily,
whereas society merely has to lean its weight a little.

DONALD WESTLAKE

12

Dialogue

Well-written dialogue does not imitate the way real people speak. Real talk is repetitive, rambling, and redundant. It is boring and often meaningless. Good literary dialogue, therefore, has to be carefully crafted. In his book, *Stein on Writing,* Sol Stein points out that the majority of published writers write dialogue instinctively with little knowledge of the craft. He defines creative dialogue this way:

> [I]t is a semblance of speech, an invented language of exchanges that build in tempo or content toward climaxes. . . . Learning the new language of dialogue is as complex as learning any new language. . . . As the writer of fiction masters dialogue, he will be able to deal with characterization and plot simultaneously.[1]

When I write dialogue, I feel as though I'm merely the typist, transcribing what the characters say inside my head. I don't have the sense that I'm making anything up.

ELIZABETH BERG

Dialog is first of all vital and interesting in itself. Readers want and need to listen to the characters interact in dialog. Human speech, because it is immediate and dramatic, is one of the things we turn eagerly to fiction to experience.

DAVID MADDEN

Adversarial dialogue is action. When characters speak, we see them as they talk, which means that dialogue is always in immediate scene. Stage plays are in immediate scene. So are films, and now, for the most part, novels.

SOL STEIN

---

1. Stein, *Stein on Writing,* 110, 111.

Dialogue is more like a movie than it is like real life, since it should be more dramatic. There's a greater sense of action.

ANNE LAMOTT

Nothing could so quickly cast doubt on, and even destroy, the author's character as bad dialog. If the people did not talk right, they are not real people.

JOHN O'HARA

Writing dialogue is a craft that demands that you *shape* what a character says so that it's representative, artful, revealing and honest. . . . Good dialogue lends the readers a sense that it is happening outside the writer's control, while clearly it is anything but outside his control.

TOM CHIARELLA

The ability of a writer to capture the speech of his characters is often overestimated or even dismissed in favor of other qualities, but in fact it is far more important than subject matter or theme if the stories are to have life.

FRANK MacSHANE

My mother looks at the dirty rug and says, "That is filthy. It ought to be cleaned." My neighbor says, "That needs washed." My cousin from Long Island: "That's gotta be cleaned." A librarian in Maine: "That needs a washing." . . . The differences in the above . . . are mostly a matter of diction, or word choice, and syntax, or word order. Diction is the key element in the initial shaping of a character's voice.

TOM CHIARELLA

New writers seem to worry a lot—probably too much—about how often you can get away with writing *he said* or *she said*. There are two opposing schools of thought on this. One, subscribed to by some of the greatest writers in the English language, affirms that *said* is the only verb of attribution needed to identify who is speaking. The other school considers *said* colorless, preferring more spirited words like *mocked, bleated, rasped, ground out,* and *hissed.* This school is heavily represented in the formula romance racks of your supermarket.

AARON ELKINS

[A]dverbs in speech tags [attributions] tend to make the author seem amateurish. Let what the character is saying tell the reader the tone of voice; don't have your character speak *coquettishly* or *snidely* or *sarcastically.*

ALLISON AMEND

When I open a book and find so and so has "answered sharply," or "spoken tenderly," I shut it. It's the dialogue itself which should express the sharpness or the tenderness without any need to use adverbs to underline them.

GRAHAM GREENE

[I]f you write, "Damn you to hell, you bastard," as a piece in conversation, it really is a waste to add "he said angrily."

NORA LOFTS

I think that a writer who can put three characters in a scene and can write several lines of dialogue without attribution and without confusing the reader has paid attention to his characters and has invested in them qualities that no amount of descriptive, expository prose can convey.

K. C. CONSTANTINE

Dialogue requires more art than does any other constituent of the novel . . . why? Because dialogue must appear realistic without being so. Actual realism—the lifting, as it were, of passages from a stenographer's take-down of "real life" conversation—would be disruptive. Of what? Of the illusion of the novel. In "real life" everything is diluted; in the novel everything is condensed.

ELIZABETH BOWEN

Dialogue presents a terrible temptation. It offers the writer a convenient platform from which to set forth his pet theories and ideas.

JOHN HERSEY

Uneducated people have a much richer language than educated people, and it is because they are forced to improvise. After you go through college, you have acquired standard, formal English that you're supposed to speak. People who are raised with parents in a neighborhood where everyone speaks standard, formal English don't understand the richness of nonstandard speech.

TIM GAUTREAUX

In spite of the exercise books and the negative approach in our schools, language stays alive; it is often more alive in the mouths of truck drivers than in the correct mouths of people who feel that there is a single proper or correct way to say everything. . . . All of us have experienced occasions when some untaught and uninhibited young man, kidding a girl or coaching at third base, has struck sparks with a casual remark— has done exactly what language ought to permit him to do, communicate vividly.

WALLACE STEGNER

If you need proof that dialogue and spoken words are not the same, go to a supermarket. Eavesdrop. Much of what you'll hear in the aisles sounds like idiot talk. People won't buy your novel to hear idiot talk. They get that free from relatives, friends, and at the supermarket.

SOL STEIN

Naturalistic or "kitchen sink" dialogue is people expressing themselves informally and the hell with grammar, if the characters knew it to begin with. . . . *Realistic* dialogue, while appearing deceptively natural, is more organized. The vast bulk of modern plays and fiction employ this style combined with naturalistic. . . . Pitfalls in realistic lines are the lack of accurate ear and the old bugaboo of educational freeze-up. One can be so organized, correct and formal that the lines go flat and lose the sound of people talking to each other.

PARKE GODWIN

An important rule of thumb, when it comes to imparting background information, is never allow the characters to tell each other anything that they already know. It's always tempting to explain things to the reader by using this technique, but it's always a mistake.

BEN BOVA

Exciting dialogue is spoken by smart characters saying important things. Beware of small talk, especially greetings, partings, and politesse. Avoid banter unless it has a clear and significant story purpose and suits the mood of what is happening between the speaking characters.

ALICE ORR

If the characters talk too much, the pace of the story is accelerated and readers can't relax. Balance your dialogue with narrative details and action.

BHARTI KIRCHNER

Writers often get carried away with dialogue, because it's fun to do and once two or three characters are chatting you can be reluctant to shut them up.

LESLEY GRANT-ADAMSON

I let them [characters] do small talk for a page or two and pretty soon they begin to come to life. They do so entirely through dialog. . . . As they chatter away, one of them, and then the other, will say something that is so revealing that I recognize the signs of created character.

JOHN O'HARA

Writing good dialect is among the most difficult of the prose acts. It demands, for one thing, uncanny skills in spelling. How do you reproduce, phonetically, one letter at a time, the sounds of accented speech? Such writing demands a keen ear for the cadence of language. . . . Cultivate a keen sense of doubt about using it, and when in doubt, don't.

JAMES J. KILPATRICK

Dialogue, when properly handled, is one of the most entertaining divisions of action. The man who speaks even one truly *significant* word is as much in action as the man who throws the villain over the cliff from the thundering express train.

ELWOOD MAREN

If you substitute "Oh sugar!" for "Oh shit!" because you're thinking about the Legion of Decency, you are breaking the unspoken contract that exists between writer and reader—your promise to express the truth of how real people act and talk.

STEPHEN KING

Don't have characters call each other by name in dialogue, unless it's for a specific effect, such as a threat. . . . In real life, people rarely use each other's names when they're talking.

CYNTHIA WHITCOMB

It is the writer's privilege to put into the mouths of his characters better speech than they would have been capable of, but only for the purpose of permitting and helping the character to justify himself or what he believes himself to be.

WILLIAM FAULKNER

People only *write* in careful flowing sentences; they don't think that way and they don't talk that way.

TOM WOLFE

The use of dialogue in fiction seems to be one of the few things about which a fairly definite rule may be laid down. It should be reserved for the culminating moments, and regarded as the spray into which the great wave of narrative breaks in curving toward the watcher on the shore.

EDITH WHARTON

[E]xclamation points in dialogue tend to make statements sound like lovesick teenage email. Try at all costs to avoid using them!

ALLISON AMEND

13

Description

How does one describe a face? This is probably one of the most difficult assignments in writing. Describing a face, real or fictitious, takes a good eye, imagination, and effort. Everyone has a forehead, two eyes, a nose, a mouth, and a chin. Other than noting eyeglasses, a moustache, a beard, or the color or condition of the character's skin, how can words be used to portray the uniqueness of a face? Perhaps this is why original and ambitious facial description is rarely seen in modern writing.

Dorothy Thompson, Sinclair Lewis's ex-wife, described the novelist this way:

> His narrow face was roughened, red, and scarred by repeated radium and electric needle burnings. There was less of the face below the hawkish nose than above it, where it broadened into a massive frontal skull, crossed by horizontal lines; reddish but almost colorless eyebrows above round, cavernously set, remarkably brilliant eyes, transparent as aquamarines and in them a strange, shy, imploring look.[1]

When it comes to describing the faces of real people—in this case writers—Virginia Woolf was no slouch. She depicted Max Beerbohm as follows: "His face is solidified; has a thick moustache; a red veined skull, heavy lines; but then the eyes are perfectly round, very large, and sky blue. His eyes become dreamy and merry when the rest of him is well groomed and decorous in the extreme."[2]

When describing Katherine Mansfield, Woolf was characteristically vivid: "She had her look of a Japanese doll, with the fringe combed quite straight across her forehead. . . . Hers were beautiful eyes—rather doglike, brown, very wide apart, with a steady slow rather faithful and sad expression. Her nose was sharp, and a little vulgar. Her lips thin and hard."[3]

---

1. Cited in Sheean, *Dorothy and Red*, 347.
2. Bell and McNeillie, eds., *Diary of Virginia Woolf*, 211.
3. Ibid., 229.

Mass murderer Dick Hickock, in Truman Capote's *In Cold Blood*, is forced upon the mind's eye this way: "But neither Dick's physique nor the inky gallery adorning it made as remarkable an impression as his face, which seemed composed of mismatching parts. It was as though his head had been halved like an apple, then put together a fraction off center."[4]

In the fields of science, linguistics, grammar and mathematics, description concerns itself with the study of things *as they exist*, which brings forth the attributes of subjects rather than simply explaining or labeling them. In literature, description refers to the language we use to bring these attributes to the reader's mind. Description is an attempt to present as directly as possible the qualities of person, place, object or event. When we describe, we make impressions, attempting through language to represent reality. Description is, in effect, *word painting*. . . . Exposition supplies background information while narration supplies the story line, the telling of events, leaving description to paint the story's word pictures.

REBECCA McCLANAHAN

Description is description. It is the portrayal of surroundings or interiors, weather, human features, reactions, and dress. But don't throw it in just because you feel it is time for a bit of it. It must be related to the sentiments, conversation, appearances, and perceptions of your character, to one or more of these elements.

A. B. GUTHRIE, JR.

Beginning writers generally find the nose more difficult to describe than the eyes, the lashes and brows. I suspect that the problem stems from two sources: the novice's unfamiliarity with names for basic nose shapes and the limited color range that can be applied to the nose.

RUTH ENGELKEN

One of the last writers in North America who believes in a description of a character's face as an index to character is Saul Bellow. . . . People still describe facial reactions, but that's not quite the same thing.

CHARLES BAXTER

---

4. Capote, *In Cold Blood*, 31.

When it comes to description, the hero requires less than the villain. The hero is essentially the reader. All he needs is a name to identify him. Sometimes he doesn't even get that.

MICHAEL GILBERT

As a reader, I dislike it when an author gives me a lengthy physical description of a character. I have to pause to visualize the specifics that the author is foisting upon me. Often I find them confusing. I would much rather have the freedom to imagine what the character looks like, and I apply this principle when I think of my own readers.

DAVID MORRELL

Recognizing the junctures at which the telling detail is important will help you not only to write in crisp, evocative prose, but also to define your story. How do you recognize those junctures? . . . Telling details crop up most often when the description addresses itself to one of two areas: a character's immediate surroundings or a character's decision to do something.

MONICA WOOD

Use omniscient descriptions only at the beginning of a chapter or during one of the breaks in the chapter. Why? Because people like getting into one character's head and seeing from his/her point of view. Suddenly switching to the author's or narrator's voice in mid-chapter or in mid-action will jar the reader and remind him that it's only a novel.

RACHAEL ANN NUNES

Describe your [romance novel] character as early as possible, so that your reader can start to build the picture you want her to see. . . . The reader wants a picture painted. She wants to know what the character looks like, and she wants this picture painted throughout the book. . . . Some publishers of romance . . . also like clothes to be described. This can be tricky, as too way-out fashions can date a book, and even though the book will only be sold in the shops for a few weeks, it may remain on library shelves for years.

DONNA BAKER

Don't spend time on lush description in the middle of an action sequence.

APRIL HENRY

The problem for the writer of popular fiction is to give sufficient description without giving too much. The best solution is to keep your type of reader in mind all the time, and follow what I call the clutter rule: If something isn't serving the advancement of the story, it needs to go.

RON ROZELLE

We have almost forgotten that descriptions of sunsets, rivers, lakes, mountains, valleys used to be one of the staple ingredients of fiction, not merely a painted backdrop for the action but a component evidently held to be necessary to the art.

MARY McCARTHY

When I wrote my first novel I thought that "good writing" meant "beautiful writing"—long descriptive passages filled with adjectives, adverbs, metaphors and similes. "Reads like poetry," I told myself with satisfaction. Then I got my first rejection letter in which the editor said, "The book is overwritten and pretentious." A second editor said, "Too much description, not enough action and dialogue."

MADGE HARRAH

[A]s my former teacher John Barth . . . used to say, description needs to be "illustrative" rather than "exhaustive," meaning that you need to give the reader information that is useful and thematically important rather than information that is merely compulsively comprehensive or too intently microscopic.

JULIE CHECKOWAY

Description begins with visualization of what it is you want the reader to experience.

STEPHEN KING

I write description in longhand because that's hardest for me and you're closer to the paper when you work by hand, but I use the typewriter for dialogue because people speak like a typewriter works.

ERNEST HEMINGWAY

[A]void the use of trite, worn-out words and phrases to describe eyes, smiles, and all the varying facial expressions. Do not say, "Her eyes were pensive"; "She smiles sweetly"; "He laughs mockingly."

ELWOOD MAREN

[A]djectives and adverbs can be very lazy words. They deceive you into thinking they're doing their job when really they're not doing much at all. . . . [A] sentence with too many adjectives and adverbs is like an unpicked apple tree, the boughs sagging from the weight. . . . If you look carefully at good description, you'll notice that writers are often quite sparing in their use of adjectives and adverbs.

CHRIS LOMBARDI

Those novelists who eschew description are probably infusing other aspects of their story with a strong sense of time and place.

DONALD MAASS

Descriptions of the setting are easily overdone, often clumsy. Through a misplaced sense of obligation to describe a setting exhaustively, many young writers get into what I call the setting fallacy—that is, they start the story with a whole paragraph describing the sky, weather, or a city street as the protagonist walks into a bar.

DAVID MADDEN

If you must write long descriptive paragraphs, your best bet today [1970] may be in the Gothics. Such passages frequently are a great help in creating a mood of suspense, an ominous background, an exotic setting, or unusual circumstances. They [the descriptive passages] should be blended into the story, however, and not stand alone as the author's tribute to purple prose.

DON JAMES

[W]e no longer describe for the sake of describing, from a caprice and a pleasure of rhetoricians. We consider that man cannot be separated from his city, his country; and hence we shall not note a single phenomenon of his brain or heart without looking for the causes or the consequence in his surroundings. . . . I should define description: "An account of environment which determines and completes man."

EMILE ZOLA

Clichés are useful bits of shorthand. . . . These are apt descriptions that have been over-used. Therefore they are regarded as poor style and a lazy way of writing. Weed them out of your text where possible.

LESLEY GRANT-ADAMSON

14

Style

As a reader, I'm put off when I suspect that a writer is too aware of his own style or is more concerned with style than communication. It's a lot like a speaker who takes on a speaker's voice when she's talking publicly. I consider this pretentious and phony. I prefer to read authors who don't recognize their own voices or, if they do, are clever enough to make their writing style appear naturally interesting and unique.

In terms of style, there is no approved way to write; and over the years, in a general way, the style of writing has changed. What passed for exciting novelistic style in the 1930s would today come off stilted and dated. In *The Art of Readable Writing*, Rudolf Flesch discusses how style has evolved over centuries. In 1893, a scholar named L. A. Sherman, in his book *Analytics of Literature*, charted the evolution of the sentence. Flesch describes Sherman's findings:

> [Sherman] discovered . . . that English sentences have grown shorter and shorter for centuries. . . . The cause was that English writers gradually learned to get along without a complete subject and predicate for each idea. First they wrote everything out in strings of sentences connected with *and*; then they discovered the subordinate clause; then they learned to cut clauses down to phrases. Result: the average Elizabethan sentence ran to about 45 words; the Victorian sentence to 29; ours to 20 and less.[1]

There is a dreadful style of writing, prose intended to sound lofty and important, found in a lot of promotional literature put out by colleges and universities. The thoughts and messages conveyed in this form are usually quite simple. An example of this style can be found in many college mission statements. In straightforward prose, one might write, "The goal of a college is the education of its students." Because this is so obvious, to say it directly and simply makes it sound kind of stupid. But when

---

1. Flesch, *Art of Readable Writing*, 61.

the mission statement is puffed up with carefully selected words and high-minded phrases, the simplicity of the message is replaced by syntax intended to make it sound profound. In my opinion, this style is pompous and false and represents writing at its worst. Colleges are probably lucky that students don't read this stuff. For example:

> The mission of _____College is to help young men and women develop competencies, commitments and characteristics that have distinguished human beings at their best. All of us who are affiliated with the College are working toward that end each day in as many different ways as there are students on this campus. Our students have unique talents and new insights that are being developed during each interaction with faculty, staff, alumni and other students. For each student, those interactions become building blocks in their foundation for living.

Ignore, if you can, the substance of this message, its unadulterated puffing and pandering, and look at the style. Note the lofty and, to my mind, cheesy alliteration that starts it off and the words *distinguished, affiliated, insights, interaction,* and *foundation,* typical university-speak vocabulary comparable to favorites such as *outcomes, challenges,* and *impact* (instead of *affect*) not used in this passage.

Style is an author's choice of words (diction), arrangement of words in each sentence (syntax), and handling of sentences and paragraph units to achieve a specific effect.

DAVID MADDEN

A man is revealed in his style, the language which he has created for himself.

HENRY MILLER

The *tone* of a novel may be described in words like comic, wry, reflective, tongue-in-cheek, bittersweet, or in compounds such as incipient fear, sense of lurking evil and sense of unease.

LESLEY GRANT-ADAMSON

I don't know what makes a writer's voice. It's dozens of things. There are people who write who don't have it. They're tone-deaf, even though they're very fluent.

PAULA FOX

I should like to put it on record that I never took the smallest pains with my style, have never thought about it, and do not know or want to know whether it is a style at all or whether it is not, as I believe and hope, just common, simple straightforwardness.

SAMUEL BUTLER

There is no satisfactory example of style, no infallible guide to good writing, no assurances that a person who thinks clearly will be able to write clearly, no key that unlocks the door, no inflexible rules by which a young writer may shape his course.

E. B. WHITE

One can derive all the principles of effective fiction from the idea that the writer must make his dream vivid and continuous. The dream is not vivid, of course, if too many words are abstract, not concrete, if too many verbs are passive, too many metaphors familiar or dull, and so on; and the dream is not continuous if some element in the writing distracts the reader from the story to thoughts about the stupidity of the writer—his inability to use proper grammar, his excessive loquacity, his deviation into sentimentality, mannerism, or frigidity, and so on.

JOHN GARDNER

Writers most often drop into passive voice when they are unsure of themselves, when they don't want anything bad to happen to one of their characters, when they don't want their characters to do anything bad.

ROGER MacBRIDE ALLEN

[T]he most durable thing in writing is style, and style is the most valuable investment a writer can make with his time. It pays off slowly, your agent will sneer at it, your publisher will misunderstand it, and it will take people you never heard of to convince them by slow degrees that the writer who puts his individual mark on the way he writes will always pay off.

RAYMOND CHANDLER

Bad style often comes when a writer is trying too hard to imitate the style of other writers.

DUANE UNKEFER

It is the beginning of the end when you discover you have style.

DASHIELL HAMMETT

A really good style comes only when a man has become as good as he can be. Style is character. A good style cannot come from a bad undisciplined character.

NORMAN MAILER

Few people realize how badly they write. Nobody has shown them how much excess or murkiness has crept into their style.

WILLIAM ZINSSER

The really popular books are full of clichés, people "flushing with anger" or "going pale with fear." Popular authors bring nothing new to their readers, and I have no wish to belong to that type of popular writer.

GRAHAM GREENE

I write in different styles because I hear different voices in my head. It would be boring to have always the same voice, point of view.

GORE VIDAL

Essentially I think of myself as a stylist, and stylists can become notoriously obsessed with the placing of a comma, the weight of a semicolon. Obsession of this sort, and the time I take over them, irritate me beyond endurance.

TRUMAN CAPOTE

If a writer cares more for his language than for other elements of fiction, if he continually calls our attention away from the story to himself, we call him "mannered" and eventually we tire of him.

JOHN GARDNER

Insecure writers want to show off their vocabulary from fear of sounding ignorant. If I don't use obscure words, they seem to wonder, how will readers know that I have a college degree? If I do use simple words, won't people think I'm a simpleton? Such attitudes make for deadly writing.

RALPH KEYES

The first thing a young writer . . . sets out to do is to show his readers that he possesses a dictionary, that he knows all the synonyms; so we get, for example, in one line, *red*, then we get *scarlet*, then we get other different words for the same color.

JORGE LUIS BORGES

American writers tend to know and use minuscule vocabulary. American writers' prose has fewer and fewer words. To use an anthropologist's expression, we are experiencing a partial *extinction* of language. And syntax, the logical spine of sentences, is losing variety.

CAROL BLY

An editor might notice an excess of "style"—if your writing is so distinctive that it's jarring with the overall feel of a magazine or publishing program—and react negatively. Even a desirable style, if too strongly expressed, might prove a hindrance in some markets.

DAVID A. FRYXELL

Those who write clearly have readers; those who write obscurely have commentators.

ALBERT CAMUS

I don't think style is consciously arrived at, any more than one arrives at the color of one's eyes. After all, your style *is* you.

TRUMAN CAPOTE

All of us recognize clichés. They fall like casual dandruff on the fabric of our prose. They are weary, stale, flat, and unprofitable.

JAMES J. KILPATRICK

[M]odern writing at its worst does not consist in picking out words for the sake of their meaning and inventing images in order to make the meaning clearer. It consists in gumming together long strips of words which have already been set in order by someone else, and making the results presentable by sheer humbug. The attraction of this way of writing is that it is easy.

GEORGE ORWELL

ACADEMIC AND OTHER FORMS OF OVERWRITING

Professors are often shy, timid and even fearful people, and under these circumstances, dull, difficult prose can function as a kind of protective camouflage.

PATRICIA NELSON LIMERICK

We sometimes speak of academic writing, of courtroom transcripts, of material that does not compel our attention or elicit a strong desire to continue reading as *dry*. What we mean by "dry" is that it does not enable use to see what we read, it does not move us, and, most important, it does not stimulate our intellect with insight, its ostensible purpose.

SOL STEIN

A few sociologists write the best English they are capable of writing, and I suspect that they are the best men in the field. There is no mystery about them. If they go wrong, their mistakes can be seen and corrected. Others, however—and a vast majority—write in a language that has to be learned almost like Esperanto. It has a private vocabulary which, in addition to strictly sociological terms, includes new words for the commonest actions, feelings, and circumstances. It has the beginnings of a new grammar and syntax, much inferior to English grammar in force and precision. So far as it has an effect on standard English, the effect is largely pernicious.

MALCOLM COWLEY

A friend of mine recently [1976] turned in a paper to a [college] course on behavior modification. She had tried to express in simple English some of her reservations about this increasingly popular approach to education. She received [the paper] back with the comment: "Please rewrite this in behavioral terms." It is little wonder that human beings have so much trouble saying what they feel, when they are told that there is a specialized vocabulary for saying what they think. The language of simplicity and spontaneity is forced to retreat behind the barricades of an official prose developed by a few experts who believe that jargon is the most precise means of communication.

LAWRENCE LANGER

Legal writers must recognize what the rest of the literary world already knows: a good style powerfully improves substance. Indeed, it largely *is* substance. Good legal style consists mostly in figuring out the substance precisely and accurately, and then stating it clearly.

BRYAN A. GARNER

One of the first signs of insecure writers is the number of phrases they use to say what could be said in just a few words. Instead of writing "now" or "then," these writers use "at this point in time."

RICHARD ANDERSON

It is easier—even quicker, once you have the habit—to say *In my opinion it is not an unjustifiable assumption that* than to say *I think*. If you use ready-made phrases, you not only don't have to hunt about for words; you also don't have to bother with the rhythms of your sentences since these phrases are generally so arranged as to be more or less euphonious.

GEORGE ORWELL

Turning out flashy, dense, complicated prose is a breeze; putting things down in simple terms that anyone can understand takes brainwork.

PATRICIA T. O'CONNER

LITERARY PRETENTIOUSNESS

Great Writing was done in a language that had nothing to do with the one you spoke. The words were similar, but arranged more cleverly, less directly. A good literary sentence was like a floor with a hole hidden in it. You got to the end and thought: "Why'd he say it that way? He must really be a great writer." Plain American language was a degraded thing, good only for getting around your dopey miniature world, cashing checks and finding restaurants and talking about television and so on.

GEORGE SAUNDERS

As one reads contemporary novelists, one can't shake the feeling that they write for one another rather than some more or less common reader. Their prose shares a showiness that speaks of solidarity and competition—the exaggerated panache with which teenaged boys shoot hoops in their driveways while pretending they don't know their neighbor is watching from across the street.

DALE PECK

As with most writers, the urge toward stylistic experimentation strikes me unpredictably and often. Usually the experiments fail, and I do the story over in more conventional ways.

FREDERIK POHL

One of the really bad things you can do to your writing is to dress up the vocabulary, looking for long words because you're maybe a little bit ashamed of your short ones.

STEPHEN KING

I think sometimes we give people a lot of credit just because they're writing nice sentences even if it isn't adding up to much.

JAMES PATTERSON

The one-sentence paragraph is a great device. You can italicize with it, vary your pace with it, lighten your voice with it, signpost your argument with it. But it's potentially dangerous. Don't overdo your dramatics. And be sure your sentence is strong enough to withstand the extra attention it's bound to receive when set off by itself. Houseplants wilt in direct sun. Many sentences do as well.

JOHN R. TRIMBLE

Style does not exist apart from the story, and, if five people tell an identical story, each one will tell it in a different style. The best style will produce the best story.

B. J. CHUTE

Style isn't something added on; it's intrinsic to the perceptions and the way you see life.

MARTIN AMIS

The best style is the *least* noticeable.

WHIT BURNETT

15

Rewriting

Writers have different attitudes toward, and methods of, revision and re-writing. Some enjoy rewriting more than the creation of the first draft, while others have to force themselves to revise. Some, when revising, mainly put in material; others take it out. A few revise sentence by sentence, revising as they advance into the story but not moving forward until they have written the best sentence they can. Others produce book-length first drafts, while still others rewrite by paragraph, page, or chapter. A few writers claim they don't rewrite at all, their first drafts being their final products. Most, however, at least according to anecdotal evidence, write several drafts before they declare their manuscripts complete. Very few published writers disagree with the literary cliché: writing is rewriting.

The beginning writer writes his first draft, reads it, and says, "This is awful. I'm screwed." The experienced writer writes his first draft, reads it, and says, "This is awful. I'm on my way!"

JERRY CLEAVER

Revision is identical with and inseparable from writing. The reader-centered writer knows that revision of subsequent drafts is as creative and enjoyable as writing the first draft.

THEODORE A. REES CHENEY

The only true creative aspect of [novel] writing is the first draft. That's when it's coming straight from your head and your heart, a direct tapping of the unconscious. The rest is donkey work. It is, however, donkey work that must be done. . . . You *must* rewrite.

EVAN HUNTER

I hate editing. I love to write, but I hate to reread my stuff. To revise. And most students do, too. It's a killer.

BARRY HANNAH

The secret is not to try to be perfect. If you try to be perfect, you procrastinate, you go over and over what you wrote, you make no forward motion. Trying to be perfect doesn't produce masterpieces, only agony and slow writing.

STEPHEN J. CANNELL

I don't write a quick draft and then revise. Instead, I write 30 or 40 drafts of each page before moving on to the next.

DEAN KOONTZ

I may rework as I go along, but when I'm done, I'm pretty much done.

LAWRENCE BLOCK

[I rewrite] the first twenty pages over and over again—because in my idea you have to get everything into them. So as I go along and the book develops, I have to go back to the beginning again and again.

HENRY GREEN

Don't try to write that perfect draft—God sakes, whatever that is. Instead, allow yourself the freedom to play. Never rein in your creativity.

FRANK McCOURT

The beautiful part of writing is that you don't have to get it right the first time, unlike, say, a brain surgeon. You can always do it better, find the exact word, the apt phrase, the leaping simile.

ROBERT CORMIER

Finish an entire book before doing a lot of editing. Too many writers spend years rewriting the first chapter. By the time you get to the end you'll have a better idea of how and where to begin.

ANNE EAMES

What I've learned through all my years of writing is that my first drafts always stink. But I can't make them sing until I've at least gotten the bones of the plot down on paper. So I keep writing, knowing that eventually I'll fix what needs to be fixed.

TESS GERRITSEN

Each time I rewrite, even if I had assumed nothing needed changing, I think of new details that might help to convince readers that this story really did happen.

ANNE TYLER

How do I approach the task of rewriting? Usually with great reluctance. But if an editor's suggestions and my own second thoughts seem to make sense, then I will set to work with renewed enthusiasm and a conviction that improvement is a worthwhile goal.

ROBERT BLOCH

When revising feels overwhelming, keep in mind that great changes are often born from small adjustments. Rewriting is more than copyediting, i.e., correcting spelling and grammar, checking references, and making sure sentences make sense, but still, for some of us it's best to start with the smallest, most rudimentary changes.

BONNI GOLDBERG

[D]o not revise in the throes of creative ecstasy, or when angry, upset, exhausted, depressed, or filled with self-doubt, dread or loathing.

PETER SELGIN

The more you go over a text the more you find that you have to add or subtract. . . . Most of our writers just give you their first wild rush and assume that because it comes from *them* it is valuable. This is the romantic fallacy of the bad writer.

GORE VIDAL

I revise until I feel I'm done, and then I am done with that section or scene. I don't often go back and change much after that.

KENT HARUF

With all your rewriting, are you making your manuscript appreciably better? There is almost nothing that can't be improved, but there are many manuscripts that are surely spoiled by too much tinkering and others that are always beyond help. You might be liberated from an unmanageable manuscript if you can set it aside and try something new.

IAN JACKMAN

I don't think anything I've written has been done in under six or eight drafts.

E. L. DOCTOROW

Everything new I write throws the rest out of kilter. It is just like a room decorated at different periods. You decide to put new chintz on those two worst chairs—"The rest aren't so bad." And then, that done, the others look shabby, and by the time you've recovered *them*, the first ones are faded again.

ANNE MORROW LINDBERGH

Revision . . . tests our ability to be honest with ourselves about our strengths and our weaknesses. Who enjoys that sort of honesty, really?

JAN BURKE

A novel is something that has to be endured by the writer. Anybody who can't go back for the fourteenth and fifteenth revision with freshness and enthusiasm ought to get out of the business.

JAMES M. CAIN

When I was in college, I revised nothing. I wrote out my papers in long-hand, typed them up and turned them in. It would never have crossed my mind that what I had produced was only a first draft and that I had more work to do; the idea was to get to the end, and once you had got to the end you were finished.

NORA EPHRON

There are writers, usually thriller writers, who claim they can only work in what I disparagingly dub the floundering method. They produce numerous drafts, making major alterations each time. But why bother when you can reach the same conclusions with no more effort than a little hard thinking? Like the majority of writers, my intention is always to do two drafts but occasionally I need three.

LESLEY GRANT-ADAMSON

No one except me could ever read one of my manuscripts in its rough state. I seldom write such length that I have to cut. Instead, I tend to write my fiction too tightly, and must then insert and elaborate, deepen and expand. Nearly every page is penciled with corrections, and on the back of most pages I write in pencil the new material that will really make the book.

PHYLLIS A. WHITNEY

I have been working hard at my novel. . . . It is nearly finished now, but I shall then have to go over it and make improvements before I am really satisfied with it. When you start to write [a novel] you always wonder if you will be able to make it long enough, but by the time you get to the end it is always too long—I love cutting out bits and crossing out whole pages.

BARBARA PYM

Fiction writers, faced with an absolute necessity to cut way back in total length, have [a] means of [cutting] words, but one that requires [great] thought: eliminating a character entirely. The character will probably be rather insignificant, but nonetheless one you've created and perhaps come to love. The trouble with pruning this kind of growth is its vines and roots are intimately entangled with the entire story. It's not simply a matter of screwing up courage and deleting every reference to the person's name. Whatever relationships this character has with any of the other characters must also be taken out.

THEODORE A. REES CHENEY

There are no rules governing the unglamorous work of rewriting, other than the fact that it is necessary and everyone does it. Rewriting is the literary equivalent of sausage-making.

IAN JACKMAN

Never correct or rewrite until the whole thing is down. Rewriting in process is usually found to be an excuse for not going on.

JOHN STEINBECK

Most of the time in speaking, we settle for the catch-as-catch-can way in which the words tumble out. In writing, however, there's a chance to try to get them right. But the opportunity to get them right is a terrible burden: you can work for two hours trying to get a paragraph "right" and discover it's not right at all. And then give up.

PETER ELBOW

I suffer agony over some of the cutting, but I realize it's got to be done. When something really good goes it's an awful wrench, but as you probably know, something really can be good and yet have no place in the scheme of a book.

THOMAS WOLFE

The main rule of a writer is never to pity your manuscript. If you see something is no good, throw it away and begin again. A lot of writers have failed because they have too much pity. They have already worked so much, they cannot just throw it away. But I say that the wastepaper basket is the writer's best friend. My wastepaper basket is on a steady diet.

ISAAC BASHEVIS SINGER

I am a rewriter. I rewrite a number of times. Imaginative richness is born in rewriting.

BERNARD MALAMUD

I write many drafts longhand, because it slows me down, gives me time to think. I change sentences, words, phrases as I write, often recopying the entire annotated draft from the first line to the point at which the corrections get so messy and confusing that I have to stop and make a fresh copy. In this way, I get to feel the rhythm of the prose, hear the tone of the narrative voice.

JOHN DUFRESNE

I think too many people rush out with a work that's half done because they want people to pat them on the back and make them feel it's OK.

ALEXANDRA STYRON

Rodin . . . said that even an achieved work is never perfect; it is always susceptible to a modification that can make it better. But I believe that with enough practice and skill and good faith, you can learn to recognize when the work is achieved. There is such a thing as fussing too much; it can deaden the work. There is also such a thing as stopping too soon; this gives the work a kind of incompleteness that is more annoying than it is mysterious. Learning when "enough is enough" is the discipline of a lifetime.

GAIL GODWIN

I write slowly because I write badly. I have to rewrite everything many, many times just to achieve mediocrity.

WILLIAM H. GASS

16

Titles

James M. Cain explained the title to his steamy crime novel, *The Postman Always Rings Twice,* this way: each time the postman delivered a rejection letter for this repeatedly rejected manuscript, he rang twice.[1]

Dan Poynter argues that a book's title has a lot to do with its commercial success or lack of sales: "In mail-order tests for the same book, a good title sold 15 percent more books than a bad title. One sales representative said titles are 33 percent of his sales package. A poorly titled book may be virtually lost and may never reach its intended audience." To illustrate his point, Poynter lists proposed titles of famous books that were rejected in favor of their eventual names. For example, *Gone with the Wind* could have been *Tomorrow Is Another Day,* and *The Great Gatsby* might have been known as *Trimalchio in West Egg.*[2]

Image is almost everything. You have four seconds to impress your potential buyer. Be clear, use metaphor and make sure your title elicits a picture or an emotion. Keep your title short, preferably 5–7 words.

JUDY CULLINS

Titles are chosen first of all to attract the eye of readers. Often the one you have given your book will not appeal to your editor. His judgment may be better, but not always. If your title means a lot to you, fight for it, and you just might win.

DORIS PICKER MARSTON

Alliteration is the occurrence within a line or phrase of words having the same initial sound. It's a device that many writers employ to create a treasure trove of tried-and-true, bread-and-butter, bigger-and-better,

---

1. Cited in Henderson and Bernard, eds., *Rotten Reviews and Rejections,* 209.
2. Dan Poynter, "Change Your Title, Change Your Sales," *Writer's Digest Magazine* (June 2003): 50.

bright-eyed and bushy-tailed, do-or-die, footloose-and-fancy-free, larger-than-life, cream-of-the-crop titles.

EDWIN NEWMAN

Book titles point up the divergence [between American and British crime fiction]: *My Gun Is Quick* strikes one note, *The Unpleasantness at the Bellona Club* quite another.

PAULINE GLEN WINSLOW

Writing a book that lacks a title feels a bit like owning a car with no license plates.

NICHOLAS WEINSTOCK

The title comes afterwards, usually with considerable difficulty. . . . A working title often changes.

HEINRICH BÖLL

I make a list of titles *after* I've finished the story or the book—sometimes as many as a hundred. Then I start eliminating them, sometimes all of them.

ERNEST HEMINGWAY

I like best to find my title before I even start writing. It's wonderful when one springs into your mind and you can fit it into your story from the beginning. Sometimes a title may even lead you to your plot.

PHYLLIS A. WHITNEY

Some authors have been know to send a whole list of suggested titles along with their manuscripts, encouraging the publisher or agent to decide which is best. This isn't a good idea. I always prefer to see *one* strong title. It's taken for granted that the title may be changed after your novel interests a publisher willing to pay for the change (and the book). But you can send a title list *after* the book has been accepted.

OSCAR COLLIER

Picking the perfect title is a distinct talent. Some authors are fortunate enough to have brains crammed with apposite quotations, or to have the knack of adapting a piece of contemporary slang or jargon. Although you may be aware that the ideal one has escaped you, don't submit your novel without a title. That creates the impression the story has you stumped. An untitled manuscript is an unfinished piece of work.

LESLEY GRANT-ADAMSON

Know exactly who your core audience is, then choose a title that will resonate with those readers. A good title should be both informative and provocative. It should tell your reader what the book is about and, at the same time, strike the right dramatic chord.

PETER RUBIE

I have peculiar ideas about titles. They should never be obviously provocative, nor say anything about murder. They should be rather indirect and neutral, but the form of words should be a little unusual. . . . As to publishers, I wonder if they know anything about titles.

RAYMOND CHANDLER

When I need a title I'll usually reread the poetry of Hart Crane. I take a copy of Crane's work with me when I travel. A phrase will catch my eye and seem right for what I'm writing. But there's no system to it.

TENNESSEE WILLIAMS

Titles as a rule do not matter much. Very good authors break down when it comes to the effort of choosing a title.

D. H. LAWRENCE

I have never been a title man. I don't give a damn what it is called. I would call it [*East of Eden*] *Valley to the Sea* which is a quotation from absolutely nothing but has two great words and a direction.

JOHN STEINBECK

An effective title is to your article or book what a good "preview of coming attractions" is to a movie. It announces what your manuscript is about in such a way that it compels your reader to sit up and take notice. And if that reader is an editor who possibly will buy your material, an enticing title can open doors for you.

JOHN McCOLLISTER

A good title is not a label, but a lure.

HAYES B. JACOBS

Watch people who are browsing in a bookstore. A catchy title grabs their interest and makes them reach for the book out of curiosity. A great title makes browsers think, "Really?" or "What does *that* mean?" or "That's what I need." Think long and hard when choosing your book's title. The title must give some clues about the book's content in a snappy "one-liner."

JONI HAMILTON

Not long ago, I walked into a bookstore. I walked past the first table, and a book caught my eye. I walked another 20 steps, stopped and went back. The title that caught my eye was *Cleopatra's Secret Diaries*. The thought of learning the most intimate secrets of one of the world's most famous lovers definitely intrigued me.

JAMES BONNET

In asking why a particular title has been used, the reader should be aware that there are many possible attitudes that a writer may assume toward his [short] story and toward his potential audience: flippant, contemptuous, ironic, soberly serious, etc.

JARVIS A. THURSTON

I'm pretty careful about titles. I always believe that a short title is better than a long title and I like (when possible) to have one-word titles such as "Nightfall" or *Foundation*. What's more, I like to have a title that describes the content of the story without giving it away, but which, when the story is finished, is seen by the reader to take on an added significance.

ISAAC ASIMOV

Three

What is it like to be a famous, or even not so famous writer? Maralyn Lois Polak, in *The Writer as Celebrity,* considers why some of us are so interested in the writing life:

> Few among us are not curious about the lives of writers. Writers are their own heroes, and sometimes ours: alone in their room, they reinvent worlds, create people, fulfill fantasies; there is almost no limit to what a writer can achieve through, or in, the imagination. . . . What interests me is the human being between the lines, behind the words: real people who have become known through their writing.[1]

If one is to believe what so many writers say, one wonders why they pursue such a lonely, difficult, and unfulfilling existence. Is being a writer really so difficult and painful, or do writers simply want people to accept that myth? Perhaps the truth is a combination of both.

---

1. Polak, ed., *Writer As Celebrity,* xiii.

The Writing Life

17

The Writing Life:
In General

Asking what it's like to be a writer is a lot like asking what it's like to be a dentist or an attorney. The answer depends on where you live, what you write, how successful you are, how old you are, if you're married, and how you think of yourself as a writer. But there is one thing that most writers do say about the writing life: it's lonely and frustrating. Writers seem to feel misunderstood by people who don't write and underappreciated or ignored by the reading public. Feeling isolated and forced to compete with other writers, many authors complain that their books are not adequately promoted by their publishers. Otherwise, they're a contented group of workers.

I am a writer as I might have been a doctor or a lawyer. It is so pleasant a profession that it is not surprising if a vast number of persons adopt it who have no qualifications for it. It is exciting and various. The writer is free to work in whatever place and whatever time he chooses; he is free to idle if he feels ill or dispirited.

W. SOMERSET MAUGHAM

[I]f I hadn't been a writer, I'd have been a bum. This would not necessarily have been unwelcome.

WILLIAM SAROYAN

The professional writer who spends his time becoming other people and places, real or imaginary, finds he has written his life away and has become almost nothing.

V. S. PRITCHETT

I find working writers to be among the happiest folks in the world. Among the unhappiest are those who are not working and have endless questions. You do not want to get within a block of these people. The Great Suck—big bottom lip, the sulk, the neurotic and despondent vortex. But the working writers are happy like un-prosecuted felons.

BARRY HANNAH

We are not geniuses, most of us who write novels, but we are, many of us, people who have chosen to live the surrogate life of the imagination. We have, perhaps, settled for that state which Wallace Stevens speaks of. "The final belief," he said, "is to believe in a fiction which you know to be a fiction, there being nothing else."

BRIAN MOORE

Writing is life. . . . Writers need their writing; they need their imaginary worlds in order to find peace in, or make sense of, the real world.

TERRY BROOKS

I'm egocentric in the sense that I live inside my own head most of the time, and I'm fascinated by my own thoughts. . . . Nothing has ever happened to me in any real sense. I haven't met famous people. I haven't been involved in world-shaking events. I haven't done unusual things like climb Mount Everest. I've led a very quiet life.

ISAAC ASIMOV

Many people hear voices when no one is there. Some of them are called mad and are shut up in rooms where they stare at the walls all day. Others are called writers and they do pretty much the same thing.

MEG CHITTENDEN

For a person to discover that she or he does *not* have a calling to write can be good news. Consider committing your life in an impossibly difficult, underpaid profession that is not right for you.

STEPHEN KOCH

Among all the home businesses touted these days, I can think of none that is easier to get into, cheaper to start, or offers more potential for recognition, respect, and reward than nonfiction book writing. It is, in my opinion, the ultimate dream job.

MARC McCUTCHEON

Most writers enjoy only two brief periods of happiness. First, when what seems like a glorious idea comes flashing into mind, and secondly, when a last page has been written and you have not yet had time to consider how much better it all ought to have been.

J. B. PRIESTLEY

Writing is not a profession but a vocation of unhappiness. I don't think an artist can ever be happy.

GEORGES SIMENON

I think aspiring writers need as much *dis*couragement as we can muster. Nobody should undertake the life of a fiction writer—so unrenumerative, so maddeningly beset by career vagaries—who has any other choice in the matter. Learn a trade! Flannery O'Connor said it best: "People are always asking me if the university stifles writers. I reply that it hasn't stifled enough of them."

GERALD HOWARD

I believe that for many writers, the hardest time is that dead spot after college (where they're wonder-children, made much of) and before their first published work.

ANNE TYLER

There is suffering in every life. There is more, perhaps, when it is our business to see it. But there can also be great beauty. If that's the way you want to play the cards, all of the struggle and loneliness of the job can be made into joy. We chose this, after all, we write because we wanted to do it more than anything else, and even when we hate it, there is nothing better.

ANN PATCHETT

Writing, like other creative and artistic pursuits, tend to be romanticized by many and vilified by some. Writers in the U.S. are seen as special, peculiar but mythical people whose lives have a certain magical charm, or, alternatively, as drunken, neurotic wastrels who sponge off the government and do no work. Sometimes, unhappily, writers themselves perpetrate these myths.

JUDITH BARRINGTON

If you're working at an outside job to support yourself while writing, something's got to give. Don't let it be sleep. Give up your social life. If you aren't prepared to put your writing first, you aren't really a writer. If you want to succeed, you've got to organize your priorities. Sleeping is more important than partying.

RITA MAE BROWN

To write is to invite angry censure from those who don't write, or who don't write in quite the way you do, for whom you may seem a threat.

JOYCE CAROL OATES

I think writing tends to deny you a full life. Writing is incompatible with everything. It's incompatible with having children, with having a job. You can't do anything.

PAUL THEROUX

Writers when they're writing live in a spooky, clamorous silence, a state somewhat like the advanced stages of prayer but without prayer's calming benefits. A writer turns his back on the day and the night and its large and little beauties, and tries . . . to fashion other days and nights with words. It's absurd. Oh, it's silly, dangerous work indeed.

JOY WILLIAMS

Genius did not need to be rootless, disenfranchised, or alienated. A writer could have a family, a job, and even live in a suburb.

JOHN CHEEVER

I don't think writers are comfortable in each other's presence. . . . There's always an acute status consciousness relating to how high or low a writer exists in the opinion of the person he's talking to.

JOSEPH HELLER

My theory is that writers don't much like each other. Nor can they— their relationships with each other are too complicated. I can't understand how two writers can be married to each other any more than I can fathom how two actors can be. It seems to me that the more contact writers have with other writers, the more vitriolic they are on the subject of one another. If a writer is only known from afar, through his or her written word or an occasional meeting at a writers' conference, the observations about that person are more restrained. It is daily contact, like stone rubbing stone, that most often produces sparks.

JAMES CHARLTON

When you write, you align yourself with others who are engaged in the same strange, exhilarating pursuit. Although you may sometimes feel alone as you sit at your desk trying to release the next phrase from your pen, you aren't alone. At the same instant, hundreds of thousands of writers are sitting at their desks or kitchen tables, speaking into tape recorders, or pacing the floor searching for a word (perhaps the word you're searching for).

REBECCA McCLANAHAN

Every time a writer tells the truth about a manuscript (or book), to a friend-author, he loses that friend, or sees that friendship dim and fade away to a ghost of what it was formerly. Every time a writer tells the truth about a manuscript (or book), to a stranger-author, he makes an enemy. If the writer loves his friend and fears to lose him, he lies to his friend. But what's the good of straining himself to lie to strangers? And, with like insistence, what's the good of making enemies anyway?

JACK LONDON

Writers don't have to destroy their friendships with people in order to write.

WILLIAM STYRON

I'm against the literary world. No cocktail parties, nothing. In France they say I have written too much. The critics don't matter to me. . . . Anyway, I'm a lone wolf and always have been.

GEORGES SIMENON

Your battle is not with other authors, your battle is with what you put on paper.

J. P. DONLEAVY

[W]riters, in their own curious way, battle for survival in a creative combat zone as tense and frustrating as anything found in the business community. Confined to a frightening solitude and battered by rejection, they had better have protection—the shrapnel is flying everywhere.

LEONARD S. BERNSTEIN

[E]nvy is a natural by-product of the achieving life. . . . If a writer sees envy as a sign of some kind of moral weakness or character failing—a view often engendered and reinforced in childhood—the effect on his or her work can be quite debilitating.

DENNIS PALUMBO

It used to be a fever with me, a compulsion, a madness: to go into a bookstore, head straight for the brand-new books, flip right to the back of the jacket and see if the author was young or old, my age or even—rats!—younger. Envy is a vocational hazard for most writers. It festers in one's mind, distracting one from one's own work, at its most virulent even capable of rousing the sufferer from sleep to brood over another's triumph.

BONNIE FRIEDMAN

[Y]ou are probably going to have to deal with it [jealousy], because some wonderful, dazzling successes are going to happen for some of the most awful, angry, undeserving writers you know—people who are, in other words, not you.

ANNE LAMOTT

Better to think of *writing*, of what one does as an activity, rather than an identity—to write; I write; we write; to keep the calling a verb rather than a noun; to keep working at the thing, at all hours, in all places so that your life does not become a pose, a pornography of wishing.

LORRIE MOORE

I still have that overlag of feeling that I am *pretending* to be an author.

AGATHA CHRISTIE

The frightening fact remains that aside from one's writer friends, *nobody cares if you write or not*. And that is the truth. Nobody but you cares whether you will ever make your mark. Nobody else gets to make their mark—what makes you think you're so goddamn special?

JANET FITCH

[Writing is] such an inessential thing. Nobody cares if you do it, and nobody cares if you don't. . . . Life tugs at you. It's not as if there's a profession for writers out there; there isn't even a fraternity. You may have friends who are writers, but they can't write your books. I don't think writers *have* careers—my work doesn't exist separately from my life.

RICHARD FORD

Writing is a painful trade with a high casualty rate. Most writers end in partial or total failure. They might fight despair in youth, fear in maturity, and the cumulative evidence of declining powers in age.

PAUL JOHNSON

The seat of my office chair, in use for 25 years, is wearing out, my office rug is wearing out, and I am wearing out. As the Chinese say, "It's later than you think."

H. L. MENCKEN

The only thing, I think, that happens to a writer as the years go by is a disturbing sense of impatience that time grows short. There's a built-in egotism to this. The quiet desperation a writer feels that he has yet to write the definitive play or book inside his head. It also assumes that a public waits with baited breath for his final and comprehensive word.

ROD SERLING

There are several compensations for growing older as a writer, as you get to know yourself better, in your writing inclinations and so on. One gets more cunning, improves one's technique slightly as one gets older.

KINGSLEY AMIS

Writers are most fortunate of all in not having to retire when they grow older. Like actors, they may have a big public, but the public does not care how writers look. The thoughts of sixty or seventy are not absurd or pitiable as faces of the same age may be when revealed to a great public. If you embrace the writing profession it is a close and long embrace. It lasts for life and may be as vital at the end of life as it was in the first young approach.

MARGARET CULKIN BANNING

A writer's life is hard. Everybody says so, and everybody is right.

STEPHEN KOCH

I happen to be in a very tough business where there are no alibis.

ERNEST HEMINGWAY

Most business and many professions thrive on good company but the writer asks people to be quiet, asks to be left alone, asks not to be called to the telephone so that he may spin out an interminable tale that will translate the pain and ecstasy of life into understandable terms.

JOHN CHEEVER

Writing is the one occupation wherein nobody else ever sees you at work. They will see you in bowling alleys, on the golf course, at parties, at meetings, at various events taking place at any time of day or night. All of which leads non-writers to Conclusion A: *Writers don't work,* and Conclusion B: *Writers are available for whatever purpose you wish to put them to.*

HILLARY WAUGH

[W]riting novels is something you have to believe in to keep going. It's a fairly thankless job when no one is paying you to do it. And you don't really know if it's ever going to get into the bookshops.

J. K. ROWLING

Male writers have always been able to study their craft in university or coffeehouse, group themselves into movements or coteries, search out predecessors for guidance or patronage, collaborate or fight with their contemporaries. But women through most of the nineteenth century were barred from the universities, isolated in their own homes, chaperoned in travel, painfully restricted in friendship. The personal give-and-take of the literary life was closed to them. Without it, they studied with a special closeness the works written by their own sex, and developed a sense of easy, almost rude familiarity with the women who wrote them.

ELLEN MOERS

My idea of being a good teacher [at Smith], writing a book on the side, and being an entertaining homemaker, cook and wife is rapidly evaporating. I want to write first, and being kept apart from writing, from giving myself a chance to really devote myself to developing this "spectacular promise" that the literary editors write me about when they reject my stories, is really very hard.

SYLVIA PLATH

Women are different from men in that they have so many small domestic things with which to occupy themselves. . . . I think I could spend my whole day doing such things, with just a little time for reading, and be quite happy. But it isn't *really* enough; soon I shall be discontented with myself, out will come the novel and after I've written a few pages I shall feel on top of the world again.

BARBARA PYM

Writing at its best is a lonely life. Organizations for writers palliate the writer's loneliness but I doubt if they improve his writing. He grows in public stature as he sheds his loneliness and often his work deteriorates. For he does his work alone, and if he is a good enough writer, he must face eternity or the lack of it each day.

ERNEST HEMINGWAY

To write, you must concentrate, concentrate long and hard, and being alone is the price of that concentration. It takes years of self-imposed quarantine to write even a bad novel.

TOBIAS WOLFF

Life is short, and the struggle that I have is not to be in touch with people; it's *not* to be in touch with people, so that I can have time to do my own work.

STEPHEN JAY GOULD

On the whole, professional writers are a lot of whining bastards who wouldn't last a day in a real job. . . . The true mortification of being a writer is having to meet other writers from time to time, and listen to their mundane egotistical rantings.

DUNCAN McLEAN

Getting Started

Writers come from different backgrounds and walks of life. Their stories of how they got started are just as varied and, in some cases, unique. Some claim to have known from early childhood that they were destined to write. Others stumbled into writing or started later in life when they had the time or economic security. For some, writing is a form of therapy or something they do to relax. Writers who have gotten published talk about overcoming rejection through hard work and persistence. They talk about gaining respect for the craft and the importance of developing a professional attitude toward one's work. In the field of commercial writing, there aren't many stories of early, overnight success.

I didn't begin to write out of political awareness. I'd been writing since I was nine years old. I published my first adult story when I was fifteen.

NADINE GORDIMER

I think I was born with the impression that what happened in books was much more reasonable, and interesting, and *real*, in some ways, than what happened in life. I hated childhood, and spent much of it sitting behind a book waiting for adulthood to arrive. When I ran out of books I made up my own.

ANNE TYLER

When I first set about, at age twenty, to write a novel, I approached the prospect with all due trepidation. It seemed a presumptuous undertaking, and indeed it was, in a number of ways. . . . I went ahead and perpetrated my maiden novel, and it was an unpublishable travesty . . . but I felt immediately at home in the form, as if my hands and feet had been unshackled.

JOHN BARTH

I wanted to write novels, but I thought it was presumptuous to think I could write them and get them published, so I thought I'd better get a job. I had a friend in advertising. I went and talked to her. She was running around her office in a T-shirt, she was funny, she was making a lot of money, and she said, this is easy. So I said, OK, I can do that while I'm trying to write novels.

JAMES PATTERSON

In the winter of 2002, I had just completed my MFA degree and was planning to write a novel. I was 25, living in a cheap Brooklyn studio, working a bunch of part-time jobs to keep afloat. I had already been in and out of several crappy relationships, and I was haunted by the question of why men do the weird, mean things they do. So I decided that the novel I was going to write would be a love story, but from a man's perspective—and he would get his heart broken (hah!).

LAUREN GRODSTEIN

Early in my writing career, I managed to turn out three novels, one right after another, while I was married, raising two children, keeping house, and working full time as a medical secretary. Those novels were never published and netted me not one red cent, but the work was essential. Writing those books prepared the way for the fourth book, which was published and got me launched as a professional writer.

SUE GRAFTON

When I first began writing, it was much more instinctive. Now, my work is much more thought out. I recognize the importance of a strong storyline in a way I didn't before.

ERICA JONG

When I read women's biographies and autobiographies, even accounts of how they got started in writing, almost every one of them had a little anecdote which told about the moment someone gave them permission to do it. A mother, a husband, a teacher . . . somebody said, "Okay, go ahead—you can do it."

TONI MORRISON

Writers need *both* some kind of permission to go ahead, *and* the will to forge ahead even without that permission.

STEPHEN KOCH

[Writing] mentors are extremely hard to come by. The ones who are generous might not really have anything to teach you. The ones who are brilliant often prefer to keep their brilliance to themselves.

ANN PATCHETT

From the beginning, writing meant freedom, a spreading of wings, and once I got the first inkling that others were reached by what I wrote, an assumption arose that some kind of public business was happening inside me, that what perplexed or moved me must move others. It was sort of a blessing I invented for myself.

ARTHUR MILLER

[A]nyone can *become* a writer. . . . The trick is not in *becoming* a writer, it is *staying* a writer. Day after week after month after year. Staying in there for the long haul.

HARLAN ELLISON

At some time or another, most everyone fancies they have a story to tell. . . . But few of these people actually manage to get the story on paper, fewer still stick with it long enough to go through several drafts, and fewer still move on to complete numerous stories.

ALEXANDER STEELE

Most writers, whether they take courses in creative writing or not, are kick-started—that is, they begin by imitating and emulating the literature that gives them the biggest kicks.

DAVID LODGE

There are people who have never studied writing who are fully capable of being writers. I know this because I am an example. I was a part-time registered nurse, a wife, and a mother when I began publishing. I'd taken no classes, had no experience, no knowledge of the publishing world, no agent, no contacts.

ELIZABETH BERG

When we start out as writers we *need* to explore our own talents. We can't possibly know where we will write most comfortably until we've followed various leads. We may not even be sure whether we are fiction or nonfiction writers. I have known successful nonfiction writers who long to write fiction but somehow lack the flair. Perhaps one of the answers to satisfaction in any creative work is to accept our own limitations, whatever they are, while still continuing to hone our skills so we can push out those limits for as long as we write. In the end, of course, we need compete only with ourselves.

PHYLLIS A. WHITNEY

Pick a subject that *means* something to you, emotionally as well as intellectually. . . . If you ignore your real feelings, which is perilously easy to do, or if you try to write with just your head, the result will be phony, bloodless prose, and the labor of writing may be excruciating.

JOHN R. TRIMBLE

I read the essays George Plimpton had done for *Paris Review* about how Hemingway and other great ones got their paragraphs hung together, and I tried to diagnose my own talents, and lack of them. I decided I was adept at description, good at moving narration along, and dialogue was no problem. I had no idea whether I could develop a plot or how I could shape characters.

TONY HILLERMAN

I remember very distinctly reading a funny ghost or terror story by Robert Bloch. He started me on my writing career. I just fell apart with laughter, and I would call my friends and read the entire story to them. And I caught fire. I wanted to write something like that.

RICHARD MATHESON

When I began to write I did so as though it were the most natural thing in the world. I took to it as a duck takes to water. I have never quite got over my astonishment at being a writer. . . . My language was commonplace, my vocabulary limited, my grammar shaky and my phrases hackneyed. But to write was an instinct that seemed as natural to me as to breathe, and I did not stop to consider if I wrote well or badly.

W. SOMERSET MAUGHAM

The most difficult, even frightening, step for an aspiring writer is transforming the marvelous creative imaginings in his head into words on a blank sheet of paper. Somehow, the imagined words become clumsy and awkward when written down. Yet, writing them down is what writing is basically all about. . . . The best way to ease into that is to keep a daily journal.

IRVING WALLACE

A writing career can begin at any point in one's life, even without prior writing experience, and any set of circumstances may give rise to it. It's never too late to start.

IAN JACKMAN

In England, a small country the size of some American states, a young writer can go to London, frequent the right Hampstead pub, meet literary people, begin to do a few of the chores of literary journalism—a book review here, a little article there, a poem, a critical essay—and in that way begin a literary apprenticeship. The United States is too big a country for that.

WALLACE STEGNER

This is how it works: You've always wanted to be a writer, but instead you decide you should become a health care worker. You go to school for four years. You are at your first day of your new job, listening to an orientation, and you realize you really did want to be a writer. You quit your job, go to the library with a notebook, and begin page one of the great American novel. You are halfway through page one when you decide it is too hard to be a writer. You want to open a café so writers can come in and sip the best *caffelatte* and write all afternoon. You open the café. You are serving *caffelatte* to all the writers in your town. It is a Tuesday. You look out at your customers and see they are writing and you are not. You want to write.

NATALIE GOLDBERG

19

Workshops, Creative Writing Classes, and Writers' Conferences

In a reader's Amazon.com review of Joyce Carol Oates's book *The Faith of a Writer*, the lay commentator expresses the view that writing workshops, creative writing classes, writers' conferences, and books on the creative process and how to write (such as the one he's commenting on) are a waste of time. Whether writing can be taught, or if people who can write understand the process well enough to teach others, is a debate that has been raging in the literary world for decades. It seems, however, that more and more writers, and those who want to learn from them, are rejecting the point of view expressed by this Amazon reviewer:

> Why exactly do writers compose these crazy self-help manuals anyway? Writing is something that can never be taught. And maxims like "explore your mind" and "discover your voice" aren't really all that helpful anyway. Most great writers . . . are gifted people. They don't now how or why they write so well, they just do it. Trying to explain how they gather inspiration is a waste of time. Hemingway said if you talk about your own writing then you will be tarnishing something sacred. And I agree with that sentiment. Stop trying to analyze your writing. Instead, just write, and be grateful that you can write. Because most of us can't. Talking about craft is stupid.[1]

As late as 1920, there weren't many, if any, good books on writing craft and there were virtually no educational programs devoted to creative writing.

---

1. The reviewer is Jerry Reynolds.

So where did James Joyce, Thomas Mann, Willa Cather, F. Scott Fitzgerald, Ernest Hemingway, and Gertrude Stein, all of whom wrote at that time, learn their craft? They read. They read a lot. And they analyzed the hell out of what they read. They also discussed things with other writers, often in cool expatriate locations, and that's also a good thing to do.

ALEXANDER STEELE

Unfortunately, the most daunting problems writers face are seldom considered at courses and conferences. These gatherings usually emphasize basic principles of good writing: show don't tell; use of active verbs; be sparing with adjectives and adverbs; make effective use of detail. Students learn about story structure and pacing and transitions and points of view. Advice is given on how to approach publishers. Such lessons are valuable, even invaluable. But mastering the elements of style can't produce the will to keep writing. The hardest part of being a writer is not getting your commas in the right place but getting your head in the right place. Where help is really needed is in the area of countering anxiety, frustration and despair.

RALPH KEYES

But you can't *teach* writing, people tell me. And I say, "Who the hell are you, God's dean of admissions?"

ANNE LAMOTT

How can anyone "teach" writing when he himself, as a writer, is never sure what he is doing? . . . Nobody can teach the geography of the undiscovered. All he can do is encourage the will to explore, plus impress upon the un-experienced a few of the dos and don'ts of voyaging.

WALLACE STEGNER

Some well-known writers are disdainful of anyone being able to teach creative writing in a meaningful way. They fear that what is being taught is mechanical "factory fiction" rather than worthwhile art that reflects the human condition in an entertaining way. In my view, this is a disingenuous attitude, because books or classes in creative writing can only point the way. There is no magic formula, and the ambitious but uninspired writer who searches for it will never succeed. Studying writing through analysis, or, more accurately diagnosis, is not a justification for encouraging or perpetuating mediocrity.

PETER RUBIE

Talent cannot be taught, but techniques of writing can be shared and thus stimulate whatever talent a writer already has. My experience has been that one of the most effective ways to teach the techniques of writing is to compare the different early versions of a writer's published work.

DAVID MADDEN

I think that out of seven years of teaching [at the University of Pennsylvania] I found maybe two [students] who had their own voice, in my judgment. There were lots who were competent but only two who were startling.

PAULA FOX

Unfortunately, all too many perfectly intelligent people, generally of the writing-can't-be-taught school, really believe that writers are supposed to teach themselves everything, all alone, and by magic.

STEPHEN KOCH

I think one reason you can't teach writing—and certainly not novel writing—is that young people haven't had enough experience. They may have enough to write a short story, but they haven't had enough *worldly* experience.

MARY McCARTHY

Creative-writing teachers, poor souls, must immerse themselves in slop and even take it seriously. . . . It is probably impossible to teach anyone to be a good writer. You can teach people how to read, possibly.

WILLIAM H. GASS

Most writers who teach in academia aren't really academics. The majority of people who teach in MFA programs, I think, tend to be working writers who just need the gig.

JAMES HYNES

When I went to writing school, I craved rules. I craved a mentor, and the revelation of secrets, and the permission to write scads, and most of all I craved the confirmation that I could write. In other words, I was like practically everyone else.

BONNIE FRIEDMAN

Go to the most celebrated writing program that you can win admission to. Its director is likelier to know which good writers are also effective mentors and coaches, and likelier to have the wherewithal to attract a staff of them.

JOHN BARTH

Ideally, a college creative writing program should accept only those applicants who have raw talent; but of course that's impossible for many reasons, one being that talent often remains hidden behind timidity until the junior or senior year.

MARTIN RUSS

If I had to say one thing about classes in writing, it would be this: You don't need them. That's not to say I don't think they are extremely valuable. I have taken classes in fiction writing, screenplay writing, and "writing from your own experience"; but I didn't take any classes until after I was published, and for me, that made a big difference. It kept me from being so vulnerable. It kept me from paying too much attention to what someone else said before I fully understood myself as a writer.

ELIZABETH BERG

One of the oddities of creative writing courses is that there exists no standard theory on how to teach creative writing.

JOHN GARDNER

Anyone who will spend the money to attend a writing course must be serious about wanting to write. If you have the motivation, the program gives you the opportunity and a ready-made community of other writers to swap ideas with or compete against, depending on your inclination. So for that period, your job is to write and nothing else. Few nonprofessionals in the outside world have that opportunity.

IAN JACKMAN

One of the great benefits of creative writing class is that it gives people deadlines where they have to produce. You give them lots of opportunities to produce. The only way to get better as a writer is to write. So it gives them chances to explore things, to make mistakes, to learn from those mistakes, to learn from the mistakes of others, to learn from the success of others. To get patted on the back when they do something well, because it's good to know when something's working.

C. J. HRIBAL

If there is one reason above others for taking a writing course, it is to go through the agonizing but indispensable recognition that one's own short story, so clear, so beautiful, so powerful, and so *true*, so definite in its meaning or so well balanced in its ambiguity, has become a hundred different things for the other writers present. Even the teacher does not get your buried symbols, or, worse, does not like them.

NORMAN MAILER

Writers string together a lifetime of writing courses and delude themselves into thinking they are writing. A quick count of their production tells the story: Writers who continually frequent courses have only a few stories and articles completed. They think of themselves as writers because a writing course sounds as if writing is going on. The proof, however, is in the manuscripts.

LEONARD S. BERNSTEIN

I can think of only a handful of well-known American writers who have not taken creative writing courses, and usually not one but several.

DOROTHEA BRANDE

Writers are endlessly taught how to write a clear declarative sentence. But ask them to try something more extensive—an article or a book—and sentences leach out all over the floor like marbles.

WILLIAM ZINSSER

It's often said of aspiring young writers in creative writing courses that they write the same six stories. Old man dies; old woman dies; why I hate my mother; why I hate my father; how I lost my virginity; how I tried to and failed. That's it.

GEORGE V. HIGGINS

Creative writing courses can help the aspirant writer to acquire a descriptive vocabulary for and explicit awareness of such technical matters as (in prose fiction, for instance) point of view, narrative voice, frame-breaking, time-shifting, etc., etc., to entertain a wider range of possibilities in these respects than the writer might have discovered independently, and to appreciate how important are the choices made in these categories to the final effect of a narrative text.

DAVID LODGE

In the practice of my trade, as writer and teacher, I lie by omission, I sometimes think, as much as I tell the truth. I note, for an eager, untalented first-year student, that her story is *interesting,* that it *shows terrific energy,* that *there's some marvelous insight here* into waking up hungover on Saturday morning after a debauched night. . . . At summer writers' conferences, I am not about to tell a seventy-year-old woman that her personal diaries, recorded since World War II and bound in leather, need to be buried or burned before she can think to write what consumes her, the story of her life.

FREDERICK BUSCH

Sometimes . . . [writing] instructors have their own jealousies and agendas. Some enjoy the process of talking about writing more than writing itself.

JAN BURKE

Recently, I've learned that I can teach a kid how to write far more efficiently if the student comes to my office where I can take a page of what he's written, put it down on my desk and rewrite it for him. Then I hand him the page and get him to admit that what I've done is better than what he's done. Then I give him another page and have him do to that page what I've just done to the other.

STANLEY ELKIN

Don't be too complimentary to the one student who is unusually intelligent and articulate and/or talented. . . . If you acknowledge the relative brilliance of such students in any way, their classmates will begin to think of them as teacher's pets.

MARTIN RUSS

On the first day in my intermediate [writing] class, I ask the students to write down their ten favorite books of fiction and their authors. A lot of them can't name ten. A lot of them fill in with genre writers, thrillers and whatnot.

T. C. BOYLE

I want my students to see that most aspects of a literary work are down-to-earth matters that are perfectly understandable to a moderately intelligent reader using common sense. Throughout my high school and undergraduate education, I encountered teachers who tried to elevate literature to a level apprehensible only to an elite few. . . . The message of that kind of teaching is that there is such an immense distance between literature and the student that the idea of any but the most gifted student having literary aspirations is absurd.

DAVID HUDDLE

You can talk to people about how they should structure their sentences or how information should unfold, but I think, in writing classes, one of the big things that people don't talk about enough is content.

A. M. HOLMES

[T]he first value of a writer's workshop is that it makes the young writer feel not only not abnormal but virtuous.

JOHN GARDNER

[Workshops are] dangerous. In some groups, nobody knows what they're doing; it's not led by someone who is knowledgeable about the craft itself. I don't know that someone leading the workshop has to be published, but it wouldn't hurt to have someone who at least has a clue about structure and rules of fiction.

TERRY McMILLAN

It's quite true that fiction can't be taught; but you can pass along a few shortcuts and get [students] interested in the craft of it. I don't think any student wastes his time in a good fiction workshop, not even the [untalented] ones.

MARTIN RUSS

[Workshop-influenced fiction] displays the hallmarks of committee effort: emotional restraint and the lack of linguistic idiosyncrasy, no vision, just voice; no fictional world of substance and variety, just a smooth surface of diaristic, autobiographical, and confessional speech.

CHRIS ALTACUISE

Workshops taught me to trust my instincts. When I was writing, I might have known that part of my story was weak, but I hoped no one would notice. People would pounce on those parts I knew needed work. Once I know something's wrong, I have to trust myself and fix it.

JUDY BUDNITZ

I think for any writer who wants to be serious about writing, just being in a workshop, if it's a good workshop, is just really the place to be.

JOHN ROWELL

When I look back at Bread Loaf from a distance of thirteen years, I can't imagine why everyone there didn't go nuts. Many did, of course. The mix—of ex-lovers, agents, editors, prize-winners, prize-losers, prize-givers, prize-takers-away, or [magazine] Auditors who hoped to be Contributors—was toxic. Envy was epidemic.

GEOFFREY WOLFF

Creative writing classes and workshops tend to be gentler than [writers'] conferences, but in all of these situations you may find yourself sitting around a table with a number of other writers who feel morally and aesthetically compelled to rip your story to threads.

ANNE LAMOTT

I've come to believe that the most important function of writers' conferences is the opportunity they afford writers to confer with one another. The company of our fellows at such gatherings far outweighs the value of what the lecturers tell us or what criticism we get of our work.

LAWRENCE BLOCK

A [writers'] conference is dependent on everyone involved, and in a workshop setting, a harsh word can be devastating. There will almost always be someone who likes to give harsh critiques for the sake of being harsh. There may be someone whose ego is simply too big for the rest of the group.

KEVIN JAMES KAGE

I'm always embarrassed when I go to writing conferences. Crowds of people who "studied English in college" and know how to diagram sentences stand around sipping espressos, chatting about their favorite authors and comparing the classics. Then, inevitably, someone will turn to me and say, "So, who's your favorite 17th century novelist?"

STEVEN JAMES

Rejection

The *Guinness Book of World Records* has a category for the highest-number of publisher rejections for a manuscript. The current record is 106 for a book called *World Government Crusade* by Gilbert Young.[1] Because one might not be proud of that distinction, however, the record is likely to be inaccurate. For example, Robert Pirsig claims to have received 121 rejections for *Zen and the Art of Motorcycle Maintenance*.[2]

In his novel *Love Warps the Mind a Little*, John Dufresne's protagonist, a struggling writer who has quit his day job to write full time, is hit hard by rejection:

> I got back two more form rejections on my stories. First, I felt de-flated. What the hell do they want anyway? And would they know it if they saw it? Does it go in one eye and out the other? My limbs were like pig iron. I couldn't move. I just sat there on the couch, staring at my pages, sluggish and thickheaded.[3]

Rejection is one aspect of the writing life that almost all writers, including successful authors, have in common. When discussing the difficulties of the creative life, dealing with rejection is often one of the first subjects an author will raise. As more people write and fewer companies publish, the odds of seeing one's work in print are not weighted in the writer's favor. As a result, more and more books are being self- and vanity-published. To some writers, this is not the proper response to rejection. Instead of breaking through the rejection wall, these authors are going around it; and in the end, they remain dissatisfied and, in reality, still unpublished.

1. Cited in Henderson and Bernard, eds., *Rotten Reviews and Rejections*, 195.
2. Burnham, *For Writers Only*, 155.
3. Dufresne, *Love Warps the Mind a Little*, 47.

I once decorated a guest bathroom all with rejection slips.

JOHN JEROME

Rejection slips are the most misunderstood part of writing. We all say we hate them when in fact we love them. Why else do we pin them on the walls or paste them in scrapbooks? We love them because in spite of their message they make a clear announcement: *We are writers.* . . . At least rejection slips indicate that something is getting written and something is getting submitted.

LEONARD S. BERNSTEIN

Over and over again, you hear stories about very famous people who suffered all kinds of rejections. These stories never did much for me. Neither did stories of people who kept all their rejection slips. Rejection slips that have encouraging messages might be worth keeping; otherwise, get rid of them.

ELIZABETH BERG

There is a story in the trade that a publisher once accepted a book and sent it to an artist for illustrations. When he had finished, the artist sent the manuscript back—and it was returned to him with a rejection slip.

ANDRE BERNARD

Pearl Buck received a rejection for one of her short stories the very week she was notified she had won the Nobel Prize for literature!

DENNIS E. HENSLEY

I have collected enough rejection slips for my short stories to paper four or five good-sized rooms. During that rejection slip period I was always reading the autobiography of writers, and in Arthur Train's *My Day in Court* I found a piece of rather wonderful advice. He said that if he were a beginning writer one of the things that he would do would be to enter Mabel L. Robinson's course in the short story at Columbia University. Needless to say I promptly applied for admission to the class.

ANN PETRY

What writer doesn't know the scene of fetching his or her precious story from the mailbox and then brooding over the rejection slip, analyzing it with a heightened sense of meaning.

JANET FITCH

Learning to deal with rejection is absolutely critical for writers because it's part of the territory. The trick is to see rejection as part of the process rather than an insurmountable obstacle.

TRAVIS ADKINS

What I clearly remember is my first rejection. . . . In it was a pre-printed postcard from *The Atlantic Monthly*. . . . I read the rejection. My heart flew up with joy! They had *read* my story! Someone had actually read my story, not thrown it in the trash! And they had spent a nickel to send me a postcard response! "We regret . . ." it said, so courteously. . . . I have also received a rejection that sent me to bed for two days, weeping, inconsolable.

SOPHY BURNHAM

[W]hen you get used to being disappointed, the recovery time gets shorter, the time you need before you get back to work gets shorter and shorter.

COLSON WHITEHEAD

[R]ejections don't distress me for various reasons: one of them is that some of my fiction many years ago was not only published but reprinted, although it was poor or no good at all. The editors who printed the work suffered from the same poor judgment as I did.

DELMORE SCHWARTZ

My favorite rejection letter was from an agent who said, "We don't have time to take on new clients, and if we did, we would not take you." But I kept trying. My second book got published. The first one never did.

LISA SCOTTOLINE

An editor rejected my first [mystery] novel with these words: "I think it would take something really unusual to convince us to take on a new mystery series—an Armenian/Jewish plumber who solves cases by listening at people's drain pipes, or something like that."

WILLIAM G. TAPPLY

Some degree of self-doubt is essential to a writer's equilibrium. The rejection of a manuscript, though painful, is also proof that [one's] work is being subjected to serious consideration, and that the writing that was not rejected must therefore be successful. Where there is nothing but rejections, then the writer can only conclude that he is a misunderstood genius or should be in another line of work.

WILLIAM MAXWELL

[A] rejection . . . may well reflect more unfavorably on the editor's ability than on yours.

JUDITH APPELBAUM

Rejection is part of any creative act. To overcome, I immediately get back to the keyboard and work harder. Then I think of Hemingway, F. Scott Fitzgerald, Jack London, all of whom were rejected hundreds of times.

CORK MILLNER

Rejection follows rejection. . . . You see the haunting thought comes that perhaps I have been kidding myself all these years, myself and other people—that I have nothing to say or no art in saying nothing.

JOHN STEINBECK

One thing about failing repeatedly: If you're still doing it after you've failed that much, you really mean it.

ALICE SEBOLD

A rejection of a story is not a rejection of the writer. It is no crime to be rejected or even a sin. Editors do not hate a writer when they reject a manuscript and do not therefore plot the writer's destruction.

ISAAC ASIMOV

The worst job in the world is writing. You're alone, you're with yourself, and either you trust your own judgment or you don't. And if your judgment is questioned enough times, you begin to question your own judgment as a writer. If enough people turn you down, you begin to question your own skill. Who else do you have to depend on? It's you against them.

ALAN LANDSBURG

Next to come to mind (as a bad memory) was my original literary agent delivering her verdict on my first novel. Don't want to show it to anyone, she said. Why not? It's a bad book. Have to think of your reputation as well as mine. Why bad? It falls between the stools, halfway betwixt mainstream and mystery. No way to promote it. And where does the book-seller shelve it? Stick to nonfiction, said my agent. I can sell that for you. How about me rewriting it? Well, if you do, get rid of the Indian stuff.

TONY HILLERMAN

The world of publishing is a potentially hostile environment, especially for the writer.

JEFF HERMAN

Virtually all magazines use printed rejection slips. Some make their points succinctly, with little attempt to soften the blow. The basic message is straightforward: "We've decided not to publish your story." Some rejection forms make a half-hearted effort to explain away the obvious: "We're not reading fiction for the time being," or, "another editor may think differently."

C. MICHAEL CURTIS

In those days [early 1960s], it was the custom at *The New Yorker* to attach a little form letter to rejected stories, but, if they were better than most, to write in, by hand, "Sorry"; if they were better still, "Sorry, thanks"; and if they were better even than that, "Sorry, thanks, try us again." The stories, two-hundred and fifty of them a week, were, with one exception, amazingly bad. . . . But I thought, these people have made this effort. You can really only judge a writer by his best work. Maybe these are all just lapses. I wrote, "Sorry, thanks, try us again," on all of them. . . . I had to stop writing the notes.

RENATA ADLER

I was trying to get my . . . work published, first with poetry, then with articles and stories. But they got nowhere at all. There was a steady flow of rejection slips. Once in awhile, a handwritten word, *Sorry*, appeared on the slips. I was grateful for even that bit of attention. My secret was that no sooner did I put something in the mail than I wrote something else and sent it off. Each rejection was cushioned by my expectations for the other manuscripts. Too many writers put their all into one script, and when it is rejected they are devastated.

LOUIS L'AMOUR

Rejection slips are never much fun, but some are better than others. In the process of sending out your stories, you may occasionally receive "good" rejection slips, ones in which the editor has taken the time to write a brief note telling you that he enjoyed the story, inviting you to try again, or offering some suggestion for improvement. Such notes are rare and good things.

WILL ALLISON

Don't take rejection slips too seriously. I don't think they ought to send them out at all.

FRANK O'CONNOR

I have had very few rejections in a long life of writing, and I have always preferred the honesty and directness of editors who said (1) "I don't like this," or (2) "This is not suitable for us." This is a good style to adopt, inoffensive to any sensible author and an effective disguise for their own dubious motives and astounding snobbery.

KATHERINE ANNE PORTER

My career was more fortunate than a lot of people's. I published first when I was eighteen. . . . Before that I picked up about sixty rejection slips. A lot of guys pick up 400, 500, or something like that.

STEPHEN KING

In some cases, editors write a sentence or two at the bottom of the rejection [letter]. Most writers make the mistake of interpreting this as a sign of encouragement. Actually, the editor is merely showing you some kindness. After poring over your manuscript . . . these editors can recognize that you have a somewhat advanced case of writing, along with an accompanying desire for fame, and that a simple form rejection might send you running amok in a bookstore.

ROBIN HEMLEY

If you wrap all your hopes up in being accepted quickly by the first one or two places you submit to, you're likely to get discouraged and quit. . . . If you see writing as a long-term commitment, you realize that there are going to be periods of rejection and discouragement. That's just part of it. Then you're much likely to stick to it and to survive in the long run as a writer.

SCOTT SANDERS

In almost every area of life, even factoring in such real variables as luck, family of origin, and where you went to school (and with whom), cause and effect seems to apply. Work hard and things happen. Except when it comes to writing.

DENNIS PALUMBO

I live in dread that the story I am currently writing resembles those (of mine) that have been rejected. They are bad, I think. When I recognize emerging on the page a rhythm similar to the rhythm of one of those "bad" stories, or when I recognize a character that turned up in one of them, I am appalled. I want to cross it out. I want to put away from me forever everything associated with those "bad" stories because frankly I do not really understand what was wrong with them. Something was probably wrong; one must be realistic enough to admit it. Yet it feels as if my new writing comes from the same place.

BONNIE FRIEDMAN

21

Work Habits, Rituals, and Daily Word Quotas

Many people have little interest in how plumbers fix sinks or how electricians wire houses. Moreover, in terms of how these skills are applied, there isn't much diversity. But when it comes to how a person produces a novel, a short story, or a work of creative nonfiction, there is plenty of interest and diversity. Published writers are always being asked when they write, how many hours a day they write, how many words they produce daily, exactly where they write, what they write with, and so forth. In the world of writing, matters such as these, referred to as work habits, are fascinating and important. Such queries often extend into the creative process itself. As John R. Trimble notes in *Writing with Style*, no two writers get the job done the same way:

> It's generally recognized that most people have highly individual ways of getting words onto paper. Writers themselves, at least, recognize this, even when their writing manuals don't. Some writers love outlines; others gag over them. Some writers dash off their drafts at high speed; others, known as "bleeders," tend to be mentally constipated or perfectionistic, and refuse to move on from one sentence to the next until the first has been mercilessly flailed. Some writers spend the bulk of their time lavishly researching their subject; others spend the bulk of their time revising—which can also mean doing their research after the fact. . . . Still, most of us are desperate enough to be always shopping for alternate strategies, bits of which we might later incorporate into our habitual method.[1]

---

1. Trimble, *Writing with Style*, 13, 14.

132

The actor works before his public, the musician plays, even the painter holds court in his studio—but the writer, the writer, what does he look like, what does he do, behind that fastened door? It can't be he just sits down at a desk, at nine o'clock, and opens his typewriter, like any junior clerk?

DAPHNE DU MAURIER

I know very little about the way in which other writers work. I would like to take a college course in creative writing and learn from a professor of literature how novelists achieve their effects.

ALEC WAUGH

If writing could be reduced to a formula or algorithm, everyone would do it.

JONATHAN FRANZEN

[R]eports of [author] writing habits are so at variance with each other that it is no wonder the young writer sometimes feels that his elders are all engaged in a conspiracy to delude and mislead him as to the actual process of literature.

DOROTHEA BRANDE

I have just spent a good week, alone like a hermit, and as calm as a god. I abandoned myself to a frenzy of literature; I got up at midday, I went to bed at four in the morning. . . . I smoked fifteen pipes in a day; I have written *eight pages*.

GUSTAVE FLAUBERT

I work almost constantly. For a novelist without hobbies, weekends don't make much difference. Most people don't enjoy weekends anyway; they don't know what to do with Sundays.

JOSEPH HELLER

I'm always quite nervous at the beginning of my workday. It takes me a great deal of time to get started. Once I get started, it gradually calms down a bit, but I'll do anything to keep postponing. . . . Anyway, one way or another, I manage to write about four hours a day.

TRUMAN CAPOTE

After I get up it takes me an hour and a half of fiddling around before I can get up the courage and nerve to go to work. I smoke half a pack of cigarettes, drink six or seven cups of coffee, read over what I wrote the day before. Finally there's no further excuse. I go to the typewriter. Four to six hours of it.

JAMES JONES

In actuality, no person, however rich or free of outside constraints, has time to write. True, some people have more money, energy, opportunity, or freedom from day-to-day duties than the rest of us. But nature abhors a vacuum, and each life, however privileged, must fill with something. And fill it does. By itself, all the time in the world will not make writing happen. . . . Writing only happens by writing, and only the person who writes the book can write the book.

REBECCA McCLANAHAN

Making writing a big deal tends to make writing difficult. Keeping writing casual tends to keep it possible. Nowhere is this more true than around the issue of time. One of the biggest myths about writing is that in order to do it we must have great swathes of uninterrupted time.

JULIA CAMERON

It's very easy to feel guilty about taking time to write because, for so long, it's a one-way street with no money or successes coming your way. Here's how I rationalize/justify it: I don't watch any TV. The average American watches over four hours of TV a day. Instead, I write for two hours each day.

A. D. HUDLER

Men writers who are married to non-working wives—that is, wives who stay at home—have a certain advantage. Every writer needs a wife!—someone to stand guard, to cook meals, to deal with the immediate problems of house and children, and keep them out of their husbands' hair. It's more difficult for women writers, who have to do all these chores *plus* their writing.

PHYLLIS A. WHITNEY

A novel is such a long involvement; when I'm beginning a book, I can't work more than two or three hours a day. I don't know more than two or three hours a day about a new novel. Then there's the middle of the book. I can work eight, nine, twelve hours then, seven days a week—if my children let me; they usually don't.

JOHN IRVING

If one wants to write, one simply has to organize one's life in a mass of little habits.

GRAHAM GREENE

There are tricks to writing full-time—to relaxing into it, basically. My trick now [1984] is to say to myself, "Okay, do one paragraph this morning." Then I'm done with it. I never actually am done with it, unless I have an particularly appalling hangover and fall back into bed again. Once I had done that one paragraph, I think, "Well, I can do another one, and the rest of this page, maybe, and then we can go over to the next page for a while."

RAMSEY CAMPBELL

I spend most of my working day in some kind of dream state. That is to say, I get up from my bed, I shower, drink my coffee and go to my desk, which is literally ten yards from my bed. I then start, on a normal day, a process which will maybe take me eight or ten hours, writing about something that my inner eye is seeing. It's not like I'm getting up in the morning, as most people do, and stepping out onto the street and being slapped into the solid problem of how I get the car to start.

CLIVE BARKER

Most writers work alone. . . . [W]ithout the routines of an office, lone workers develop quirky work habits. Deprived of a boss or coworkers to apply the lash, they learn how to apply their own. As creative people, writers come up with imaginative ways to goose themselves, summon the muse, and avoid stepping out for a newspaper.

RALPH KEYES

I write on vacations, I write on weekends, and, occasionally, I write early in the mornings. It's going to be a long time between books.

LINDA FAIRSTEIN

Once I start work on a project, I don't stop and I don't slow down unless I absolutely have to. If I don't write every day, the characters begin to stale off in my mind—they begin to seem like characters instead of real people.

STEPHEN KING

My only ritual is to sit close enough to the typewriter so that my fingers touch the keys.

ISAAC ASIMOV

I am a completely horizontal author. . . . I can't think unless I'm lying down, either in bed or stretched on a couch with a cigarette and coffee handy. I've got to be puffing and sipping.

TRUMAN CAPOTE

As for me, I have founded what maybe a new school of writing, the peripatetic-dart-throwing school. I write for fifteen minutes, then walk about and throw darts at my dartboard to free the caged sedentary animal. . . . Next month I may go further *and write standing up!*

DELMORE SCHWARTZ

I write in the nude most of the time. We live in total isolation out in the country. . . . And it's warm most of the year in Alabama, so why wear clothes? I mean, they're just a bother.

FORREST McDONALD

When I'm working well, I wear a moving man's zip-up uniform because I perspire so freely.

ALLAN GURGANUS

I prefer to work on novels in cold weather. . . . When I can look out my window and see snow on the ground, I am impelled to go right to the typewriter; and a miserable, gloomy, raw rainy day has the same effect.

JOHN O'HARA

I write when I can and I don't write when I can't; always in the morning or the early part of the day. You get very gaudy ideas at night but they don't stand up.

RAYMOND CHANDLER

I like to start early before I can be distracted by people and events. . . . I rise at first light . . . and I start by rereading and editing everything I have written to the point I left off. That way I go through a book I'm writing several hundred times. Then I go right on . . . because I always stop at a point where I know precisely what's going to happen next. So I don't have to crank up every day.

ERNEST HEMINGWAY

I work on a manual typewriter because I like the feeling of making something happen with my hands. I like paper. I like to see the key come up and hit that paper.

DAVID McCULLOUGH

[C]onsider the pen you write with. It should be a fast-writing pen because your thoughts are always much faster than your hand. You don't want to slow up your hand . . . with a slow pen. A ballpoint, a pencil, a felt tip, for sure, are slow.

NATALIE GOLDBERG

I work on one project at a time, until it's completed, whether that takes a month like some of my stories, or seven years like some of my novels. I've never been able to think about the next thing I'm going to write while I'm writing.

JOHN BARTH

I myself cannot write with people around me—I need solitude both for concentration and for the freedom to go through without embarrassment the kind of gesturing, wincing, and mumbling I often need to get a scene right.

JOHN GARDNER

I've always worked in the room where I usually sleep, so that I sleep near my desk. . . . I write with a "dip pen," which causes all kinds of problems—everything from finding blotters to pen points—but it makes me take my time, and it gives me a real feeling of satisfaction.

SHELBY FOOTE

When it's time to get the first draft of a new book on paper—I check into a hotel and stay from Monday through Friday until it's done. I write all day. My husband joins me each evening for dinner and we catch up on the day's news. Then he goes back home and I go back to work. Once the first draft is finished, I return home and work at my computer, making revisions, adding scenes, enhancing plot.

JANETTE OKE

[T]each yourself to work in busy places, under the barrage of noises the world makes—work in rooms where children are playing, with music on, even with the television on.

RICHARD BAUSCH

What the writer needs is an empty day ahead. A big round quiet space of empty hours to, as it were, tumble about in.

CATHERINE DRINKER BOWEN

I write a lot—every day, seven days a week—and I throw a lot away. Sometimes I think I write to throw away. It's a process of distillation.

DONALD BARTHELME

What I do now [1966] is write something like an average of 8,000 words a sitting, in the middle of the night, and another about a week later, resting and sighing in between. I really hate to write. I get no fun out of it because I can't get up and say I'm working, close my door, have coffee brought to me, and sit there camping like a "man of letters" "doing his eight hour day of work" and thereby incidentally filling the printing world with a lot of dreamy self-imposed cant and bombast.

JACK KEROUAC

I keep to what amounts to a seventy-hour week, if you count all the ancillary jobs of proofreading, indexing, research and so on. In the past six years, I have averaged a book a month. . . . I'm not sure if my work habits should be imitated. I don't have set hours for working. I just write whenever I feel like, but I feel like it all the time. . . . I do very little research, because I have been reading avidly all my life and remember virtually everything I read. To back me up, however, I have developed a personal reference library in my office of some two thousand books or so in all fields.

ISAAC ASIMOV

I get up at 6:30 and work until 8:30, drinking coffee and from time to time eating a little more bread and honey; and it is delightful. Not a bell, not a bore, not a telephone; and a sense of virtue that keeps me in good temper all day.

SYLVIA TOWNSEND WARNER

I write every day from about nine in the morning to one in the afternoon. I set myself to the task of writing ten pages a day in longhand, which comes out to about five typewritten pages. The rest of the day I spend talking on the phone with my publishers, promoting my books and answering the mail.

ERICA JONG

I usually write a chapter then revise it the next day. I've gone from writing four solid hours a day to writing for one to two hours a day. I think about the next section for 24 hours, then write it quickly.

STUART WOODS

When I'm in a writing mode (eight months of the year), I am at my computer at least six days a week from 10 a.m. to about 7:30 p.m., and I require ten pages a day—my personal commitment.

ANN RULE

I write at night, from about midnight until dawn. Nights are more beautiful than days, and I feel "alive" at night. I'm a night person. Moreover, there are no interruptions at night—no telephones, no doorbells. I avoid these by sleeping during the day. It's too bad—in my opinion—that nights are so short and days are so long.

TAYLOR CALDWELL

I write from 10 AM to 6 PM, Monday to Friday. I try to write eight pages a day. When I had a 9-to-5 job, I used to write at night and on weekends, but not anymore.

ED McBAIN

On a good working day when all goes well I can complete six or seven pages, between 7:30 A.M. and 12:30 P.M., never in the afternoon and not more than three or four nights a month. I get it done in the morning or I don't get it done.

JAMES A. MICHENER

When I'm in writing mode for a novel, I get up at 4:00 AM and work for five to six hours. In the afternoon, I run for 10km or swim for 1500m (or do both), then I read a bit and listen to some music. I go to bed at 9:00 PM. I keep to this routine every day without variation.

HARUKI MURAKAMI

[I]n my 20s and 30s I usually wrote at night, roughly 10 PM to 4 AM, alone in my lit room, like a solitary balloon sailing through the night. I loved it, but social reality impeded. Now I wander [into my office] at 9 in the morning or so, and come back for awhile in the afternoon. I am a very lenient boss.

DONALD WESTLAKE

I don't structure my work in terms of hours, finding it more useful to aim at producing a certain amount of work, usually somewhere between five and ten pages depending on the sort of material I'm working on, the deadline I'm facing, and phases of the moon. My work usually takes me somewhere between two and three hours. If I'm done in an hour, I'm delighted to call it a day. If I am not done in three hours, I generally call it a day anyway; though I'm by no means delighted about it.

LAWRENCE BLOCK

22

Money, the Day Job, and the Economic Realities of Writing

Thinking you'll get rich by writing books is like thinking you'll get rich by growing corn in West Virginia. For the great majority of published authors, writing is a vocation supported by a primary occupation—the dreaded day job. During the day, writers are cops, reporters, lawyers, physicians, office clerks, bureaucrats, sales associates, receptionists, and real estate agents. The lucky ones, although they seem to complain the most, are the college professors teaching in English (Richard Russo calls them "Anguish") departments. The poet and novelist Delmore Schwartz gleefully declared himself "self-employed" after quitting his professorship at Harvard. A few years later, however, economic reality drove him back into teaching at Kenyon, then later at Princeton. Still, the Stephen Kings and J. K Rowlings of the writing world keep the dream of literary wealth and fame alive. And so do stories like this one:

> Conan Doyle, after five years as a struggling medical student, graduated from Edinburgh University in 1881. He nailed up his oculist shingle and waited for patients. Six years later he was still waiting. Lacking a practice, desperate for any kind of income, Doyle turned to writing. . . . [H]e decided to try a detective story.[1]

---

1. Irving Wallace, "The Incredible Dr. Bell," in Editors of the *Saturday Review*, eds., *Saturday Review Gallery*, 111.

Being a writer is a little bit like being a shepherd: it's quaint, people envy the solitude, but everyone knows the real money is in synthetic fibers.

ROB LONG

My generation was maybe the last in which you could set up shop as a writer and hope to make a living of it.

JOHN UPDIKE

I didn't want to write what people would pay me to write, and no one wanted to pay me for what I wanted to write.

SOPHY BURNHAM

There are only three ways in which the writing of fiction is economically feasible. One is for the writer to be born rich or to have married rich. The second is for the writer to have a full- or part-time job and write during his free time, and the third is for him to be versatile enough to write for various media.

MERLE MILLER

For every writer who makes a good living, there are 50 or so who simply make a little spare change and 5,000 who go nowhere at all. And there's simply nothing anyone can do about it.

ISAAC ASIMOV

There's a difference between a vocation and a profession. A vocation is a calling—something you are called to. A profession is something that you practice. . . . In the states, I think about 10 percent of the novel writers actually make a living out of their novel writing. The others have the vocation, but they can only partly have the profession, because they have to spend the rest of their time making money in order to keep themselves in their habit. They are word junkies. They've got to pay for their fix. I chose university teaching because there was a long summer vacation, and also because you could fake it.

MARGARET ATWOOD

I hate to hear writers complain about how hard it is to write, because anybody who can make a living at it is so lucky. I don't care how good they are, but anybody who can actually make a decent living at writing has no right to complain. That said, I hate to write.

ANDREW FERGUSON

More likely, the writer will have to find a job. Almost all full-time jobs are hard on writing, even office work where one has practically nothing to do.

JOHN GARDNER

Almost nobody makes serious money by writing fiction. Real serious means earning an advance of maybe $75,000, for a three-book deal. You'll probably have to make that advance last for three years, and you're unlikely ever to see another penny for those particular books. If you don't earn the advance—and many don't earn the advance—you won't be asked for it back—but you'll never get that sort of sum again.

REBECCA TOPE

When people ask me what I do for a living, I try to change the subject. If they persist, I tell them I teach writing, judge writing contests, edit manuscripts, and give lectures and readings. These are not lies; I do all these things. They are, in fact, what I do for a living—that is, to pay the rent and health insurance. What I do for a *life* is write, and that's the part that's hard to explain.

REBECCA McCLANAHAN

You would-be Thomas Wolfes and Gertrude Steins out there should understand *one* thing above all: likely you ain't gonna make no money as a writer. *Real* money I mean.

LARRY L. KING

[Economic] security is a kind of death, I think, and it can come to you in a storm of royalty checks beside a kidney-shaped pool in Beverly Hills or anywhere at all that is removed from the conditions that made you an artist, if that's what you are or were or intended to be. Ask anyone who has experienced the kind of success I am talking about—what good is it?

TENNESSEE WILLIAMS

[S]ome writers find their first book, written on the sly during coffee breaks at their day job, easier than their second, with the success of the first has allowed them to become full-time professional writers, with all the attendant anxieties.

DR. ALICE W. FLAHERTY

I'd advise a young writer to make a living any way he can, rather than depend entirely on his writing. That way, he can be absolutely free in his choice of subject matter, and he doesn't have to worry if he writes a book that doesn't sell.

BERNARD MALAMUD

Perhaps the worst consequence of turning full-time too soon is the cynicism that creeps into the outlook of writers who undergo repeated financial crises. While you may not vanish from the creative process, the business half can become an unendurable misery.

DONALD MAASS

My advice is that in general, no writer, no matter how talented or potentially so, should give up his or her primary source of income to pursue a full-time writing career, as there are too many possible pitfalls along the way to be reliable.

R. BARRIE FLOWERS

The truth is, having a day job often facilitates not only doing work [writing], but also the quality of the work that gets done. Artists thrive on structure, and we need regularity to our days.

JULIA CAMERON

I think there is a danger in getting all the right credentials and staying in university settings. I think a lot of young writers, developing writers, don't understand that a lot of energy can be drained out of their writing.

NANCY PEACOCK

I am sacrificing my energy, writing and versatile intellectual life for grubbing over 66 Hawthorne papers a week [at Smith] and trying to be articulate in front of a rough class of spoiled bitches. If I knew *how* to teach a short story, or a novel, or a poem I'd at least have that joy. But I'm making it up as I go along, through trial and error, mostly error. . . . I see too well the security and prestige of academic life, but it is Death to writing.

SYLVIA PLATH

I've been trying to get away from teaching for eight years now, but without any real success. . . . The trouble with [with nonteaching jobs] is that one spends so much time thinking of money and making it only in makeshifts that one is more distracted than ever.

DELMORE SCHWARTZ

Teaching is entirely different from writing, you're always up to it, or more or less up to it; there's no question of its clogging, of its not coming. It's much less subjective, and it's a very pleasant pursuit in itself. In the kind of teaching I do, conversational classes, seminars, if the students are good, which they've been most of the time, it's extremely entertaining.

ROBERT LOWELL

I've always worried that if I had to write for my job, either as an ad copywriter or a journalist or pretty much anything other than a fiction writer, I would burn out that part of my brain I need for fiction.

CHRISTIAN BAUMAN

The bookstore [I own] is a good balance to my writing. It's intellectually challenging but not emotionally demanding, and unlike writing you don't reach a peak and then dry up.

LARRY McMURTRY

Occasionally, a beginning writer will run into grave danger. Lightning will strike—he will sell a story. Once he has seen himself in print, he is a "goner." On the strength of the few hundred dollars he has earned, he will give up his job, move his wife and family into humble quarters, sit down at the typewriter and strike out as a free-lance. The chances are that he will not sell another story for months, or even years, if at all. His ability to sell a story every thirty months or so does not mean that he has "arrived." Yet, having drawn blood, he will never abandon the illusion that he is a "pro."

EDWARD UHLAN

I admire honest hacks, ghosts and pulp writers who make no claim to literary distinction, but are content selflessly to batter out reading matter for the semi-educated millions on an old typewriter, and raise large, happy families on the proceeds.

ROBERT GRAVES

I never found any money; I never won any prizes; I was never helped by anyone, aside from an occasional encouraging word. . . . No fellowships or grants came my way, because I was not eligible for any and in no position to get anything of the sort. I never expected it to be easy.

LOUIS L'AMOUR

I believe . . . that the writer who loafs after he has made a financial success is confessing that the money was all he was after in the first place.

JOHN O'HARA

New fiction writers rarely cite money as their primary motive. Indeed, even most established novelists are not in the game to get rich.

DONALD MAASS

Writing a best-seller with conscious intent to do so is, after all, a state of mind that is not without comparison to the act of marrying for money only to discover that the absence of love is more onerous than anticipated.

NORMAN MAILER

We writers are the most severely taxed group that I know of, with so few ways to take deductions.

GORE VIDAL

It is easy to say that the writer should have an occupation that provides him with his bread and butter and write in such leisure as this occupation affords him. . . . The English-speaking writer has the potentiality of such an enormous public that writing can very reasonably be adopted as a profession.

W. SOMERSET MAUGHAM

[I]f I didn't have to do it, I wouldn't [teach]. It's how I support my family, but once that initial reluctance to do anything but write and indulge in one's natural hedonism has been overcome, and you make the commitment to teach, you may as well do the best job you possibly can. I feel a considerable obligation to give those kids their tuition's worth. They pay a lot of money to come sit in the classroom with me a couple of times a week.

VANCE BOURJAILY

Being a professional writer would be like being a porn star, compelled to be combed and pointy at 9:00 sharp every morning, ready to perform private pleasures in public.

STEVEN CONNOR

It is a very American notion that being paid to do something makes us somehow more legitimate. We would actually do well to take a cue here from the world of sports and realize that just as some of our best athletes are amateurs, some of our most gifted writers may be too. They may never choose to "go professional."

JULIA CAMERON

23

Productivity

In America, writing a bestselling novel that is also critically acclaimed is not enough. In order to be regarded as a truly successful author, the writer must also be prolific. The dreaded one-book-author disease is a leper-like malady that has mainly infected American writers. Among the most famous one-book authors are Ralph Ellison, Harper Lee, Margaret Mitchell, Fred Exley, and J. D. Salinger. Yet highly prolific writers such as Stephen King, Isaac Asimov, and Joyce Carol Oates are often criticized for attenuating their talent and product by publishing too much.

If you apply to writing the same standards and methods that people regularly apply to other professions, you will take a lot of weight off your subconscious and increase your productive capacity.

AYN RAND

Evaluate how you're using your free time every day for a week—talking on the phone, reading the newspaper, watching TV, listening to the radio. All these things are bleeding away from your writing time, thinking time, preparation time. You have to structure your life to allow yourself to write.

ELIZABETH GEORGE

To be productive, we have to make writing part of our daily lives. The problem is that we view writing as a luxury, something special to allow ourselves as soon as we've taken care of the countless nagging duties that seem to come first.

SUE GRAFTON

[D]uring the past five years . . . I have managed . . . to do a lot of work. Since my sixtieth birthday I have published five books . . . and two of them have been of formidable size. All have got good notices and sold well.

No other lustrum of my life has been so productive. I often wonder, looking back over my years, whether I have got out of myself all that was there. In all probability I have.

H. L. MENCKEN

I've written about 2,000 short stories; I've only published about 300 and I feel I'm still learning. Any man who keeps working is not a failure. He may not be a great writer, but if he applies the old-fashioned virtues of hard, constant labor, he'll eventually make some kind of career for himself as a writer.

RAY BRADBURY

I don't feel very rapid or prolific to myself. Looking back [from 2001] on the alleged 50 books that I've written, many of them are quite short, some are children's books, some are collections of material that appear in other books, so in a way it's a fraudulent appearance of muchness. Some of the books are sequels, which, again, is a kind of cheating. I feel always on the edge of my last effort, my last invention, my last book.

JOHN UPDIKE

I wish I had written more. I wish I had been more prolific. I wish I had had less fear of writing, more self-confidence, less terror of it. . . . There are writers who are quite fearless, and they are prolific. But I'm a fearful writer and I don't know how to become brave.

CYNTHIA OZICK

Productivity is the *only* path to confidence.

STEPHEN KOCH

I can go months, sometimes even years, without writing a solitary word. . . . I'm just baffled, baffled, by those people who seem to publish a new book every nineteen days. There's a kind of compulsion there, or need, that I simply do not possess to any degree whatsoever.

DAVID MARKSON

A mystery writer who waits patiently for a mood to encompass him, for an idea to strike, may find starvation, or other employment, striking first. The professional in this field cannot . . . write one book every three or four years. Three or four a year would be more like it.

RICHARD LOCKRIDGE

It looks as if [mystery writer John] Creasey is in no danger of being dethroned as the king of sheer bulk, with 560 titles; his bibliography takes up ten very large pages.

JAY PEARSAL

I've slowed down. I'm now doing a book every fifteen to eighteen months. I couldn't keep that pace up.

SUE GRAFTON

I like my own writing—another secret to prolificity, since I can't wait till I write something so I can *read* it.

ISAAC ASIMOV

If a full-time writer averages a book every five years, that makes seventy-five usable pages a year, or a usable fifth of a page a day. The years that biographers and other nonfiction writers spend amassing and mastering materials match the years novelists and short story writers spend fabricating solid worlds that answer to immaterial truths. On plenty of days the writer can write three or four pages, and on plenty of other days he concludes he must throw them away. These truths comfort the anguished. They do not mean, by any means, that faster-written books are worse books. They just mean that most writers might stop berating themselves for writing at a normal, slow pace.

ANNIE DILLARD

If I work two years on one of my large books, having done a wealth of work prior to starting, that's 730 workdays, and if the book contains 730 pages, it's obvious that I produce one page of work a day. Of course I do better than that, counting the heavy rewriting I do and the time I must take off for non-writing obligations.

JAMES A. MICHENER

As for my "productivity," I used to write a book in nine months . . . but now it's one every three years. I'm writing more slowly and I'm spending more and more time on holiday.

GRAHAM GREENE

[M]any writers who hate themselves every winter for their sluggishness and lack of productivity could be aided not by "more motivation," but by bright full-spectrum light for half an hour every morning to treat their brain's seasonal response to the shortened days.

DR. ALICE W. FLAHERTY

Most writers write too much. Some writers write way too much, gauged by the quality of their accumulated oeuvre.

RICHARD FORD

I've been annoyed less by sneers at my alleged overproduction than by the imputation that to write much means to write badly. I've always written with great care and even some slowness. I've just put in rather more hours a day at the task than some writers seem able to.

ANTHONY BURGESS

I would work furiously day after day until my creative energies were utterly exhausted, and although at the end of such a period I would have written 200,000 words, enough in itself to make a very long book, I would realize with a feeling of horrible despair that what I had completed was only one small section of a single book.

THOMAS WOLFE

If [novelists] keep writing fiction much past sixty, they usually become their own recycling unit, reworking, with less verve, veins already well explored. Self-repetition, if not self-parody, are the traps that await elderly novelists—yet few novelists voluntarily flip off the switch, either because they can't afford to financially or because they simply don't know what else to do with themselves. They grow old, they grow weak, they wear the bottoms of their trousers rolled, but they keep writing.

LARRY McMURTRY

I think there's a period in a writer's life when he is, well, simply for lack of any other word, fertile and he just produces. Later on, his blood slows, his bones get a little more brittle, his muscles get a little stiff, he gets perhaps other interests, but I think there's one time in his life when he writes at the top of his talent plus his speed, too. Later the speed slows, the talent doesn't necessarily have to fade at the same time.

WILLIAM FAULKNER

When writers get together, the subject often turns to productivity. How does Joyce Carol Oates—whose name is synonymous with productivity—

do it? What about Stephen King or Anthony Burgess? . . . What seems true is that serious writers who write a lot of books and who experiment with different kinds of writing will suffer for it. The critics won't keep up with them. Their books will be reviewed in isolation from previous works, and their careers will resist categorization. Overproduction can also damage the quality of a writer's prose. . . . Virtually every prolific writer has dull passages, even whole books worth tossing out.

JAY PARINI

[T]here is a prejudice against prolific writers. Joyce Carol Oates, who has published [as of 2004] thirty-eight novels, twenty-one story collections, nine books of poetry, and twelve essay collections, and who also teaches full time at Princeton, has had to answer rude questions about her rate of production.

JOAN ACOCELLA

I think I do like to work under the pressure of a deadline. There's something exciting about knowing you have to get something done by a certain time. It's not at all like having months to write in.

TRUMAN CAPOTE

I am twenty-eight years old now and I must have at least one book a year from now on if I can manage it.

JOHN STEINBECK

There are several reasons why so many American writers have only one book in them. One is that it is very hard to be a writer of serious fiction in this country, not merely because we have so little respect for such work but because we throw up so many distractions in the way of it. All the hullabaloo attendant to writing a book to which other people respond intensely can be hugely flattering and can make it difficult to get on with one's work.

JONATHAN YARDLEY

They [young writers] write two or three books that are not only brilliant, but mature, and then they are done for. But that is not what enriches the literature of a country. For that you must have writers who can produce not just two or three books, but a great body of work. Of course it will be uneven, because so many fortunate circumstances must go together to produce a masterpiece, but a masterpiece is more likely to come as the culminating point of a laborious career than as the lucky fluke of untaught genius.

W. SOMERSET MAUGHAM

[T]hose few who gain public notice in early youth with seeming ease are the beneficiaries of whimsical fortune that almost never lasts long enough to get them successfully through completion of a third book contract.

GEORGE V. HIGGINS

No one is waiting for you to write your first book. No one cares if you finish it. But after your first, if it goes well, everyone seems to be waiting. . . . You go from having nothing to lose to having everything to lose, and that's what creates the panic.

JEFFREY EUGENIDES

[T]here is the writer who has had an early success but is unable to repeat it. . . . There is a cant explanation which is offered whenever this difficulty is met: this type of writer is a "one-book author"; he has written a fragment of autobiography, has unburdened himself of his animus against his parents and his background, and, being relieved, cannot repeat his tour de force. But obviously he does not consider himself a one-book author, or we should hear nothing more from him. Moreover, all fiction is, in the sense used here, autobiographical, and yet there are fortunate authors who go on shaping, recombining, and objectifying the items of their experience into a long series of satisfactory books or stories. . . . But [the one-book author's] first impatience at being able to repeat his success can pass into discouragement and go on to actual despair; and an excellent author may be lost in consequence.

DOROTHEA BRANDE

One of the curiosities of our publishing world is the boom and bust of the one-shot novelist. . . . The number of one-shot novelists living in this country who are never heard from after a spectacular debut is amazing.

EDWARD UHLAN

A man can write one book that can be great, but this doesn't make him a great writer—just the writer of a great book.

ANTHONY BURGESS

The thing about writing is not to talk, but to do it; no matter how bad or even mediocre it is, the process and production is the thing, not the sitting and theorizing about how one should write ideally, or how well one should write if one really wanted to or had the time. As [Alfred] Kazin told me: "You don't write to support yourself; you work to support your writing."

SYLVIA PLATH

The far greater danger, at least among the women writers I know, is that they stop writing. It seems to me that many of them fall into silence. From what I've seen, it's very hard to continue working, especially if you have a family.

GISH JEN

I wonder if many novelists have their desks as full as mine of—I will not say rejected manuscripts because no editor has had the opportunity of rejecting them; abandoned efforts would be as better word—for which I confidently expect to finish or use some day.

ALEC WAUGH

Always I have been weak. Vacillating and miserable. I wish I wouldn't. I wish I weren't. I'm so lazy, so damned lazy.

JOHN STEINBECK

A bad novel is better than an unwritten novel, because a bad novel can be improved; an unwritten novel is defeat without a battle.

PAUL JOHNSON

24

Reviews

It's hard to imagine how a review—say, in *Kirkus Reviews*—could, in a substantial way, affect the commercial success of a book. Other than writers and a handful of literary types, who reads book reviews? Book reviews, however, are important to the authors under review and to people in the business of dust-jacket blurbs, review excerpts that carry no credibility whatsoever. Still, in the life of a writer, a bad review is a terrible thing; and writers who say they don't read the reviews of their books or don't care if a review is good or bad are generally not believed.

Authors are also upset when their books are not reviewed. Isaac Asimov complained that none of his books were ever reviewed in *The New Yorker*, even though, as a well-known writer, he had been mentioned in the magazine many times. The reason: he was not taken seriously as a novelist because most of his writing was science fiction. Wallace Stegner, a brilliant novelist and nonfiction writer who lived in and wrote about the American West, was never reviewed in the *New York Times* even though his novels, *Angle of Repose* (1971) and *Spectator Bird* (1976), won the Pulitzer Prize and the National Book Award respectively. Why did the *Times* ignore Wallace Stegner? Probably because he was not a part of the Manhattan literary scene.

I have a friend who says that reviewers are the tickbirds of the literary rhinoceros—but he is being kind. Tickbirds perform a valuable service to the rhino and the rhino hardly notices the birds.

JOHN IRVING

Criticism and rejection are not personal insults, but your artistic component will not know that. It will quiver and wince and run to cover, and you will have trouble in luring it out again to observe and weave tales and find words for all the thousand shades of feeling that go to make up a story.

DOROTHEA BRANDE

Is it not clear that a reviewer's psyche, like an iceberg, is seven-eighths beneath the surface?

DELMORE SCHWARTZ

I am never much interested in the effects of what I write. . . . I seldom read with any attention the reviews of my . . . books. Two times out of three I know something about the reviewer, and in very few cases have I any respect for his judgments. Thus his praise, if he praises me, leaves me unmoved. I can't recall any review that has even influenced me in the slightest. I live in sort of a vacuum, and I suspect that most other writers do, too. It is hard to imagine one of the great ones paying any serious attention to contemporary opinion.

H. L. MENCKEN

People who aren't writers might think that authors would be well advised to study their negative reviews with care, rather than letting a protective skin form. After all, isn't there something to be learned from the thoughtful analysis of intelligent and knowledgeable critics? Well, maybe, but most of the writers I know don't take them seriously, and neither do I. It's not that I don't respect reviewers. It's that reviewers don't write their columns for writers. They write them . . . with readers in mind, and that's a different thing.

AARON ELKINS

I can get very depressed by a review that is unfair, unreasonable, and totally destructive.

JOHN O'HARA

I get angry at the stupidity of critics who willfully refuse to see what my books are really about. I'm aware of malevolence, especially in England. A bad review by a man I admire hurts terribly.

ANTHONY BURGESS

A recent review of one of my books was kind of horrific. It described my work as some sort of terrorist mission—and yet I *like* it, I like to be controversial in that way. It's proof I'm alive.

ROBERT COOVER

I am not alone in bearing grudges against reviewers who have doomed a book's chances because they've missed the point, the tone, *everything*.

ANN BEATTIE

A lady who was once married to Salman Rushdie had one of her novels published just as the famous *fatwa* was handed down on him. I gave the book a bad review. I was surprised that her pretty awful novel got a solemn, respectful review in the *New York Times* and everywhere else I looked. I was probably the only literate person in America who hadn't heard about the *fatwa*, and when I found out, I was sorry for what I had written. The poor woman had enough to worry about. A few years later, she got hold of one of my novels to review for the *Washington Post* and she *killed* me! She said I wrote "embarrassing surfer prose." Oh, the agony!

CAROLYN SEE

I'd never dream of not reading reviews. It's like not looking at a naked woman if she happens to be standing in front of her open window.

NORMAN MAILER

Very often adverse criticism goes to craft, and that sounds an alarm to which attention should be paid.

DOROTHY SALISBURY DAVIS

It's discouraging to be criticized because you can't contend with it. It's like someone saying, "Sorry, Jim, but you just don't measure up. We're looking for someone a bit more handsome than you."

JAMES LEE BURKE

It isn't infrequent that reviewers get the plot wrong. Am I naïve to have expected more consideration, am I naïve to be disappointed? Even "positive" criticism so often seems uniformed, ignorant.

JOYCE CAROL OATES

The critics don't interest me because they're concerned with what's past and done, while I'm concerned with what comes next.

ALDOUS HUXLEY

You're always looking—and it's very foolish, it really would be better not to read the reviews—but you're always looking for some reviewer who will tell you something about your book that you didn't know yourself and at the same time that you think is true. And that very, very rarely happens.

MARY McCARTHY

Rotten reviews are the lot of the writer, and selling well is the best revenge.

ISAAC ASIMOV

Never demean yourself by talking back to a critic, never. Write those letters to the editor in your head, but don't put them on paper.

TRUMAN CAPOTE

My favorite *Kirkus* review labeled my writing as "awkward and repetitious." I framed that one.

CHARLES KNIEF

I am often called a "storyteller" by flippant and unadmiring critics. I revel in the title. I bathe in the lotions and unguents of that sweet word.

PAT CONROY

I quit writing after *Publishers Weekly* told me my first novel was "just terrible." Something broke, you see. I was 29 and I'd worked for ten years at that novel, and I didn't see the point of spending another ten years only to be told the same thing again. So I tend bar here in North Plainfield, New Jersey, and try to encourage the other writers who come by now and then. We don't get many writers in North Plainfield.

LUKE WALTON

I've known writers who are absolutely destroyed by adverse opinion, and I think this is a lot of shit. You shouldn't allow that to happen to yourself, and if you do, then it's *your* fault.

JAMES DICKEY

Books are savaged and careers destroyed by surly snots who write anonymous reviews and publishers can't be bothered to protest this institutionalized corruption.

WARREN MURPHY

[G]ood reviews aren't helpful, and the bad reviews are less. . . . They're not creatively critical. I don't think there's really any point in reading them. You don't learn anything from them.

THOMAS TRYON

As a writer my feeling is that the critic can help me only when I am writing the book. I don't read reviews of my novels. They're too late to do me any good.

RITA MAE BROWN

The writer is on leg four of his seven-leg book tour of the U.S.A. He has done New York, Washington, and Boston and is about to head for Cleveland, Ohio, when he receives the bad news. His latest, ambitious, big novel has received a lengthy, sniffy review in the Sunday book section of the *New York Times*. Even on the telephone he can sense the awful plunge in morale at his American publishers: the gloom is palatable, bitter disappointment practically drips from the telephone receiver. For a foreign writer in America there is really only one review that counts: the Sunday *New York Times* book supplement. If that's bad, to put it bluntly, then everything else—including all the other good reviews . . . is a waste of time.

WILLIAM BOYD

In general, never choose your critic from your immediate family circle: they have usually no knowledge of the process of writing, however literary they may be as consumers; and in their best-natured act of criticism one may hear the unconscious grinding of axes sounding like a medieval tournament.

JACQUES BARZUN

If you ever write something, and it is reviewed, and the reviewer includes a photo of you, and both the photo and the review are bad, you will find that the photo is more painful.

DIANE JOHNSON

25

Readers

Writers have differing views on subjects such as what readers want and expect from a writer; whether or not it is wise to write for a specific audience; the quantity and quality of readership in America; the writer's duty to, and relationship with, his or her readers; and the type of people who read their books. Writers are also readers and, as such, usually have strong opinions about books that have influenced them. Many of them also have strong feelings about the books they discovered when they were young.

As you are writing you get no clues as to how readers will react. You have to write the whole thing out, keep going till the end, even though you have no idea whether the reader is lost or thinks you are crazy at the end of the first paragraph. Not only that, you don't even know *who* will read it. Once your words are on paper, they can be easily transported before the eyes of anyone—no matter how you feel about him, no matter how little he knows or understands you.

PETER ELBOW

We in the mass audience require characters who surprise us, but we also want their feelings to resemble our own—after all, that's what we mean when we call a character human. We demand originality, but we don't much like anything that catches us entirely unawares. . . . As an audience we accept strange and exotic settings, yet we want to feel comfortable as soon as a story takes us there. . . . Above all, we require that plots be made the way we think plots have always been made, with heroes and heroines, and villains, and a side we can take.

ROBERT FULFORD

I suppose most people read works of fiction because they have nothing else to do. They read for pleasure, which is what they should do, but different

159

people look in their reading for different kinds of pleasure. One is the pleasure of recognition.

W. SOMERSET MAUGHAM

The chief difference between good writing and better writing may be measured by the number of imperceptible hesitations the reader experiences as he goes along.

JAMES J. KILPATRICK

[A] writer *must* knock readers down. This is what he must constantly have in mind: to make people listen, to catch their attention, to find ways to make them hold still while he says what he so passionately wants to say.

WALLACE STEGNER

Never forget that the reader of fiction reads to feel. He doesn't read to think and most certainly doesn't read to be bored.

ELWOOD MAREN

[A]s long as one works hard to keep his work interesting and literate, he needn't become unduly worried about whether the reader will command all the complexities of the novel, . . . A writer, if he's lucky, will be aware of that delicate point where he had better not tax the reader's patience too much.

JOHN BARTH

I want my readers to have every advantage; that's why I make a comfortable place for them, give them a couch, a lap robe and a bowl of cherries and pistachios.

ALLAN GURGANUS

My own view is that if you write with an audience in mind, you are involved in useless speculation. I don't believe you should think about audience.

SUSAN SONTAG

I made the decision very early on in my career to put everyone out of my mind when I write. Relatives, editors, Hollywood, critics. I have no reader in mind. I think it's death to a writer to consider how anyone will view their work. One writes for oneself in much the same way one daydreams for oneself.

ANITA SHREVE

The natural audience of the novelist is not a crowd, but single individuals in armchairs, and they are absolutely faceless, they can't be safely imagined or predicted—if they could there would be a great deal more pressure by publishers upon authors to satisfy the definable wants of these definable readers.

WALLACE STEGNER

I write for me. For the audience of me. If other people come along for the ride then it's great.

EDWARD ALBEE

I don't write for stupid people.

ROBERT A. HEINLEIN

[R]eaders will be put off by a manuscript that's written with pretension rather than warmth and sincerity.

JUDITH APPELBAUM

The writer and the reader are involved in a creative relationship. The writer must provide the materials with which the reader will construct bright pictures in his head. The reader will use those materials as a partial guide and will finish the pictures with the stuff from his own life experience.

JOHN D. MacDONALD

[A] writer owes a debt of authenticity to his readers. . . . Readers wish to believe the printed word . . . and I believe when we deal with history or anything factual, it should be with care. We may be the only source they have for such information.

LOUIS L'AMOUR

The only catty letters I get are from men. They come from different men, but they all sound like the same man.

JAMES THURBER

The country is swarming with . . . lunatics. I receive letters from them constantly, and now and then one pops up in Baltimore, and I have a dreadful time getting rid of him—or her, for they are often women. . . . Such maniacs constitute one of the chief afflictions of an author's life.

H. L. MENCKEN

I received anonymous letters full of vilification and abuse, one which threatened to kill me if I came back home, others which were merely obscene. One venerable old lady, whom I had known all my life, wrote me that although she had never believed in lynch law, she would do nothing to prevent a mob from dragging my "big overgroan karkus" across the public square. She informed me further, that my mother had taken to her bed "as white as a ghost" and would "never rise from it again."

THOMAS WOLFE

[T]he most intense relationship anybody can have with a writer is by reading their work, alone, in silence. Yet readers seek writers in search of something additional. It was J. D. Salinger's hero, Holden Caufield, who said that what really knocked him out was a book that when you're done reading it, you wish the author that wrote it was a terrific friend of yours and you could call him up on the phone whenever you felt like it. It was also J. D. Salinger who, when *The Catcher in the Rye* achieved its enormous success, made himself as inaccessible to his readers as any living author has ever been.

SEAN FRENCH

It is important for a writer to say all that he can to anyone who is interested in his work.

JOHN HAWKES

Most of us who write are neither wildly popular nor particularly controversial. We are surprised at first to get any letters at all, a little bit disbelieving that anyone is actually reading what took such a long and mysterious route from our desks to the bookseller's counter. Far from being indifferent to individual readers, we are eager to make contact with them, to find out just who they are.

THOMAS MALLON

People *are* deeply affected by certain books if they read them at the right time, at the right stage in their development.

MICHAEL FABER

I will be perfectly willing to autograph and oblige my readers in any way possible. I don't know what other writers are like, but I am always aware that it is from my readers that my income ultimately derives.

ISAAC ASIMOV

I think I know most of my readers by name.

STANLEY ELKIN

If you can't annoy somebody, there's little point in writing.

KINGSLEY AMIS

The ideal reader of my novels is a lapsed Catholic and failed musician, short-sighted and color-blind . . . who has read the books that I have read. He should also be about my age.

ANTHONY BURGESS

I know that I am not writing to everybody. I assume an intelligent reader. I assume that my reader is going to be up to any little tricks I pull. I assume that my reader has a sense of humor, which is not always the case. I assume all kinds of things about the reader that won't necessarily be true. Otherwise I would be writing down to people, and I have no interest in that.

MARGARET ATWOOD

I wrote for 14 years before I finally sold something, so it is clear that I am not writing totally for an audience. . . . I write what I have to write — and then I find out who might be interested in reading it.

DONNA JO NAPOLI

Too many male writers are writing for critics. I don't write for men with pipes and leather on their elbows. I write for the public.

JACQUELINE SUSANN

A good novel needs all the attention the reader can give it. . . . The reader, you should premise, will always dislike you and your book. He thinks it an insult that you should dare to claim his attention, and if lunch is announced or there is a ring at the bell he will welcome the digression.

FORD MADOX FORD

In my view, curiosity is the great quality that binds writers to readers. Curiosity sends [nonfiction] writers on their quests, and curiosity is what makes readers read the stories that result. These days, when there is increasing competition for people's time, writers cannot count on anyone to read their work out of a sense of obligation, moral duty, or abstract dedication to "being informed." They will not read because someone else deems a subject to be important. They will read because they want to, and they will want to because they are curious.

JAMES B. STEWART

People need books with an epic background. They are bored with books that tell only one story on one level. They need something fantastic, something that gives them a sense of living in history. As it is, most novels aren't giving readers a chance to use their sense of fantasy.

GÜNTER GRASS

Men and women who do not find good books interesting are either too dull or too vivid. Either their imaginations cannot be kindled, or their real life is too intense to permit them even for a moment to step out of it.

HENRY SEIDEL CANBY

Most science-fiction fans like to think of themselves as special people. They especially like to picture themselves as being on top of the latest issues, but most of them are reactionary escapists. The average fan probably started as a high school misfit who discovered pulp magazines as a way of avoiding reality.

HARLAN ELLISON

I think detective novel readers are very ordinary people, conservative in their outlook.

PETER DICKINSON

Mystery readers unconsciously indulge in murdering mama vicariously. We soberly enjoy revenge at arm's length, momentarily releasing our primitive, pent-up urge to kill. This release invariably brings pleasure.

LUCY FREEMAN

I can think of no more gracious and enthusiastic an audience than young readers. Children identify strongly with characters in their books and often want the same book read to them over and over again.

ALIJANDRA MOGILNER

I have never met an author who admitted that people did not buy his book because it was dull.

W. SOMERSET MAUGHAM

I think personal catharsis is a terrible reason for writing fiction. It's a great reason to keep a diary but a lousy reason to write fiction, because really, who cares? What reader cares that I feel better for having written this story? They want to know what's in it for *them*, how are you going to make *them* feel better. And that's a perfectly valid response.

AMY HEMPEL

The decline in reading among every segment of the adult population reflects a general collapse in advanced literacy. To lose the human capacity—and all the diverse benefit it fosters—impoverishes both cultural and civic life.

DANA GIOIA

When I despair it is not because I think the time will come when people can't tell a good book from a bad one (though there are always signs of that) but that there won't be any readers.

WILLIAM MAXWELL

Every writer has a particular book that unlocked the desire to write. For me, I think *Ethan Frome* was that book. I read it when I was in junior high school. I consider it a nearly perfect novel. It's a framed story and contains within it the delicate thread of literary suspense.

ANITA SHREVE

A reader, I think, should make her own trail, each book leading to the next, so that a chronology of all the books one reads in one's life forms kind of a map, a measure of an individual, irreplaceable life. Sometimes it's the books we discover on our own, with no blogger or auntie or librarian whispering down our necks, that we love the most, that we find ourselves flipping back through long after we've finished, wistfully, longingly, as we might an old and happy diary.

ANTHONY DOERR

After reading those Rabbit books—something like 1,500 pages total, which I cruised through in two weeks—I had to suppress the urge to locate [John] Updike's home address, head over, thank him, and then slip some cleaning fluid into his coffee on the way out, because I was never going to be able to write like that and no aspiring writer wants his career snuffed out before it's ever begun.

DAVID AMSDEN

Alice in Wonderland, which I read when I was 9 or 10, has had the most profound influence in my life. Alice has bizarre adventures but she never gets frightened. She's thoughtful, she's skeptical, she has a sense of humor, and she's rational. Her calmness made a strong impression. That's the way I am. I can write about nightmares and bizarre things in a coherent, calm way.

JOYCE CAROL OATES

On the bookshelves of my house in London are the books I read as a child: Robert Louis Stevenson's *Kidnapped,* Kenneth Grahame's *The Wind in the Willows,* Lewis Carroll's *Alice's Adventures in Wonderland,* George MacDonald's *The Princess and the Curdie,* and a strange book called *The Pheasant Shoots Back* by Dacre Baldson. The last, an account of how a family of pheasants outwitted the hunters and lived to fly another season.

MARGOT LIVESEY

At the library I made the acquaintance of [J. D.] Salinger, who influenced me greatly, and, if I remember correctly, it was Salinger who suggested that being an author of fiction was the most noble occupation of all.

THOM JONES

As a high school student I fell in love with crime novels. I was living in Kobe [Japan], which is a port city where many foreigners and sailors used to come and sell their paperbacks to the secondhand bookshops. I was poor, but I could buy paperbacks cheaply. I learned to read English from these books, and that was so exciting.

HARUKI MURAKAMI

Most writers, I believe, contrary to the old classroom saw, write before they read. Writing teaches them how to read, and as their writing matures so does their ability to read deeply and well, which may be the principal benefit of pursing this [writing] vocation.

ROBERT COOVER

I have heard writers declare that they are in love with words. I do not understand what they mean. Words are tools, like bricks. I can be in love with a great house, but the materials themselves do not interest. I do not pore over dictionaries. . . . But I am made passionate, stirred to admiration and new visions, by great fictional prose, mighty descriptive passages, that create new worlds, paint great pictures.

SUSAN HILL

When I was fifteen I read *All the King's Men* by Robert Penn Warren for the first of many times—I must have read this book once a year for the following ten years. I loved it for its visual treatment of the Southern scene I came from, and for the infectious power of the style.

MADISON SMARTT BELL

Robert Penn Warren's *All the King's Men* is one of my favorite books. I read a lot of Southern writers—Faulkner, Eudora Welty—and a lot of Dickens. It seems I stole something from everybody I ever read. I hope in a good way.

RICK BRAGG

I think my sense of right and wrong, my feeling of noblesse oblige, and any thought I may have against the oppressor for the oppressed, came from this secret book [*The Acts of King Arthur and His Noble Knights*]. I was not frightened to find that there were evil knights, as well as noble ones. In my own town there were men who wore the clothes of virtue whom I knew to be bad. In pain or sorrow or confusion, I went back to my magic book.

JOHN STEINBECK

What should I do? Read, or write? . . . There is not much of a record, in the memoirs of writers, about the tension . . . between reading and writing. I don't know if many writers feel it. I do know that some writers seem to resent reading, to resent literature even—as if it were unfair competition. . . . On the rare occasions when I visit another writer's home I always immediately look at their books, which in too many cases consist mainly, if not exclusively, of books they've been sent to blurb or perhaps review.

LARRY McMURTRY

I get the most inspiration from—and this is soon to be an obsolete genre—collected letters. I have a huge shelf of collected letters. My favorites are Flannery O'Connor's and E. B. White's. The intimacy and the immediacy and the eloquence with which they write are reflected in those letters. It's reflected in their work as well. Of course, those collections are soon to be gone because we don't write letters any more. We send e-mail.

LOIS LOWRY

26

Literary Awards

As Anthony Arthur points out in *Literary Feuds,* literary awards are lightning rods for controversy. Prominent in the history of the Nobel Prize are stories of writers who should have won the prize but were passed over. Arthur writes: "The Swedish selection committee had given the first prize, in 1901, to the mediocre Sully Prudhomme, over Leo Tolstoy, and the list of other great writers who have not won the prize included Marcel Proust, Henry James, and Joseph Conrad."[1]

While many writers scorn literary prizes, few ever turn them down. In 1926, Sinclair Lewis refused the Pulitzer Prize for his novel *Arrowsmith,* but only because he was miffed about not winning it earlier for *Main Street.* Four years later, however, he accepted the Nobel Prize, becoming the first American so honored. In winning the Nobel, Lewis beat out Theodore Dreiser. Many American writers and critics considered his selection an insult, believing that Lewis had been awarded the prize because his novels were so critical of American culture. (As a side note, Irish playwright George Bernard Shaw turned down a Nobel Prize.)

Any author who gets a swelled head because he has been given a prize or a plaque is a foolish man.

JOHN O'HARA

A would-be writer [Alfred Nobel] had little talent for writing. In his forties he was rich, lonely, and bothered by stomach trouble and an unhappy love affair. As a final ignominy, even the famous prizes are not being awarded in the manner he intended.

HARLAND MANCHESTER

1. Arthur, *Literary Feuds,* 52.

The Nobel Prize is like that purse they give in Verona for the shot who bags the most sitting ducks on a clear day. There are other kinds of shooting, but they don't give prizes for it.

JOHN CHEEVER

I do something truly innovative, and who gets the prizes? Norman Mailer, who told me that what I was doing with *In Cold Blood* was stupid and who then sits down and does a complete rip-off. . . . But I resent only one thing, and that Mr. Mailer nor all the others who copied me . . . ever said, "We owe Truman Capote something; he really invented this form." They got all the prizes and I got nothing!

TRUMAN CAPOTE

While the giving and receiving of [literary] prizes usually induce from all sources an unhealthy uprising of false modesty, backbiting, self-torture and envy, my own view is that certain awards [the Prix del Duca], though not necessary, can be very nice to receive.

WILLIAM STYRON

The Nobel Prize, to me, is a joke. They give it year after year to one absolutely nonexistent writer after another.

TRUMAN CAPOTE

Just in case you should ever want to get a National Book Award I think I can give you some advice. First you have to have at least three good friends among the judges and then you have to have strong nerves, a commodious bladder and a good supply of bourbon.

JOHN CHEEVER

Winning the National Book Award for your first book . . . is an efficient way to lose your writer friends. People are cheered by your success—but only up to a point.

RON CHERNOW

The two most prestigious groups of American literary awards, the National Book Awards and the Pulitzer Prizes, no longer bestow instant celebrity on their winners, as they did in decades past. Last year [2004], judges for the National Book Awards were widely criticized after the selection of a group of largely unknown authors as the finalists for the fiction prize, the most visible category of the awards.

EDWARD WYATT

I should be scared to death to receive [the Nobel Prize], I don't care how coveted it is . . . [for] it has seemed to me that the receivers never do a good nor courageous piece of work afterwards. It kind of retires them.

JOHN STEINBECK

Prizes, awards, rave reviews are, after all, snares, and perhaps they are more destructive to one's sense of creative independence than the systematic discouragement the perpetual outsider receives.

ERICA JONG

My definition of a worthwhile literary prize is that now and then one will be awarded to a writer *despite* the fact that he deserves it.

JOHN BARTH

[W]hile it's lovely to receive awards, they should be appreciated for what they mean: that a certain number of people like your work. Don't expect any more than that, and certainly don't make the slightest change in your writing or your behavior in an attempt to win one. If you win, fine; if you don't, that's also fine. The awards rarely go to the most innovative writers until long after their best work is done.

ORSON SCOTT CARD

[Sinclair] Lewis . . . made a great mistake in not refusing the Nobel Prize, as he some time ago refused . . . the Pulitzer Prize. If I had got to him in time I'd have tried to induce him to do so. . . . Winning the Nobel Prize will probably make him cautious, and so hobble him. He has a very active inferiority complex, and will be sure to remember his responsibilities as a Nobel Prizeman.

H. L. MENCKEN

[Literary] prize committees have always been unreliable judges of quality . . . and any reader silly enough to buy a book for the stamp on the cover deserves a ghastly read.

B. R. MYERS

The awards are generally gutless, and the criticism that they are discredited is all right, as far as it goes. But the term Pulitzer Prize has a prestige that the National Book Award has never had and never will.

JOHN O'HARA

People tend to take you more seriously when you have award nominations, if not outright wins, on your CV [curriculum vitae]. One can spout off all one likes about awards being meaningless, or mere popularity contests, or no reflection of worth, but—hell yes, it's grand to get your name on that list.

KAGE BAKER

I told people that if I didn't win this time, I was not going to any more award ceremonies. You go from not caring about awards to being all caught up in the excitement. And the fact of the matter is that I always wanted to win an Edgar [Edgar Allan Poe Award], so I was thrilled [to win].

ERIK LARSON

The only possible attitude one can have to literary prizes is that they are worthless appendages, gratifying to collect should one be lucky, not to be confused with literary merit but thank you, anyway, and this is the number of the appropriate bank account.

JOHN HARTLEY WILLIAMS

England [as of 1971] has three literary prizes of any consequence, none of which, so far as I can discover, has ever been awarded to a volume of [short] stories. . . . In England there are no Pulitzer prizes, no O. Henry Memorial Award.

H. E. BATES

27

Despair

A good many writers are odd, high-strung, emotional wrecks. Many slip into despair, some go mad, a number get hooked on booze or drugs, and a few end their desperate lives with suicide.[1] To writers, there is nothing more morbidly fascinating than the tormented life and self-inflicted death of a fellow author. Case in point: Ross Lockridge, Jr. In February 1949, about a year after the publication of his first book, *Raintree County,* a bestselling Book-of-the-Month-Club selection, the thirty-three-year-old writer gassed himself to death in his garage while seated in his newly purchased car. Nanette Kutner, who had interviewed Lockridge six months before his suicide, wrote after his death: "He was no one-book author; he never would have been content to live as Margaret Mitchell [*Gone with the Wind*] lived. But he could not find a remedy for the letdown that invariably comes after completing a big job, the letdown [Anthony] Trollope understood so well he never submitted a novel until he was deep into the next."[2]

Do writers end their lives more often than other professionals do? There is no way to know. Experts say that statistics on suicide by occupation are not clear because there is no national data set based on this variable. Experts also believe that because occupation is not a major predictor of suicide, it does not explain much about why a person takes his or her life.[3] But writing is more of a vocation than an occupation, so it may not fit this theory.

---

1. The following writers killed themselves: John Berryman, Richard Brautigan, Hart Crane, John Gould Fletcher, Romain Gary, Ernest Hemingway, William Inge, Randall Jarrell, Jerzy Kosinski, Primo Levi, Ross Lockridge, Jr., Vachel Lindsay, Jack London, Malcolm Lowry, Charlotte Mew, Cesare Pavese, Sylvia Plath, Anne Sexton, Hunter S. Thompson, John Kennedy Toole, and Virginia Woolf.
2. Nanette Kutner, "Ross Lockridge, Jr.—Escape from Main Street," in Editors of the *Saturday Review,* eds., *Saturday Review Gallery,* 393.
3. K. Foxhall, *Monitor on Psychology* (January 2001): 32.

Despite depression's eclectic reach, it has been demonstrated with fair convincingness that artistic types (especially poets) are particularly vulnerable to the disorder.

WILLIAM STYRON

Every writer goes through this period of despair. Without doubt many promising writers, and most of those who were never meant to write, turn back at this point and find a lifework less exacting. Others are able to find the other bank of their slough of despond, sometimes by inspiration, sometimes by sheer doggedness. Still others turn to books or counselors.

DOROTHEA BRANDE

Summer is a discouraging time to work—you don't feel death coming on as the way it does in the fall when the boys really put pen to paper.

ERNEST HEMINGWAY

Like most new writers, I was startled to discover how quickly I slipped into a black trough of despair after mailing my first book manuscript.

RALPH KEYES

To be a writer is to be a shuttlecock in a badminton game, one racquet of which is naïve optimism and the other a cynical despair.

JOHN JEROME

[U]nless the author has the great good luck to visit the best-seller lists or wallow in unusual critical adulation, book writing often seems an exercise in futility. After a short burst of reviews, the comments of one's close friends and a smattering of letters from strangers who care enough to write, a disturbing silence descends. It is like a small death. Something that has long been alive in us struggling to breathe is suddenly without discernible pulse. Nothing looks quite so dusty and dead as yesterday's book on the shelf; the author likely will begin to brood that the months or years invested in his work have gone for naught. It is at this point that writers become difficult to live with. They may take up drink, flirt with Godless religions or seek to run with stray blondes. One's worth and how one has chosen to spend one's day are called into question.

LARRY L. KING

Sometimes I feel so stupid and dull and uncreative that I am amazed when people tell me differently.

SYLVIA PLATH

At the age of thirty-four I am weary, tired, dispirited, and worn out. I was a decent-looking boy six years ago—now I am a bald, gross, heavy, weary-looking man. I wanted fame—and I have had for the most part shame and agony.

THOMAS WOLFE

I write a scene and I read it over and think it stinks. Three days later (having done nothing in between but stew) I reread it and think it is great. So there you are. You can't bank on me. I may be all washed up.

RAYMOND CHANDLER

[F]or the last ten days I have been almost *non compos mentis*. . . . I sit for hours before my paper, not doing my book, but incapable of doing anything else, and thinking upon that subject always, working with it, walking about with it, and going to bed with it. Oh, the struggles and bothers—oh, the throbs and pains about this trumpery.

WILLIAM THACKERAY

I've been working, working, working, and you know, sometimes you look back at your work and you see that it just isn't any good.

TRUMAN CAPOTE

I get moments of gloom and pessimism when it seems as if nobody could ever like my kind of writing again [social-comedy novels]. . . . I get depressed about my writing, and feel that however good it was it still wouldn't be acceptable to any beastly publisher.

BARBARA PYM

Frankly, I don't think writing is where it's at these days. Neither the fat-bellies nor the crazies believe anything they read anyway, and most of the others are too stoned to even talk, much less read. This book I'm supposed to have been working on for 2 years strikes me as the most monstrous waste of time I've ever got bogged down in. Even if I manage to finish the goddamn thing, I can't see any reason why anybody should read it, even for free.

HUNTER S. THOMPSON

If you are exasperated, burned out, getting nowhere, and cynical about this novel writing "crap," then quit. Life is tough enough.

DONALD MAASS

Some writers I know who are successful are no longer happy with the writing process. They're dropping out, burning out.

TERRY BROOKS

My latest tendency is to collapse about 11:00 and with the tears flowing from my eyes or the gin rising to their level and leaking over, and tell interested friends or acquaintances that I haven't a friend in the world and likewise care for nobody.

F. SCOTT FITZGERALD

American writers, more than any others, are haunted by the fear of failure, because it's such a common pattern in America. The ghost of Fitzgerald, dying in Hollywood, with his comeback book unfinished, and his best book, *Tender Is the Night*, scorned—his ghost hangs over every American typewriter.

IRWIN SHAW

[O]ne *does* get depressed sometimes, has anyone ever done [a study] on why memories are always unhappy? I don't mean really unhappy, as of blacking factories, but sudden stabbing memories of especially absurd or painful moments that one is suffused and excoriated by—I have about a dozen, some 30 years old, and once *one* arrives, all the rest follow. I suppose if one lives to be old one's entire working life will be spent turning on the spit of recollection over the fires of mingled shame, pain or remorse.

PHILIP LARKIN

Nothing more horrible, no failure of nerve more acute, than to be a writer and not write, to never write, perhaps, to stop, *to decide to stop*, not to hope for writing or want it, to let go of writing, to swear it off like drugs or sex with the wrong party, or some other terrible compulsion that will finally tear one apart—decimating the room and maiming anyone in the house. The writer not writing is a wholly guilty party, like someone who through anger or neglect has killed off his own life's mate, counterpart, reason to live.

JAYNE ANNE PHILLIPS

Many people ask why a writer commits suicide. But I think that people who ask don't know the vanity and the nothingness of writing. I think it is very usual and natural for a writer to commit suicide, because in order to keep on writing he must be a very strong person.

ABE KOBO

At the moment I'm so exhausted that I feel like cutting my throat, so the next news may well be that I am across the river and under the trees: what is the meaning and purpose of life? Death.

DELMORE SCHWARTZ

Because in fact I only lived to write, see no sense in life, have only forced "interests," wish every night, not urgently but quite definitely I could just not wake up tomorrow.

JAMES GOULD COZZENS

And there was Aaron Klopstein. Who ever heard of him? He committed suicide at the age of 33 in Greenwich Village by shooting himself with an Amazonian blow gun, having published two novels . . . two volumes of poetry, one book of short stories and a book of critical essays.

RAYMOND CHANDLER

We've always had a tradition in America of hounding our artists to death. Look at the list of our great artists, you see a continual history of defeat, frustration, poverty, alcoholism, drug addiction. The best poets of my generation are all suicides.

JAMES DICKEY

I spent a hell of a lot of time killing animals and fish so I wouldn't kill myself. When a man is in rebellion against death, as I am in rebellion against death, he gets pleasure out of taking to himself one of the god-like attributes; that of giving it.

ERNEST HEMINGWAY

The first time we heard of Ernest Hemingway's death was a call from the *London Daily Mall*. . . . I find it shocking. He [Hemingway] had only one theme—only one. A man contends with the forces of the world, called fate, and meets them with courage. Surely a man has a right to remove his own life but you'll find no such possibility in any of Hemingway's heroes. The sad thing is that I think he would have hated accident much more than suicide. He was an incredibly vain man.

JOHN STEINBECK

I slipped a bullet into a chamber and, holding the revolver behind my back, spun the chambers [cylinders] round. . . . I put the muzzle . . . into my right ear and pulled the trigger. There was a minute click, and looking down at the chamber I could see that the charge [the bullet] had moved into the firing position.

GRAHAM GREENE

I often thought of killing myself but then I wanted lunch.

PAULA FOX

[Albert] Camus . . . occasionally hinted at his own despondency and had spoken of suicide. Sometimes he spoke in jest, but the jest had the quality of sour wine.

WILLIAM STYRON

I see a world of monsters and beasts; my grasp on creative and wholesome things is gone. To justify this I think of the violence of the past; an ugly house and exacerbating loneliness. How far I have come, I think, but I do not seem to have come far at all. I am haunted by some morbid conception of beauty-cum-death for which I am prepared to destroy myself. And so I think that life is a contest, the forces of good and evil are strenuous and apparent, and that while my self-doubt is profound, nearly absolute, the only thing I have to proceed on is an invisible thread. So I proceed on this.

JOHN CHEEVER

Life seems . . . a horrible fact. Sometimes I wonder how long I shall support it. . . . I am not strong enough to live without happiness. . . . I struggle through each new day working with suicidal thoughts early in the morning. . . . Eight-and-twenty [years old], and living without hope.

BEATRICE WEBB

[Anne] Sexton [who killed herself] saw [Sylvia] Plath's suicide as a career move, one that had been taken from her because Plath beat her to it. . . . Sexton saw suicide as a kind of death that had a lot of resonance for a literary career and also helped with the marketing of the work. Her prediction about Sylvia Plath came true: Plath was relatively unknown when she killed herself, but shortly after that she became the best-known woman writer in America and probably in England as well.

DIANE WOOD MIDDLEBROOK

Virginia [Woolf]'s suicide letter to Leonard [Woolf] is the most moving and noble letter I think anybody could write. She is utterly concerned for him. She tells him that he's been wonderful to her, has done everything for her, and that they have been the happiest couple there could be. But she cannot again face going into the madness alone.

JANE DUNN

It turned out that putting together a suicide note, which I felt obsessed with a necessity to compose, was the most difficult task of writing that I had ever tackled. There were too many people to acknowledge, to thank, to bequeath final bouquets. And finally I couldn't manage the sheer dirge-like solemnity of it; there was something I found almost comically offensive in the pomposity of such a comment as "For some time now I have sensed in my work a growing psychosis that is doubtless a reflection of the psychotic strain tainting my life."

WILLIAM STYRON

[T]he writings of authors . . . on the brink of suicide often are cogent and they give us insights into the human condition, in both inclusion and exclusion of what they write. Suicidal writers often treat us to skewed perspectives, where everything is out of place in the world, and only the act of writing, in the reflection of fiction to reality does the funhouse mirror of perception cease to distort the perspective. But this most intimate of revelings, this sharing of perspective is a grim task, as it takes a great deal of pain to have knowledge of such a skewed perspective. . . . The suicide notes, suicide diaries, the novels and poems of depressive writers are all pornography, and we are but sadistic voyeurs who transform a writer's pain into a reader's pleasure.

PATRICK EARNEST

28

Booze

William Faulkner, Sinclair Lewis, and F. Scott Fitzgerald are probably three of the most notorious falling-down drunks in the literary history of twentieth-century America. They were followed by Tennessee Williams, Truman Capote, and John Cheever, whose drinking habits became well-known components of their literary lives. Rita Mae Brown, in *Starting from Scratch,* believes that all this drinking among male writers stems from the fact that, in American culture, creative writing is not considered masculine. In other words, real men don't write. She attributes Hemingway's rugged outdoor lifestyle to this perception of men who create. Noting that Hemingway was a heavy drinker himself, she writes:

> Alcohol is associated with writers. The list of famous literary drunks could fill pages. Most of them are male but there are enough females to make one worry. Boozing is an occupational hazard for the male writer. What a pity masculinity wasn't defined as having a forty-two-inch chest instead of the ability to wench and hold liquor.[1]

Of the seven native-born Americans awarded the Nobel Prize in literature, five were alcoholic [Sinclair Lewis, Eugene O'Neill, William Faulkner, Ernest Hemingway, and John Steinbeck].

TOM DARDIS

Boozing does not necessarily have to go hand in hand with being a writer, as seems to be the concept in America. I therefore solemnly declare to all young men trying to become writers that they do not actually have to become drunkards first.

JAMES JONES

---

1. Brown, *Starting from Scratch*, 31.

Writers have always used drugs and drink to disinhibit themselves. In the beginning, the intoxicating effects of alcohol and drugs can prove prodigious. But once the tail is wagging the dog, the effects are generally deleterious.

BETSY LERNER

[T]he writer's life is inherently an insecure one. Each project is a new start and may be a failure. The fact that a previous item has been successful is no guard against failure this time. . . . It's no wonder writers so often turn misanthropic or are driven to drink to dull the agony.

ISAAC ASIMOV

Many writers use alcohol to help themselves write—to calm their anxieties, lift their inhibitions. This may work for a while . . . but eventually the writing suffers. The unhappy writer then drinks more; the writing then suffers more, and so on.

JOAN ACOCELLA

I used alcohol as the magical conduit to fantasy and euphoria, and to the enhancement of the imagination. There is no need to either rue or apologize for my use of this soothing, often sublime agent, which had contributed greatly to my writing; although I never set down a line while under its influence. . . . Alcohol was an invaluable senior partner of my intellect, besides being a friend whose ministrations I sought daily— sought also I now see, as a means to calm the anxiety and incipient dread that I had hidden away for so long in the dungeons of my spirit.

WILLIAM STYRON

In 1978, I got sober. I discovered I associated writing and drinking a little bit like scotch and soda: They went together. I needed to find a method of writing that was more grounded.

JULIA CAMERON

It's unfortunate that I learned something through booze. Everybody does, but ultimately on the level I was using, it was sickness. Jail, hospitals, DUIs. Briefly it worked, to be frank, but that was on three beers and exactly where, if I were to appear on television today as a spokesman for anti-alcohol, I'd say, Listen, if you need more than three beers, worry.

BARRY HANNAH

Faulkner drank himself to death; Hemingway's body was banged to bits, the booze had saturated him and he couldn't write; he had nothing to live for, so he shot himself.

PHILIP ROTH

Raymond Chandler is reported to have said he couldn't find an ending to one of his excellent stories unless he took time to get drunk. Up to a point I accept this report. For alcohol can stimulate imagination. It can find inventions. But I'll lay my bottom dollar, as one not unacquainted with booze, that Chandler had to sober up to write that ending.

A. B. GUTHRIE, JR.

I've gone on the wagon, but my body doesn't believe it. It's waiting for that whiskey to get in there . . . to get me going. I never drink while I'm working, but after a few glasses, I get ideas that would never come to me dead sober.

IRWIN SHAW

I can go three or four months without having a drink. And then suddenly I'm walking down the street and I feel that I'm going to die, that I can't put one foot in front of the other unless I have a drink. So I step into a bar. Someone who's not an alcoholic couldn't understand. But suddenly I feel so tired. I've had this problem with alcoholism for about fifteen years. I've gone to hospitals, I've tried Anatabuse, I've done everything. But nothing seems to work.

TRUMAN CAPOTE

I was . . . addicted to compulsive exercise. . . . One night, with a case of beer on hand, I did ten thousand sit-ups in sets of five hundred. . . . I could pick up the entire stack of weights on the Universal machine. Weight lifting merely requires a doggedness bordering on obsession. After two years of this, nearly every joint in my body was injured. Drinking killed the pain and tedium of it, but long-term spasms would force me into weeks of recuperation. I kept on drinking. My hand-to-mouth action was never impaired, and the drinking got out of hand. . . . Ultimately the drinking pushed me to type 1 diabetes, and I had no choice but to stop. . . . From the first, sobriety did not seem like a friendly place. I could accomplish only a small amount of physical work and would then be forced to lie on the floor for a time to recover from these small exertions. . . . The man of ten thousand sit-ups now barely had the strength to get through a single night of work.

THOM JONES

I used to drink a lot. I was never somebody who sat in bars drinking alone or because I was sad; I just did it for fun—fun stuff happened in bars. But it's no fun to sit there drinking Cokes, and if you don't hang out anymore, you've got an extra 30 hours a week [to work].

PETE DEXTER

Now working is terribly painful and I'm still having a fight with the booze. I've enlisted the help of a doctor but it's touch and go. A day for me; a day for the hootch.

JOHN CHEEVER

Although none of us ever policed his drinking—in fact we rarely even mentioned it—part of my father's addiction to alcohol seemed to involve a need for secrecy. He had to be getting away with something. No one could know. There were always bottles of gin and whiskey in full view in the pantry, but he also kept a bottle in his closet, a bottle in the desk where he worked, a bottle behind the New York Edition of Henry James in the library, and in warm weather, a bottle outside in the hedge near the driveway.

SUSAN CHEEVER

You usually can tell when a writer is going downhill by the size of his liquor bill.

JAMES M. CAIN

The town [Baltimore] is full of tales about his [Faulkner's] incessant boozing. He had a roaring time while he was here, and will go back to prohibition Mississippi with enough alcohol in his veins to last him a year.

H. L. MENCKEN

I haven't reached a point yet where I've had to be confined, but I can see that coming unless I watch myself very carefully. I reached a point where I don't even like alcohol. I don't drink for enjoyment. . . . I don't like the taste anymore.

FRED EXLEY

I didn't join Alcoholics Anonymous. I didn't seek out other help. I just stopped. My goal was provisional and modest: one month without drinking. For the first few weeks, this wasn't easy. I had to break the habits of a lifetime. But I did some mechanical things. I created a mantra for myself, saying over and over again, *I will live my life from now on, I will not perform it.* I began to type pages of private notes, reminding myself that writers were rememberers and I had already forgotten material for twenty novels. I urged myself to live in a state of complete consciousness, even when that meant pain or boredom.

PETE HAMILL

I often wonder if all the writers who are alcoholics drink a lot because they aren't writing or are having trouble writing. It is not because they are writers that they are drinking, but because they are writers who are not writing.

NATALIE GOLDBERG

It was a vicious circle. The more miserable and inadequate I felt about what I saw as my failure as a writer, the more I'd try to escape into a bottle, which would only exacerbate the domestic stress and make me even more depressed. . . . I'd lie awake at night seeing myself at fifty, my hair graying, my jowls thickening, a network of whiskey-ruptured capillaries spiderwebbing across my nose — "drinker tattoos," we call them in Maine — with a dusty trunkful of unpublished novels rotting in the basement, teaching high school English for the rest of my life and getting off what few literary rocks I had left for advising the student newspaper or maybe teaching a creative-writing course.

STEPHEN KING

I was released four days ago after 40 days in the drunk looney bin. Turned myself in for treatment to kick alcohol and light drugs right after the July 4th [1980] weekend, which I barely remember. Detoxed at Washington Hospital Center and then spent a month at a plush drunk tank for rich folks, Melwood Farm, near Olney, MD. Feel better than I have in a long time and have experienced no strange cravings. Believe I'm gonna be O.K.

LARRY L. KING

29

Hollywood

Referring to serious writers who sell out to Hollywood, a character in Rod Serling's play *Velvet Alley* says:

> They give you a thousand dollars a week. And they keep on giving you a thousand dollars a week until that's what you need to live on. And then every day you live after that, you're afraid they'll take it away from you. It's all very scientific. It's based on the psychological fact that a man is a grubbing, hungry little sleaze. . . . In twenty-four hours you can develop a taste for caviar. In forty-eight hours fish eggs are no longer a luxury, they're a necessity.[1]

A friend just back from the coast [in 1953] tells us that Hollywood is in shock—cameras aimed but not grinding, actors dressed but not performing, writers poised but not creating, and all top-level people studying charts and omens, convinced that TV is the enemy and that a miracle has to happen to save the day.

E. B. WHITE

If you write a novel, and you get X for your labors, that sets up a value system: you put in a certain amount of effort, you receive a certain amount of reimbursement, just like any other worker. However, if you are lucky or talented enough to become in demand as a screenwriter, the amounts you are paid are so staggering, compared to real writing, that it's bound to make you uneasy.

WILLIAM GOLDMAN

"Writers are a pain in the ass," notes a producer friend of mine. . . . "They whine about money so we pay them well, then when the script

---

1. Engel, *Rod Serling*, 162.

undergoes changes they whine it isn't their original vision. Tough. They sold their vision to us, and now *we* do all the work."

DONALD RAWLEY

The big fear is if you work in film, you may stop writing novels. Or, you'll become like all those writers who were ruined by Hollywood, Faulkner and Fitzgerald, who go over to the dark side and may never come back.

RICHARD RUSSO

I knew her name—Madam Hollywood. I rose and said good-by to this strumpet in her bespangled red gown; good-by to her lavender-painted cheeks, her coarsened laugh, her straw-dyed hair, her wrinkled fingers bulging with gems. A wench with flaccid tits and a sandpaper skin under her silks; shined up and whistling like a whore in a park; covered with stink like a railroad station pissery and swinging a dead ass in the moonlight.

BEN HECHT

In the picture business intelligence and taste are to be found only among the office help.

JOSEPH HANSEN

In the thirties and forties the movie industry was "Hollywood," and in that district of Los Angeles the major studios were giant factories producing movies at the rate of one a week at their busiest. Like any factory geared to mass-produce a product, the movie studio had a huge roster of salaried employees, from makeup experts to famous stars. Script writers were often on a weekly salary and, like every other worker in the factory, were expected to keep their output flowing.

STEWART BONFELD

Because there's little established hierarchy (even studio heads often don't hold their coveted jobs for long), many show business people spend a lot of time and money trying to look like A-players even if they aren't. This is the reason for the ostentatious display of wealth and power in the Hollywood game. It's not that industry folks lack modesty and subtle taste (although that can certainly be true for many). It's a matter of how they appear in the town. It's business. You have to look and act like a player or your club membership could be revoked very quickly at the first sign of a slipping career.

LINDA BUZZELL

I realized . . . that Hollywood was worse than a rat race, it was a *trap*. It lured a person into a lifestyle of sunshine and tans, of barbecues and swimming pools—a life you couldn't afford unless you kept on working in Hollywood. So you kept on working. It was a pact with Mephistopheles that could not be broken.

ISAAC ASIMOV

If you are ever in a situation where you've had enough commercial success to be dealing with a movie company—don't worry about the number-one man or woman. Do your best to have Number Two approve of what you are doing. Because if Number One likes what you offer him and Number Two doesn't, Number One will almost never give the go-ahead. It is to his or her advantage to go along with Number Two's declared opinion.

NORMAN MAILER

[A]s an older [over thirty-five] screenwriter, by virtue of a few . . . gray hairs, crow's feet and a mid-life bulge, you risk turning potential deal makers off simply because you'll be perceived as old. There's a peculiar kind of thinking in Hollywood that if you're older and haven't sold a script nor had one made [into a movie], that somehow you can't possibly be any good.

D. B. GILLES

What happens when the career [in Hollywood] begins to slide? It's a myth that when people in this town lose their viability, they long for some motion-picture relief home. This is Hollywood! There is no relief. No one leaves without a fight, and no one ever thinks he's too old.

ART LINSON

Like most managers, TV execs want to work with people who are just like them. For many that means YOUNG. For almost as many that means NEW. . . . Once you've become an expert in the hip and trendy, it's time to move to L.A. Just as you can't be a cowboy if you live in the Bronx, you can't be a TV writer if you don't live in L.A. It's not a freelance business anymore. You've got to go where the industry is.

LARRY BRODY

Celebrities focus on the minutiae of self all the time—and they make sure that no distractions like airplane reservation snafus or colicky babies interrupt this singular focus. This often extremely lucrative self-obsession invariably becomes downright pathological. That is why Hollywood is a veritable triage center for psychiatry. . . . It is . . . why psychiatry's arch-nemesis, Scientology, has made Hollywood central to its base of operations. . . . The competition for the dollars of damaged celebrity souls is stiff—may the best man win, Freud or Hubbard.

ANDREW BREIBART AND MARK EBNER

I just despise it [Hollywood]. . . . It isn't even a city. It's nothing. It's like a jumble of huts in a jungle somewhere. I don't understand how you can live there. It's really, completely dead. Walk along the street, there's nothing moving.

TRUMAN CAPOTE

I went to Hollywood to make money. It's very simple. The people are friendly and the food is good, but I've never been happy there, perhaps because I only went there to pick up a check.

JOHN CHEEVER

Hollywood is the only industry in the world that pays its workers the kind of money only capitalists and big executives make in other industries. If it [Hollywood] is something less than ideal, it is the only industry that even tries for idealism; if it makes bad art, no other makes any art, except as a by-product of money-making. If it makes money out of poor pictures, it could make money out of good ones, and it knows it and tries to make them. There is simply not enough talent in the world to do it with, on any such scale. Its pictures cost too much and therefore must be safe and bring in big returns; but why do they cost so much? Because it pays the people who do the work, not the people who cut coupons. If it drains off all the writing talent in the world and then proceeds to destroy it the way it treats it, then why is it able to drain off that talent? Because it knows how to pay for talent.

RAYMOND CHANDLER

I once lucked into a situation where I made thirty-five thousand dollars a week (for three weeks) revamping one of the worst pictures ever shot. Numbers like this addle the mind. In fact, the price paid to movie writers has probably done more to alter the face of American narrative than any other factor.

MARK JACOBSON

If Hollywood wants to prostitute me by buying one of my books for the movies, I am not only willing, but eager for the seducers to make their first dastardly proposal.

THOMAS WOLFE

Films help the novels they're based on, which I both resent and am grateful for. My *Clockwork Orange* paperback has sold over a million in America [1975], thanks to dear Stanley [Kubrick]. But I don't like being beholden to a mere film maker. I want to prevail through pure literature. Impossible, of course.

ANTHONY BURGESS

My own belief is that pictures needn't hurt a writer, but that they probably will. If he could merely work for them they would teach him a lot, particularly about concision and the necessity for building a story before trying to sell it. But he rarely stops there. Having as a rule little critical sense, he begins to believe in them, talk of the screen as a "great medium," and so on, and that sinks him. Pictures are entertainment if they entertain you, but to allow them any validity beyond that one night is to be silly.

JAMES M. CAIN

It's said in Hollywood that if you experience a creative dream, you don't even tell the person you're sleeping with. Certainly if you conceive a commercial media idea, you don't discuss it in restaurants or public places. Such is the paranoia of the movie world, where ideas and dreams are stolen every day.

STANLEY J. CORWIN

Producers of films tend to involve writers of books in the moviemaking process as little as possible, for the sensible reason that it's hard enough to make a film without having an interested amateur meddling in the process.

TONY HILLERMAN

I'm not interested in getting a job in Hollywood. I have no desire in the world to write a movie script. Why the hell should I write a movie script? Scriptwriting has nothing to do with writing. The best scriptwriter in the world, ideally, would be a film editor with a novelistic gift. And those are qualities that don't usually go together.

NORMAN MAILER

I'm not a good screenwriter. Maybe I have too much ego that just won't let me bend to the form.

BARRY HANNAH

The screenwriter Andrew Kevin Walker once said that no one in Los Angeles is ever more than fifty feet from a screenplay. They're stowed in the trunks of cars. In desk drawers at work. In laptop computers. Always ready to be pitched. A winning lottery ticket looking for its jackpot. An uncashed paycheck.

CHUCK PALACHNIUK

[W]hen you write a book you have the final and ultimate voice if there's a conflict with the editor over copy, and pretty much the same situation exists on stage. But if you write a movie, you don't have any more power than a stage grip.

LARRY L. KING

I simply don't want to do any more work for Hollywood. There is nothing in it but grief and exhaustion and discontent. In no real sense is it writing at all. It carries with it none of the satisfactions of writing. None of the sense of power over your medium. None of the freedom, even to fail.

RAYMOND CHANDLER

The attitude that writers are a special class, that really alienates me. They talk about stress and how awful it is to be a writer—you hear that talk a lot in Hollywood. . . . I had to catch a flight out of L.A. at 11 the night before last, so I walk around a little bit goofy for a couple of days 'cause I'm sleepy, but that is nothing like unloading trucks for 20 years.

PETE DEXTER

The chaotic nature of the entertainment industry has done what no amount of melodramatic Oscar-night speeches, fifties-era blacklist reminiscences, or embittered and disorganized Writers Guild meetings have yet been able to achieve. The writer in Hollywood, thanks to the explosion of mini-studios, new media, and high-stakes competition, is actually an important commodity.

ROB LONG

In Hollywood . . . writers seem to gravitate naturally toward a buddy. This is usually, but not always, another writer; someone who understands the vocabulary of the town, the particular joys and pains of pitch meetings, rewrites, and development deals.

DENNIS PALUMBO

Hollywood is a long shot on the best of days. To let it influence the novel is a disservice to you and your readers.

DAVID BALDACCI

The course of making movies is strikingly instructive about all forms of collaborative work. It is a Petri dish that grows through its high stakes and public adulation every imaginable type of cell, both healthy and malignant. Ego problems are endemic in every walk of life, but in the movie business egomaniacs are megalomaniacs. Greed is a universal factor. In Hollywood it's the whole factor, a way of life. Every business is hard to break in to. In Hollywood there's a Darwinian hazing ritual. Competition is the impulse of capitalism; in the movie business it's the impulse to homicide.

LYNDA OBST

I was offered a lot of money to do a book on Jackie Gleason. I get a lot of crap offers like that—biographies of morons from L.A.—I won't touch any of that stuff. And I won't do movies for people I dislike, you know, or cheap movies.

WILLIAM PRICE FOX

Why do Hollywood stars, the most attractive, admired, and highly compensated citizens of the world, have families more screwed up than even the notoriety-driven mongrels loitering around the green room at the "Jerry Springer Show"? The short answer is *ego*. Insatiable ego. Constantly massaged ego. 24-hour-a-day concierge ego. 400-thread-count linen at the five-star luxury dog kennel ego. Trading in your pre-fame spouse for a world-class model ego. Ego. Ego. Ego. For every celebrity, by design and necessity, is a narcissist. The desire to become a star requires an incredible appetite for attention and approval. To achieve fame and its accoutrements takes laser-like focus, and a nearly commendable ability to stay self-centered in the service of a dream.

ANDREW BREIBART AND MARK EBNER

30

Fame

A character in B. Traven's story "The Night Visitor," who has written several books he has chosen not to publish, contemplates fame: "What is fame, after all? It stinks to hell and heaven. Today I am famous. Today my name is printed on the front page of all the papers in the world. Tomorrow perhaps fifty people can still spell my name correctly. Day after tomorrow I may starve to death and nobody cares. That's what you call fame."[1]

B. Traven, the pen name of the mysterious author of dozens of novels—notably, *The Treasure of the Sierra Madre*—believed that all books should be published anonymously. He based this belief on the notion that readers, by knowing in advance who the author is, will expect and demand a certain kind of book.

Most people who become suddenly famous overnight will find that they lose practically eighty percent of their friends. Your old friends just can't stand it for some reason.

TRUMAN CAPOTE

My idea of fame is to get the books out to the public so they read them.

T. C. BOYLE

For a writer, the conduct of life is not easy. Should he encounter too many worldly disappointments, then he runs the risk of seeing his spirits dampened by anxiety and his heart invaded by bitterness. Should success make him a person of consequence, then social life engulfs him and his working hours are consumed by time-wasters. Celebrity . . . creates duties he can hardly escape.

ANDRÉ MAUROIS

---

1. Wyatt, *Man Who Was Traven*, 161.

I find myself getting "famous," but no richer than I was before people started recognizing and harassing me almost everywhere I go.

HUNTER S. THOMPSON

A very large percentage of mankind seems to live in imaginary proximity to famous people with whom they carry on complex relationships, illusory conversations, scenes of conflict, and love affairs that even include heartbreaking partings and joyous reconciliations. The famous are balloons far up in the sky, to be envied for their quiet freedom or shot down as enemies.

ARTHUR MILLER

Fame is a worthless distraction.

PHILIP ROTH

[I]t's nice to be asked how it felt to write *God's Little Acre* [by Erskine Caldwell] and *Farewell to Arms* [by Ernest Hemingway].

JOHN STEINBECK

Fame is a kind of death because it arrests life around the person in the public eye. If one is recognized everywhere, one begins to feel like Medusa. People stop their normal life and actions and freeze into staring mannequins. "We can never catch people or life unawares," as I wrote to my mother, in an outburst of frustration. "It is always looking at us."

ANNE MORROW LINDBERGH

One dreams of the goddess Fame and winds up with the bitch Publicity.

PETER DE VRIES

I was famous too young. I pushed too hard too soon. I wish somebody would write what it's really like to be a celebrity. People come up and ask me for autographs in airports, and I give them 'cause otherwise I think they'll hit me over the head.

TRUMAN CAPOTE

Learn to spot and avoid "writer groupies." The writer's self-sufficiency and our love for our work tend to attract insecure people who never can get enough love. They grow jealous of our work and come to regard it as a rival. These people can destroy you, so kick them out of your life or don't admit them in the first place.

FLORENCE KING

People say, "Well, you went on television, it enlarged your readership." It did not at all, not at all. I might as well tell you, I *lost* some readership, because the profound audience felt somehow bothered by my too easy manner.

JERZY KOSINSKI

Unless he [a writer] can get himself noticed, he is nothing; but if he gets himself noticed by cheating, or out of mere vanity, he is less than nothing.

WALLACE STEGNER

Every time a story about me appears in a newspaper, I am injured professionally.

NORMAN MAILER

One bull's-eye and you're rich and famous. The rich get more famous and the famous get rich. You're the talk of the town. . . . The sense of so much depending on success is very hard to ignore, perhaps impossible. It leads to disproportionate anxiety and disproportionate relief or disappointment.

TOM STOPPARD

I never cease to be amazed why some of my friends became famous and others, just as talented, didn't. I've come to suspect it's a matter of wanting fame or not, and those who don't want it, don't get it.

MALCOLM COWLEY

I have a great ambivalence about interviews [of writers]. I believe writers should be read and not heard from. There are certain writers whose personalities are more responsible for their reputations than their writing. And who use their personalities to make their works popular. I resent that, because they get far more attention than their work merits. And other writers who are really much better, but who are quiet and invisible souls, are not noticed at all. Part of me wants to be totally anonymous. The writer who I really admire most for his image is B. Traven, who wrote *The Treasure of the Sierra Madre*; he was totally unidentified in his lifetime. I admire that.

DENNIS ETCHISON

I have come to regard this matter of fame as the most transparent of all vanities.

HERMAN MELVILLE

A writer is nothing but a gray dirt-covered root. The works he sends up into the sunlight are his fruits, and only those are worthy of attention.

HERMAN WOUK

Of all the questions I'm asked, the most difficult is, "How does it feel to be famous?" Since I'm not, that question always catches me with a feeling of surrealism. . . . I've got three kids and I've changed all their diapers, and when it's two o'clock in the morning and you're changing something that's sort of special delivery with one eye open and one eye shut you don't *feel* famous.

STEPHEN KING

The fame thing is interesting because I never wanted to be famous, and I never dreamt I would be famous. . . . You know I didn't think they'd rake through my bins, I didn't expect to be photographed on the beach through long lens. I never dreamt it would impact my daughter's life negatively, which at times it has. It would be churlish to say there's nothing good about being famous; to have a total stranger walk up to you as you're walking around Safeways, and say a number of nice things that they might say about your work.

J. K. ROWLING

Whatever fame a novelist may attain, it's always kind of an anonymous one. I can go anywhere, and no one knows who I am.

JONATHAN KELLERMAN

[Literary fame] is a fourth tier kind of celebrity thing, and how to most of the world, you're absolutely nobody, but to a few, you're somebody, and you're really somebody.

AUGUSTEN BURROUGHS

Authors lead obscure lives. . . . Not for them is the honour of breaking a bottle of champagne against the hull of an ocean-going liner soon to set out on her maiden voyage. Crowds do not assemble, as they do with film stars, to see them emerge from their hotel to leap into a Rolls-Royce. . . . But they have their compensations. . . . Throughout the ages artists have found their complete satisfaction in producing works of art.

W. SOMERSET MAUGHAM

Yeah, I think I'll be remembered. . . . I think I'll be remembered as the voice of the 1960s . . . Andy Warhol, the Beatles and me.

JACQUELINE SUSANN

You write one book and you're ready for fame and fortune. I don't know that people are spending the time and attention on learning how to write—which takes years. Everybody sees the success stories.

SUE GRAFTON

You get the fun, the pleasure, the agony, the horror of writing the god-damned thing. That should be all that you get. If you get money besides, terrific. If you get the other things of the success syndrome, the fame and all of those things, that's terrific too. But I've had the fame [the author was an actor before he wrote novels] so I know how ephemeral and how silly all that is and it really doesn't matter. What matters to me is getting up at six o'clock and hitting the keys.

THOMAS TRYON

The best thing about celebrity is it gets your books read, because people say, "I'm interested in him; I know something about how his mind works—and what does he think about this?" So to the extent that it serves to get people to open books and read the columns, then it's wonderful.

GEORGE WILL

Journalists are now celebrities. Part of this has been caused by the abil-ity and willingness of journalists to promote themselves. Part of this has been caused by television: the television reporter is often more famous than anyone he interviews.

NORA EPHRON

When you're a famous person and cease to be active—particularly in journalism and politics—when you're no longer a mover or a shaker, the world quickly forgets or is too busy for you.

RICHARD STEEL

There is . . . a new sort of fame in our day that has never quite been known before. It is a fame seemingly invented out of whole cloth, based on nothing and needing only a press agent to keep it alive. This new spe-cies of fame does not wait for a man to win a race or a worldly prize. . . .

People in our day become famous who are no more than advertisements, and they advertise not genius but existence.

BEN HECHT

The Devil comes to the writer and says, "I will make you the best writer of your generation. Never mind generation—of the century. No—this millennium! Not only the best, but the most famous, and also the richest; in addition to that, you will be very influential and your glory will endure for ever. All you have to do is sell me your grandmother, your mother, your wife, your kids, your dog and your soul." "Sure," says the writer, "absolutely—give me the pen, where do I sign?" Then he hesitates. "Just a minute," he says. "What's the catch?"

MARGARET ATWOOD

Sources of Quotations

Chapter One. Creativity

Creativity is. . . . Julia Cameron, *Writer's Digest* (March 2003).
I believe. . . . Joyce Carol Oates, in Dembo, ed., *Interviews with Contemporary Writers*.
A would-be. . . . Elizabeth McCracken, in Conroy, ed., *Eleventh Draft*.
In going. . . . Ernest Hemingway, *Short Stories of Ernest Hemingway*.
Those of us. . . . Rebecca McClanahan, *Write Your Heart Out*.
Many people. . . . Edith Wharton, *Writing of Fiction*.
For the vast. . . . Mark Robert Waldman, in Waldman, ed., *Spirit of Writing*.
The idea of. . . . Dennis Palumbo, *Writing from the Inside Out*.
Only writers. . . . Ed McBain, www.bestsellersworld.com (30 June 2002).
A lot of. . . . Robert Anderson, in Murray, ed., *Shoptalk*.
I find that. . . . Tom Wolfe, in *Writers at Work*, 2d series.
We must be. . . . Truman Capote, in Clarke, *Capote*.
I don't know. . . . William Faulkner, in *Writers at Work*, 5th series.
Many undergrads. . . . Martin Russ, *Showdown Semester*.
Oh, it is. . . . Gore Vidal, in Stanton and Vidal, eds., *Views from a Window*.
An idea isn't. . . . William G. Tapply, *Elements of Mystery Fiction*.
Whenever there's. . . . Patricia T. O'Conner, *Words Fail Me*.
Ask a professional. . . . Richard Curtis, *Beyond the Bestseller*.
[I]deas are everywhere . . . . Louis L'Amour, *Education of a Wandering Man*.
For me, ideas . . . . Elizabeth George, *Write Away*.
Many times . . . . Flannery O'Connor, in Appelbaum, *How to Get Happily Published*.
One of the . . . . Martin P. Levin, *Be Your Own Literary Agent*.
I have a big . . . . James Patterson, in *Writer's Digest* (July 2001).
People say to . . . . Thomas Tryon, in Duggan et al., eds., *Conversations with Writers*.
Ideas, concepts. . . . Dee Brown, *When the Century Was Young*.
If you're a doctor. . . . Isaac Bashevis Singer, in Mitgang, ed., *Words Still Count with Me*.
Writers who say . . . . Dorothy Allison, in *Writer's Digest* (May 2003).
I have rarely . . . . James A. Michener, *James A. Michener's Writer's Handbook*.
Novelists—most of . . . . Patricia Highsmith, *Plotting and Writing Suspense Fiction*.
I have never claimed . . . . W. Somerset Maugham, *Writer's Notebook*.
I never begin . . . . Eleanor Clark, in McCullough, ed., *People, Books, and Book People*.
In the author's mind . . . . C. S. Lewis, in Brown, ed., *Opinions and Perspectives from the "New York Times Book Review."*
To me, the . . . . Ted Conover, in Sims and Kramer, ed., *Literary Journalism*.
There is, I. . . . V. S. Pritchett, *Midnight Oil*.
In the writing process. . . . Doris Lessing, in Henry, ed., *Fiction Writer's Market, 1987*.
[A] writer is working. . . . Lawrence Block, in Fredette, ed., *Handbook of Short Story Writing*.
I never mention. . . . Agatha Christie, in *Writer* (August 1966).
I like to discuss. . . . Gail Godwin, in Staff of the *New York Times*, eds., *Writers on Writing*.
A certain. . . . Nelson Algren, *Nonconformity: Writing on Writing*.
I think melancholy. . . . Susanna Kaysen, in Casey, ed., *Unholy Ghost*.
Freud wrote somewhere. . . . Peg Bracken in Daigh, *Maybe You Should Write a Book*.
I write best. . . . Sylvia Plath, in A. S. Plath, ed., *Letters Home*.

When I'm writing. . . . Ayn Rand, in Branden, *Judgment Day*.
[A] person's best. . . . Peter Elbow, *Writing without Teachers*.
[W]hile you're. . . . Philip Roth in Murray, ed., *Shoptalk*.
The terrible thing. . . . Natalie Goldberg, *Writing down the Bones*.
How does the. . . . Brenda Ueland, *If You Want to Write*.
Harsh criticism. . . . Gayle Brandeis, *Fruitflesh*.
Reverie is the. . . . W. Somerset Maugham, *Summing Up*.
The one thing. . . . Robert Olen Butler, interview by Jessica Murphy, www.
    atlanticmonthly.com (20 May 2004).
I don't think. . . . Elizabeth Hardwick, in *New Yorker* (14 and 21 June 2004).
[D]eadlines do more. . . . Chris Baty, *No Plot? No Problem!*
Are crop circles. . . . Amy Hempel, in Blythe, ed., *Why I Write*.

Chapter Two. Talent
Writing is like. . . . Julia Cameron, *Right to Write*.
Everyone has talent. . . . Erica Jong, in Shaughnessy, *Walking on Alligators*.
I believe that. . . . Wallace Stegner, *On Teaching and Writing Fiction*.
Everybody is talented. . . . Brenda Ueland, *If You Want to Write*.
I never felt. . . . Paula Fox, in *Paris Review* (winter 2004).
Writers may not. . . . William Stafford, in Muscatine and Griffith, eds., *Borzoi College
    Reader*.
One of the most. . . . William Boyd, in Steinberg, ed., *Writing for Your Life*.
Everybody has [talent]. . . . John Gardner, in Brande, *Becoming a Writer*.
I just think. . . . Stephen King, in Underwood and Miller, eds., *Bare Bones*.
Be it modest. . . . Stephen Koch, *Writer's Workshop*.
Talent is like. . . . Loretta Burrough, in Hull and Drury, eds., *Writer's Roundtable*.
A writing gift. . . . Deena Metzger, *Writing for Your Life*.
Would I like more. . . . Jerzy Kosinski, in Polak, ed., *Writer As Celebrity*.
I believe that. . . . Dee Brown, *When the Century Was Young*.
I've been increasingly. . . . Lawrence Block, *Write for Your Life*.
Writers like to think. . . . Tom Wolfe, in Scura, ed., *Conversations with Tom Wolfe*.
[An] indicator of. . . . John Gardner, *On Becoming a Novelist*.
Really, talent is. . . . Christopher Isherwood, in *Writers at Work*, 4th series.
The one talent. . . . Tom Clancy, in *Writer's Digest* (January 2001).
The consensus. . . . Dr. Alice W. Flaherty, *Midnight Disease*.
Talent cannot be. . . . Robert DeMaria, *College Handbook of Creative Writing*.
Writing is at. . . . Jacques Barzun, *Jacques Barzun on Writing, Editing, and Publishing*.
Talent is not. . . . Marc McCutcheon, *Damn! Why Didn't I Write That?*
All you need. . . . Ernest Hemingway, in Hotchner, *Papa Hemingway*.
Personally, I think. . . . James M. Cain, in Hoopes, *Cain*.
Most people who. . . . Norman Mailer, in *Writer's Digest* (January 1998).
What are the. . . . H. L. Mencken, in Mencken and Joshi, eds., *H. L. Mencken on
    American Literature*.
Fiction, first of. . . . William H. Gass, in McCormack, ed., *Afterwords*.
If you write. . . . Stephen King, in Burack, ed., *Writer's Handbook, 1998*.

Chapter Three. The Difficulty of Writing
If you have . . . . Ayn Rand, in Rand and Mayhew, eds., *Art of Nonfiction*.
I do find. . . . Tom Wolfe, in Scura, ed., *Conversations with Tom Wolfe*.
[T]here's always. . . . William E. Blundell, *Art and Craft*.
Oh God! how. . . . Katherine Anne Porter, in Givner, *Life of Katherine Anne Porter*.

In addition to the. . . . Dennis Palumbo, *Writing from the Inside Out*.
I have never. . . . Ward Just, in Staff of the *New York Times*, eds, *Writers on Writing*.
[T]he assumption. . . . David Morrell, *Lessons from a Lifetime of Writing*.
There is nothing. . . . Leonard S. Bernstein, *Getting Published*.
Line by line. . . . Hilary Mantel, in Boylan, ed., *Agony and the Ego*.
I have never. . . . Reynolds Price, in *New York Times* (27 March 1966).
[B]eing a true. . . . Ellen Glasgow, in Haverstick, ed., *Saturday Review Treasury*.
I'm in my. . . . Ralph Ellison, in Murray and Callahan, eds., *Trading Twelves*.
To learn to. . . . James Gould Cozzens, in Bruccoli, *James Gould Cozzens*.
The aesthetic gift. . . . James M. Cain, in Hoopes, *Cain*.
In case no . . . . Sheldon Russell, in *Byline* (January 2000).
Writing should be. . . . John Dufresne, *Lie That Tells a Truth*.
Large numbers of . . . . Larry L. King, *None but a Blockhead*.
[M]ost people secretly. . . . Margaret Atwood, *Negotiating with the Dead*.
Some kinds of. . . . John Jerome, *Writing Trade*.
The most enjoyable. . . . Abe Kobo, in Dembo, ed., *Interviews with Contemporary Writers*.
While working on. . . . Richard Ben Cramer, in Lamb, ed., *Booknotes*.
The difficulty of. . . . Marvin Bell, in Pack and Parini, eds., *Writers on Writing*.
I get a fine. . . . William Styron, in *Writers at Work*, 1st series.
[W]hat you ultimately. . . . Ernest Hemingway, in Hotchner, *Papa Hemingway*.
Writing is hard. . . . George V. Higgins, *On Writing*.
There are much. . . . John Jakes, in Burack, ed., *Writer's Handbook*, 1988.
Writing is a nerve-flaying. . . . Joan Acocella, in *New Yorker* (14 and 21 June 2004).
Writing a book. . . . Tom Clancy, in Leder and Heffron, eds., *Complete Handbook of Novel Writing*.
The anxiety involved. . . . Anthony Burgess, in *New Yorker* (14 and 21 June 2004).
Every book I. . . . Nora Roberts, in Gee, ed., *Novel and Short Story Writer's Market*, 1994.

Chapter Four. Why Writers Write
[A] blank sheet. . . . E. B. White, in Elledge, *E. B. White*.
[Elementary, middle school . . . .] Peter Elbow, *Writing without Teachers*.
[T]here are many. . . . Donald Maass, *Career Novelist*.
There are writers. . . . bell hooks, *Remembered Rapture*.
Some of us want. . . . Lawrence Block, *Write for Your Life*.
[I write because. . . .] James Jones, in *Writers at Work*, 3d series.
Many of us. . . . Barry Hannah, in *Paris Review* (winter 2004).
Many people. . . . William Maxwell, *Outermost Dream*.
I write because. . . . Isaac Asimov, in S. Asimov, ed., *Yours, Isaac Asimov*.
I do it for. . . . Frederick Busch, *Dangerous Profession*.
I write because. . . . S. D. Williams, in *Leader* (4 June 1987).
I write because. . . . Elizabeth George, *Write Away*.
There is only. . . . Barbara Taylor Bradford, in Burack, ed., *Writer's Handbook*, 1988.
I think the urge. . . . Natalie Goldberg, in *Writer's Digest* (August 2000).
I write basically. . . . James Thurber, in *Writers at Work*, 1st series.
I suppose I write. . . . Norman Mailer, in Lennon, ed., *Conversations with Norman Mailer*.
It is easy. . . . Judith Guest, in Natalie Goldberg, *Writing down the Bones*.
It's a nervous. . . . James Gould Cozzens, in Bruccoli, *James Gould Cozzens*.
My interest is in. . . . Philip Roth, in *Guardian* (11 September 2004).
I write to please. . . . Molly Gloss, interview by Dave Weich, www.powells.com (31 July 2000).

The fact that. . . . Ben Marcus, interview by Dave Weich, www.powells.com (16 April 2002).

What I want. . . . Jonathan Lethem, interview by Dave Weich, www.powells.com (23 September 2003).

I write, as. . . . Ira Levin, *Mystery Writers Annual, 2003*.

Reading usually. . . . Susan Sontag, in Staff of the *New York Times*, eds., *Writers on Writing*.

Neurologists have found. . . . Dr. Alice W. Flaherty, *Midnight Disease*.

Why I write. . . . George Orwell, *Collected Essays, Journalism and Letters of George Orwell*.

I am a compulsive. . . . Richard Marius, in Murray, ed., *Shoptalk*.

[B]efore you have. . . . Margaret Culkin Banning, in Hull, ed., *Writer's Book*.

I write to keep. . . . Bob Shacochis, in Waldman, ed., *Spirit of Writing*.

The first question. . . . Jacques Barzun, *Jacques Barzun on Writing, Editing, and Publishing*.

Nothing ever seems. . . . Gore Vidal, in Stanton and Vidal, eds., *Views from a Window*.

Anyone who has. . . . Mitchell Ivers, *Random House Guide to Good Writing*.

My preoccupation with. . . . Franz Kafka, in Brod, *Franz Kafka*.

A true writer's. . . . Graham Swift, in Boylan, ed., *Agony and the Ego*.

Writing is thinking. . . . Anne Morrow Lindbergh, *Locked Rooms and Open Doors*.

I don't feel. . . . Rod Serling, in Engel, *Rod Serling*.

[W]riting is the. . . . Ernest Hemingway, in Hotchner, *Papa Hemingway*.

It isn't the money. . . . Don Marquis, in Uhlan, *Rogue of Publishers' Row*.

[T]here are dozens. . . . Rebecca McClanahan, *Write Your Heart Out*.

Chapter Five. Writer's Block

I can't understand. . . . Anthony Burgess, in *Writers at Work*, 4th series.

I know I am. . . . Peter Elbow, *Writing without Teachers*.

I think that. . . . Terry McMillan, in Abbe, ed., *Writer's Handbook, 2003*.

What is one to do. . . . Sigmund Freud, in Jones, *Life and Work of Sigmund Freud*.

There are few. . . . Anne Lamott, *Bird by Bird*.

When I can't. . . . John Steinbeck, in Parini, *John Steinbeck*.

[P]ublishers always begin. . . . Katherine Anne Porter, in Givner, *Katherine Anne Porter*.

When we try. . . . Tess Gerritsen, in *Mystery Writers Annual, 2004*.

Some people, especially. . . . Scott Edelstein, *No-Experience-Necessary Writer's Course*.

I get stuck. . . . James M. Cain, in Hoopes, *Cain*.

For me. . . . Oliver Sacks, in Abbe, ed., *Writer's Handbook, 2003*.

After depression. . . . Dr. Alice W. Flaherty, *Midnight Disease*.

The extraordinarily. . . . Victoria Nelson, *On Writer's Block*.

Regardless of the issues. . . . Dennis Palumbo, *Writing from the Inside Out*.

The trail of literary. . . . Ralph Keyes, *Courage to Write*.

When you are stuck. . . . Annie Dillard, *Writing Life*.

I have always felt that. . . . James A. Michener, *James A. Michener's Writer's Handbook*.

No writer has. . . . Jacques Barzun, *Jacques Barzun on Writing, Editing, and Publishing*.

[Writer's block is]. . . . Stephen King, in Underwood and Miller, eds., *Bare Bones*.

Blocked writers are. . . . Joan Acocella, in *New Yorker* (14 and 21 June 2004).

My cure for. . . . Don Webb, in Olsen, *Rebel Yell*.

Sometimes the. . . . Sophy Burnham, *For Writers Only*.

The best way. . . . John Gardner, *On Becoming a Novelist*.

Chapter Six. The Writer's Personality

[Writers are] a. . . . Roger Rosenblatt, in *Time* (24 January 2000).

There are lots. . . . Allan Gurganus, in Epel, ed., *Writers Dreaming*.

Do you have a. . . . Betsey Lerner, *Forest for the Trees.*
I like routine. . . . Anne Tyler, in Sternburg, ed., *Writer on Her Work.*
I have a growing. . . . Anaïs Nin, in Schuller, ed., *Diary of Anaïs Nin.*
The studio where. . . . Peter Selgin, in Steele, ed., *Gotham Writers' Workshop.*
Writers mainly fall. . . . Brian W. Aldiss, in Maren, ed., *Epoch.*
Most writers I know. . . . Anne Lamott, interview by Dave Weich, www.powells.com (26 September 2003.
A surprising. . . . Dr. Alice W. Flaherty, *Midnight Disease.*
Apparently, it's. . . . Dennis Palumbo, *Writing from the Inside Out.*
One has to be. . . . James Jones, in Mitgang, ed., *Words Still Count with Me.*
Writers are such. . . . Ann Beattie, in Casey, ed., *Unholy Ghost.*
Unsurprisingly, a psychological. . . . Tom Grimes, *Workshop.*
Writers as a class. . . . Raymond Chandler, in Gardiner and Walker, eds., *Raymond Chandler Speaking.*
[T]o reach the. . . . Noah Lukeman, *First Five Pages.*
Writing is a great. . . . Agatha Christie, in *McCall's* (February 1969).
[Sigmund Freud] said. . . . Tom Wolfe, in Scura, ed., *Conversations with Tom Wolfe.*
You might want. . . . Josip Novakovich, in Novakovich, ed., *Fiction Writer's Workshop.*
The most essential. . . . Ernest Hemingway, in Plimpton, ed., *Writer's Chapbook.*
Most great writers. . . . Frank O'Connor, in Brown, ed., *Opinions and Perspectives from the "New York Times Book Review."*
I don't think. . . . Ross MacDonald, in Murray, ed., *Shoptalk.*
I have the wrong. . . . Janet Burroway, in Sternburg, ed., *Writer on Her Work.*
[T]he [writer] . . . possesses. . . . Dr. Beatrice Hinkle, in Hull, ed., *Writer's Book.*
It is no accident. . . . Richard D. Altick, *Lives and Letters.*
Arguably the biggest. . . . Dr. Alice W. Flaherty, *Midnight Disease.*
To be a good. . . . Czeslaw Milosz, in Mitgang, ed., *Words Still Count with Me.*
Novelists are oxymorons. . . . Norman Mailer, in *New Yorker* (23 and 30 December 2002).
Writers' minds, I. . . . Patricia Highsmith, in Winn, ed., *Murderess Ink.*
Any person who. . . . Merle Miller, in Hull and Drury, eds., *Writer's Roundtable.*
There are very. . . . Paul Theroux, in Polak, ed., *Writer As Celebrity.*
I cannot get drunk. . . . W. Somerset Maugham, *Summing Up.*
I'm a loner. . . . Haruki Murakami, in *Paris Review* (summer 2004).
Stupid people do. . . . George V. Higgins, *On Writing.*
My findings show. . . . Arnold Ludwig, *The Price of Greatness.*
[T]he manic-depressive. . . . Dr. Jablow Hershman, in Hershman and Lieb, *Manic Depression and Creativity.*
The fiery aspects of. . . . Kay Redfield Jamison, *Touched with Fire.*
My greatest. . . . John Steinbeck, in *Writers at Work*, 4th series.
Psychologist Anthony. . . . Bonni Goldberg, *Beyond the Words.*
Writers should have. . . . Leonard S. Bernstein, *Getting Published.*

Chapter Seven. Outlining
By writing an. . . . Tom Wolfe, in Scura, ed., *Conversations with Tom Wolfe.*
The danger of. . . . Michael Connelly, in *Writer's Digest* (September 1999).
There are two. . . . Jean Auel, in Strickland, ed., *On Being a Writer.*
Being forced. . . . Susan Elizabeth Phillips, in Abbe, ed., *Writer's Handbook, 2004.*
There's nothing. . . . Donald Hamilton, in Daigh, *Maybe You Should Write a Book.*
Another of my. . . . Raymond Chandler, in Gardiner and Walker, eds., *Raymond Chandler Speaking.*

I almost know. . . . William Boyd, in Steinberg, ed., *Writing for Your Life*.
I don't plot. . . . Nora Roberts, in *Writer's Digest* (June 2001).
The liability of. . . . David Morrell, *Lessons from a Lifetime of Writing*.
Sometimes, in a book. . . . Lawrence Block, in *Writer* (July 2003).
I think with. . . . Sue Grafton, www.writerswrite.com (October 1999).
I sit down. . . . Jeffery Deaver, in *Writer's Digest* (November 2000).
The plot outline. . . . Elizabeth George, in *Writer's Digest* (February 2003).
Why not an. . . . Jacques Barzun, *Jacques Barzun on Writing, Editing, and Publishing*.
If you are. . . . Ian Jackman, *Writer's Mentor*.
You can either do. . . . Terry Brooks, *Sometimes the Magic Works*.
I learned that. . . . Tracy Chevalier, in *Writer's Digest* (August 2002).
I have these. . . . J. K. Rowling, interview by Jeremy Paxman, *BBC News* (19 June 2003).
I haven't the. . . . Henry Miller, in Moore, ed., *Henry Miller on Writing*.
I rarely have. . . . James Thurber, in Fensch, ed., *Conversations with James Thurber*.
I always plan. . . . Elizabeth George, *Write Away*.
Structure is often. . . . David Madden, *Revising Fiction*.
[T]he most important. . . . Daniel Boorstin, in Lamb, ed., *Booknotes*.

Chapter Eight. Plots and Plotting

If you read . . . . J. Madison Davis, *Novelist's Essential Guide to Creating Plot*.
I define . . . . Ursula K. LeGuin, in Abbe, ed., *Writer's Handbook*, 2003.
Plots are nothing. . . . Louis L'Amour, *Education of a Wandering Man*.
Most successful fiction. . . . Jack M. Bickham, *Scene and Structure*.
Plot is the. . . . Ansen Dibell, *Plot*.
When I plot. . . . Dorothy Eden, in Daigh, *Maybe You Should Write a Book*.
Most writers think. . . . Raymond Chandler, in MacShane, ed., *Selected Letters of Raymond Chandler*.
You can begin. . . . Elizabeth George, *Write Away*.
Plot-driven commercial. . . . James Scott Bell, in *Writer's Digest* (December 2003).
MFA's [masters of fine arts] write. . . . Donald Maass, *Career Novelist*.
If you look. . . . Ian Jackman, *Writer's Mentor*.
A woman never. . . . James M. Cain, in Hoopes, *Cain*.
Starting in the. . . . Dennis Lehane, in *3rd Degree* (January 2003).
Many writers spend. . . . Noah Lukeman, *First Five Pages*.
I think plots. . . . Stuart Woods, in *3rd Degree* (January 2003).
A plot isn't. . . . Robert Kernen, *Building Better Plots*.
An idea is. . . . John Dufresne, *The Lie That Tells a Truth*.
Since a novel. . . . Ayn Rand, in Branden, *Judgment Day*.
[T]heme is not. . . . Rhona Martin, *Writing Historical Fiction*.
I distrust plot. . . . Stephen King, *On Writing*.
Know the story. . . . John Irving, in Pack and Parini, eds., *Writers on Writing*.
Probably more than. . . . Stephanie Kay Bendel, *Making Crime Pay*.
Never raise expectations. . . . Patricia T. O'Conner, *Words Fail Me*.
A reader can. . . . Michael C. Eberhardt, in Murphy, ed., *Their Word Is Law*.
[D]on't distract. . . . Florence King, in *Writer's Digest* (July 1990).
[O]nce you have. . . . Jay Brandon, in Murphy, ed., *Their Word Is Law*.
As far as I'm. . . . David Morrell, *Lessons Learned from a Lifetime of Writing*.
[S]how me a. . . . William Noble, *Writing Dramatic Nonfiction*.
I'm incapable of. . . . Stanley Elkin, in Dembo, ed., *Interviews with Contemporary Writers*.
The best plot. . . . David King, in *Writer's Digest* (July 1998).

A good ending. . . . David Michael Kaplan, *Revision.*
Contemporary popular. . . . Michael Seidman, *Complete Guide to Editing Your Fiction.*
Flashbacks come in. . . . Ron Rozelle, *Description and Setting.*
Flashbacks [in dramatic nonfiction]. . . . William Noble, *Writing Dramatic Nonfiction.*
If you feel. . . . Orson Scott Card, in Clark, ed., *Handbook of Novel Writing.*
[A]ny gain made. . . . Nancy Kress, in Clark, ed., *Handbook of Novel Writing.*
Beginning a story. . . . David Michael Kaplan, *Revision.*
A work of. . . . Thomas Mallon, *In Fact.*

Chapter Nine. Setting

One of the. . . . Ron Rozelle, *Description and Setting.*
The setting of. . . . Stephanie Kay Bendel, *Making Crime Pay.*
Ideas can come. . . . Elizabeth George, *Write Away.*
To avoid confusion. . . . Lou W. Stanek, *Story Starters.*
Stories must happen. . . . Jarvis A. Thurston, *Reading Modern Short Stories.*
When readers read. . . . Caren Gussoff, in Steele, ed., *Gotham Writers' Workshop.*
When you choose. . . . Jack M. Bickham, *Setting.*
If the setting. . . . Robert DeMaria, *College Handbook of Creative Writing.*
[M]any writing teachers. . . . William Noble, *Writing Dramatic Nonfiction.*
I have always. . . . Ngaio Marsh, in Winn, ed., *Murderess Ink.*
A real location. . . . Phyllis A. Whitney, *Guide to Fiction Writing.*
Environment includes. . . . Elwood Maren, *Characters Make Your Story.*
Many writers make. . . . Robert DeMaria, *College Handbook of Creative Writing.*
Generally, in a. . . . Mary McCarthy, *The Writings on the Wall and Other Literary Essays.*
Many of the. . . . Rust Hills, in Fredette, ed., *Handbook of Short Story Writing.*
Natural settings. . . . Jarvis A. Thurston, *Reading Modern Short Stories.*
For most novelists. . . . Joyce Carol Oates, *Where I've Been, and Where I'm Going.*
The great novelists. . . . Donald Maass, *Writing the Breakout Novel.*
Almost anything drawn. . . . Elizabeth Bowen, in Allen, ed., *Writers on Writing.*
Setting is as. . . . Bob Mayer, in *Writer's Digest* (March 2004).
A good novel. . . . Helen Haukeness, in Clark, ed., *Handbook of Novel Writing.*
If I had to. . . . Robert Penn Warren, in Duggan et al., *Conversations with Writers.*
In scenes, events. . . . Renni Browne, *Self-Editing for Fiction Writers.*
[I enjoy] creating. . . . Charles Baxter, in Levasseur and Rabalais, eds., *Novel Voices.*

Chapter Ten. Point of View

Perhaps the single. . . . Kit Reed, in Henry, ed., *Fiction Writer's Market, 1987.*
[M]y friend Richard. . . . Raymond Carver, in Strickland, ed., *On Being a Writer.*
When a novelist. . . . Robert C. Meredith and John D. Fitzgerald, *Structuring Your Novel.*
I like the. . . . Toni Morrison, in Zinsser, ed., *Inventing the Truth.*
For me narrative. . . . Jonathan Lethem, in Olsen, *Rebel Yell.*
It is always. . . . Anthony Trollope, in Allen, ed., *Writers on Writing.*
I beg the. . . . W. Somerset Maugham, in Haverstick, ed., *Saturday Review Treasury.*
First-person narratives. . . . Lesley Grant-Adamson, *Writing Crime and Suspense Fiction.*
[I]f a story. . . . Sol Stein, *Stein on Writing.*
The first-person. . . . Jim Thompson, in Polito, *Savage Art.*
Even in the. . . . Stephen Koch, *Writer's Workshop.*
A useful variant. . . . Joel Rosenberg, in Clark, ed., *Handbook of Novel Writing.*
When I write. . . . Andre Dubus, in Levasseur and Rabalais, eds., *Novel Voices.*
The appeal of. . . . Thomas Mallon, in *New Yorker* (5 July 2004).

Quite a few. . . . Elizabeth George, *Write Away.*
A first-person. . . . Raymond Chandler, in MacShane, ed., *Selected Letters of Raymond Chandler.*
Just write your. . . . Donald Hamilton, in Burack, ed., *Writer's Handbook, 1988.*
Third-person singular. . . . Barry Hannah, in *Paris Review* (winter 2004).
A story told. . . . David Madden, *Revising Fiction.*
Whether I write. . . . Phyllis A. Whitney, in Grafton et al., *Writing Mysteries.*
Point of view. . . . Mary Kay Andrews, www.HarperCollins.com (2004).
Omniscient point. . . . Nancy Kress, in *Writer's Digest* (November 1998).
If the author. . . . Sherri Szeman, *Mastering Point of View.*
If you have. . . . Graham Greene, in Allain, ed., *Conversations with Graham Greene.*
A particularly strong. . . . William Noble, *Writing Dramatic Nonfiction.*
When a writer. . . . Patricia T. O'Conner, *Words Fail Me.*
I don't like. . . . Christopher Keeslar, in Abbe, ed., *Writer's Handbook, 2002.*
Beginning writers. . . . Sherri Szeman, *Mastering Point of View.*
The twentieth-century. . . . Anne Dillard, *Living by Fiction.*
If it's crucial. . . . Nancy Kress, in *Writer's Digest* (May 1995).
Most nonfiction. . . . Sherri Szeman, in Leder and Heffron, eds., *Complete Handbook of Novel Writing.*

Chapter Eleven. Characterization

The first step. . . . Linda Seger, *Creating Unforgettable Characters.*
My stories write. . . . Isaac Asimov, in S. Asimov, ed., *Yours, Isaac Asimov.*
My characters write. . . . Ray Bradbury, in Busch, ed., *Letters to a Fiction Writer.*
Whenever characters. . . . Alberto Moravia, in *Writers at Work,* 1st series.
Fictional characters. . . . John Banville, in Boylan, ed., *Agony and the Ego.*
The notion that. . . . Jerome Weidman, *Praying for Rain.*
I try to get. . . . Elmore Leonard, in Mitgang, ed., *Words Still Count with Me.*
[A]void wishy-washy. . . . Brandi Reissenweber, in Steele, ed., *Gotham Writers' Workshop.*
The writer, like. . . . Jack Higgins, in *Writer's Journal* (March/April 2000).
You are a minor. . . . Susan Isaacs, in *3rd Degree* (May 2001).
It's very hard. . . . James Gould Cozzens, in Bruccoli, *James Gould Cozzens.*
Some [characters] come. . . . Ernest Hemingway in *Writers at Work,* 2d series.
I should say. . . . W. Somerset Maugham, in Allen, ed., *Writers on Writing.*
In practice I. . . . Norman Mailer, in Lennon, ed., *Conversations with Norman Mailer.*
When we speak. . . . Brandilyn Collins, *Getting into Character.*
If you can't. . . . James N. Frey, *How to Write a Damn Good Novel, II.*
If you were. . . . Sol Stein, *Stein on Writing.*
Let your characters. . . . Gayle Brandeis, *Fruitflesh.*
[T]he most difficult. . . . Christopher LaFarge, in Hull, ed., *Writer's Book.*
The schlemiel story. . . . Robert Silverberg, *New Dimensions II.*
Your characters must. . . . Orson Scott Card, in Fredette, ed., *Handbook of Short Story Writing.*
Avoid the strange. . . . Elwood Maren, *Characters Make Your Story.*
Ruling sympathy. . . . Elizabeth Bowen, in Allen, ed., *Writers on Writing.*
I like to. . . . Haruki Murakami, in *Paris Review* (summer 2004).
Any story has. . . . Christopher Tilghman, in *Literary Review* (winter 1995).
Characters take on life. . . . Eudora Welty, *One Writer's Beginnings.*
You often have. . . . Robert Olen Butler, in Gee, ed., *Novel and Short Story Writer's Market, 1995.*
For characters to. . . . Sonia Levitin, in *Writer* (December 1997).

Your protagonist. . . . Laurie Henry, *The Novelist's Notebook*.
Too often, in. . . . Orson Scott Card, in Clark, ed., *Handbook of Novel Writing*.
Every character must. . . . Lajos Egri, *Art of Creative Writing*.
On page 3. . . . Ann Hood, *Creating Character Emotions*.
One great difference. . . . W. Somerset Maugham, *Summing Up*.
One of the most. . . . Donald Maass, *Writing the Breakout Novel*.
I once had to. . . . Carrie Brown, in Levasseur and Rabalais, eds., *Novel Voices*.
I have never. . . . Robert Crichton, in McCormack, ed., *Afterwords*.
You'll have to. . . . James Alexander Thom, in *Writer's Digest* (March 1998).
My female characters. . . . John Fowles, in McCormack, ed., *Afterwords*.
I'm not a good. . . . Elmore Leonard, in Prescott, *Never in Doubt*.
It's a mistake. . . . Georges Simenon, in Marnham, *The Man Who Wasn't Maigret*.
If, after you. . . . James N. Frey, *How to Write a Damn Good Novel, II*.
To even begin. . . . Noah Lukeman, *Plot Thickens*.
Most people, though. . . . Elwood Maren, *Characters Make Your Story*.
A stream of complaints. . . . William Noble, *Conflict, Action and Suspense*.
In society the. . . . André Maurois, *Memoirs 1885–1967*.
In the course of. . . . Norman Mailer, in *New Yorker* (23 and 30 December 2002).
Since almost every. . . . Harry Fenson, in Fenson and Kritzer, *Writing about Short
    Stories*.
Change in fortune. . . . David Madden, *Revising Fiction*.
The over-thirty. . . . Martin Russ, *Showdown Semester*.
I find characters. . . . Donald Westlake, interviewed by Joe Hartlaub, www.
    bookreporter.com (3 May 2002).

Chapter Twelve. Dialogue
When I write. . . . Elizabeth Berg, *Escaping into the Open*.
Dialog is first. . . . David Madden, *Revising Fiction*.
Adversarial dialogue. . . . Sol Stein, *Stein on Writing*.
Dialogue is more. . . . Anne Lamott, *Bird by Bird*.
Nothing could so. . . . John O'Hara, in MacShane, *Life of John O'Hara*.
Writing dialogue is a. . . . Tom Chiarella, *Writing Dialogue*.
The ability of a. . . . Frank MacShane, in MacShane, ed., *Collected Stories of John
    O'Hara*.
My mother looks. . . . Tom Chiarella, *Writing Dialogue*.
New writers seem. . . . Aaron Elkins, in Grafton et al., *Writing Mysteries*.
[A]dverbs in speech. . . . Allison Amend, in Steele, ed., *Gotham Writers' Workshop*.
When I open. . . . Graham Greene, in Allain, ed., *Conversations with Graham Greene*.
[I]f you write. . . . Nora Lofts, in Daigh, *Maybe You Should Write a Book*.
I think that. . . . K. C. Constantine, in Winks, ed., *Colloquium on Crime*.
Dialogue requires. . . . Elizabeth Bowen, in Allen, ed., *Writers on Writing*.
Dialogue presents a. . . . John Hersey, in Hull, ed., *Writer's Book*.
Uneducated people have. . . . Tim Gautreaux, in Levasseur and Rabalais, eds., *Novel
    Voices*.
In spite of the. . . . Wallace Stegner, *On Teaching and Writing Fiction*.
If you need. . . . Sol Stein, *Stein on Writing*.
Naturalistic or "kitchen. . . . " Parke Godwin, in Mettee, ed., *Portable Writers'
    Conference*.
An important rule. . . . Ben Bova, *Notes to a Science Fiction Writer*.
Exciting dialogue is. . . . Alice Orr, *No More Rejections*.
If the characters . . . . Bharti Kirchner in *The Writer* (August 2004)

Writers often get. . . . Lesley Grant-Adamson, *Writing Crime and Suspense Fiction.*
I let them. . . . John O'Hara, in MacShane, ed., *Collected Stories of John O'Hara.*
Writing good dialect. . . . James J. Kilpatrick, *Writer's Art.*
Dialogue, when. . . . Elwood Maren, *Characters Make Your Story.*
If you substitute. . . . Stephen King, *On Writing.*
Don't have characters. . . . Cynthia Whitcomb, in *Writer's Digest* (August 1999).
It is the writer's privilege. . . . William Faulkner, in Blotner, *Faulkner.*
People only *write.* . . . Tom Wolfe, in Scura, ed., *Conversations with Tom Wolfe.*
The use of dialogue. . . . Edith Wharton, in Lubbock, ed., *Craft of Fiction.*
[E]xclamation points. . . . Allison Amend, in Steele, ed., *Gotham Writers' Workshop.*

Chapter Thirteen. Description

In the fields. . . . Rebecca McClanahan, *Word Painting.*
Description is. . . . A. B. Guthrie, Jr., *Field Guide to Writing Fiction.*
Beginning writers. . . . Ruth Engelken, in Dickson and Smythe, eds., *Handbook of Short Story Writing.*
One of the last. . . . Charles Baxter, interviewed by Dave Weich, www.powells.com (15 September 2003).
When it comes. . . . Michael Gilbert, in Winks, ed., *Colloquium on Crime.*
As a reader. . . . David Morrell, *Lessons from a Lifetime of Writing.*
Recognizing the. . . . Monica Wood, *Description.*
Use omniscient. . . . Rachael Ann Nunes, www.rachelannnunes.com.
Describe your [romance]. . . . Donna Baker, *Writing a Romantic Novel.*
Don't spend. . . . April Henry, in *Writer's Digest* (July 2003).
The problem. . . . Ron Rozelle, *Descriptions and Setting.*
We have almost. . . . Mary McCarthy, *Writings on the Wall and Other Literary Essays.*
When I. . . . Madge Harrah, in Gee, ed., *Novel and Short Story Writer's Market, 1994.*
[A]s my former . . . . Julie Checkoway, in Eiben and Gannon, eds., *Practical Writer.*
Description begins. . . . Stephen King, *On Writing.*
I write description. . . . Ernest Hemingway in Hotchner, *Papa Hemingway.*
[A]void the use. . . . Elwood Maren, *Characters Make Your Story.*
[A]djectives and adverbs. . . . Chris Lombardi, in Steele, ed., *Gotham Writers' Workshop.*
Those novelists. . . . Donald Maass, *Writing the Breakout Novel.*
Descriptions of the setting. . . . David Madden, *Revising Fiction.*
If you must. . . . Don James, in Dickson and Smythe, eds., *Handbook of Short Story Writing.*
[W]e no longer. . . . Emile Zola, in Allen, ed., *Writers on Writing.*
Clichés are useful. . . . Lesley Grant-Adamson, *Writing Crime and Suspense Fiction.*

Chapter Fourteen. Style

Style is an. . . . David Madden, *Revising Fiction.*
A man is. . . . Henry Miller, in Moore, ed., *Henry Miller on Writing.*
The *tone* of. . . . Lesley Grant-Adamson, *Writing Crime and Suspense Fiction.*
I don't know. . . . Paula Fox, in *Paris Review* (summer 2004).
I should like. . . . Samuel Butler, in Allen, ed., *Writers on Writing.*
There is no. . . . E. B. White, in Strunk and White, *Elements of Style.*
One can derive. . . . John Gardner, *On Writers and Writing.*
Writers most often. . . . Roger MacBride Allen, www.sfwa.org.
[T]he most durable. . . . Raymond Chandler, in MacShane, ed., *Selected Letters of Raymond Chandler.*

Bad style often. . . . Duane Unkefer, *Basic Fiction*.

It is the beginning. . . . Dashiell Hammett, in Layman, *Shadow Man*.

A really good. . . . Norman Mailer, in Lennon, ed., *Conversations with Norman Mailer*.

Few people realize. . . . William Zinsser, *On Writing Well*.

The really popular. . . . Graham Greene, in Allain, ed., *Conversations with Graham Greene*.

I write in. . . . Gore Vidal, in Stanton and Vidal, eds., *Views from a Window*.

Essentially I think. . . . Truman Capote, in Plimpton, ed., *Truman Capote*.

If a writer cares. . . . John Gardner, *On Becoming a Novelist*.

Insecure writers want. . . . Ralph Keyes, *Courage to Write*.

The first. . . . Jorge Luis Borges, in *Writers at Work*, 4th series.

American writers tend. . . . Carol Bly, *Beyond the Writer's Workshop*.

An editor might. . . . David A. Fryxell, in *Writer's Digest* (March 2000).

Those who write. . . . Albert Camus, in Anderson, *Powerful Writing Skills*.

I don't think. . . . Truman Capote, in *Writers at Work*, 1st series.

All of us. . . . James J. Kilpatrick, *Writer's Art*.

[M]odern writing at. . . . George Orwell, in Malarkey, ed., *Style*.

Professors are often. . . . Patricia Nelson Limerick, in *New York Times Book Review* (31 October 1993).

We sometimes speak. . . . Sol Stein, *Stein on Writing*.

A few sociologists. . . . Malcolm Cowley, in Malarkey, ed., *Style*.

A friend of mine. . . . Lawrence Langer, in Muscatine and Griffith, eds., *Borzoi College Reader*.

Legal writers must. . . . Bryan A. Garner, *Elements of Legal Style*.

One of the first. . . . Richard Anderson, *Powerful Writing Skills*.

It is easier. . . . George Orwell, in Muscatine and Griffith, eds., *Borzoi College Reader*.

Turning out flashy. . . . Patricia T. O'Conner, *Words Fail Me*.

Great Writing was. . . . George Saunders, *Writers under Influence*, www.amazon.com (2004).

As one reads. . . . Dale Peck, *Hatchet Job*.

As with most. . . . Frederik Pohl, in Maren, ed., *Epoch*.

One of the really. . . . Stephen King, *On Writing*.

I think sometimes. . . . James Patterson, in *Writer's Digest* (July 2001).

The one-sentence. . . . John R. Trimble, *Writing with Style*.

Style does not. . . . B. J. Chute, in Burack, ed., *Writer's Handbook*, 1998.

Style isn't something. . . . Martin Amis, interviewed by Dave Weich, www.powells.com (20 November 2003).

The best style. . . . Whit Burnett, in Burnett and Burnett, eds., *Modern Short Story in the Making*.

Chapter Fifteen. Rewriting

The beginning writer. . . . Jerry Cleaver, *Immediate Fiction*.

Revision is identical. . . . Theodore A. Rees Cheney, *Getting the Words Right*.

The only. . . . Evan Hunter, in Abbe, ed., *Writer's Handbook*, 2003.

I hate. . . . Barry Hannah, in *Paris Review* (winter 2004).

The secret is not. . . . Stephen J. Cannell, in *Esquire* (February 2003).

I don't write. . . . Dean Koontz, in *Writer's Digest* (March 2000).

I may rework. . . . Lawrence Block, in *Writer's Digest* (July 2003).

[I rewrite] the first. . . . Henry Green, in *Writers at Work*, 5th series.

Don't try to. . . . Frank McCourt, in *Writer's Digest* (February 1999).

The beautiful part. . . . Robert Cormier, in Murray, ed., *Shoptalk*.

Finish an entire. . . . Anne Eames, www.writersreview.com.
What I've learned. . . . Tess Gerritsen, in *Writer's Digest* (November 2002).
Each time I rewrite. . . . Anne Tyler, in *Writer* (April 2004).
How do I. . . . Robert Bloch, in Henry, ed., *Writer's Market, 1987.*
When revising feels . . . . Bonni Goldberg, *Beyond the Words.*
[D]o not revise. . . . Peter Selgin, in Steele, ed., *Gotham Writers' Workshop.*
The more you. . . . Gore Vidal, in Stanton and Vidal, eds., *Views from a Window.*
I revise until. . . . Kent Haruf, in Darnton, ed., *Writers on Writing.*
With all your. . . . Ian Jackman, *Writer's Mentor.*
I don't think. . . . E. L. Doctorow, in *Writers at Work,* 8th series.
Everything new I. . . . Anne Morrow Lindbergh, *Locked Rooms and Open Doors.*
Revision . . . tests our. . . . Jan Burke, in Grafton et al., *Writing Mysteries.*
A novel is. . . . James M. Cain, in Hoopes, *Cain.*
When I was. . . . Nora Ephron, in *Writer* (April 1987).
There are writers. . . . Lesley Grant-Adamson, *Writing Crime and Suspense Fiction.*
No one except. . . . Phyllis A. Whitney, *Guide to Fiction Writing.*
I have been. . . . Barbara Pym, in Holt, *Lot to Ask.*
Fiction writers. . . . Theodore A. Rees Cheney, *Getting the Words Right.*
There are no rules. . . . Ian Jackman, *Writer's Mentor.*
Never correct or. . . . John Steinbeck, in *Writers at Work,* 4th series.
Most of the time. . . . Peter Elbow, *Writing without Teachers.*
I suffer agony. . . . Thomas Wolfe, in Berg, *Max Perkins.*
The main rule. . . . Isaac Bashevis Singer, in Murray, ed., *Shoptalk.*
I am a. . . . Bernard Malamud, in Lasher, ed., *Conversations with Bernard Malamud.*
I write many. . . . John Dufresne, in Abbe, ed., *Writer's Handbook, 2002.*
I think too. . . . Alexandra Styron, in *Writer's Digest* (August 2001).
Rodin . . . said that. . . . Gail Godwin, in Sternburg, ed., *Writer on Her Work.*
I write slowly. . . . William H. Gass, in *Writers at Work,* 5th series.

Chapter Sixteen. Titles

Image is almost. . . . Judy Cullins, www.independentpublisher.com (April 2004).
Titles are chosen. . . . Doris Picker Marston, *Guide to Writing History.*
Alliteration is the. . . . Edwin Newman, *Literary Trivia.*
Book titles point up. . . . Pauline Glen Winslow, in Wynn, ed., *Murderess Ink.*
Writing a book. . . . Nicholas Weinstock, in Eiben and Gannon, eds., *Practical Writer.*
The title comes. . . . Heinrich Boll, in Plimpton, ed., *Writer's Chapbook.*
I make a list. . . . Ernest Hemingway, in Plimpton, ed., *Writer's Chapbook.*
I like best. . . . Phyllis A. Whitney, *Guide to Fiction Writing.*
Some authors have. . . . Oscar Collier, in Collier and Leighton, *How to Write and Sell Your First Novel.*
Picking the perfect. . . . Lesley Grant-Adamson, *Writing Crime and Suspense Fiction.*
Know exactly who. . . . Peter Rubie, in *Writer's Digest* (March 2004).
I have peculiar. . . . Raymond Chandler, in MacShane, ed., *Selected Letters of Raymond Chandler.*
When I need a. . . . Tennessee Williams, in Plimpton, ed., *Writer's Chapbook.*
Titles as a rule. . . . D. H. Lawrence, in Pack and Parini, eds., *Writers on Writing.*
I have never. . . . John Steinbeck, in *Writers at Work,* 4th series.
An effective title is. . . . John McCollister, *Writing for Dollars.*
A good title. . . . Hayes B. Jacobs, *Complete Guide to Writing and Selling Nonfiction.*
Watch people who. . . . Joni Hamilton, www.sarahsmiley.com (2004).

Not long ago. . . . James Bonnet, www.writersstore.com (2003).
In asking why. . . . Jarvis A. Thurston, *Reading Modern Short Stories*.
I'm pretty careful. . . . Isaac Asimov, *I Asimov.*

Chapter Seventeen. The Writing Life: In General

I am a writer. . . . W. Somerset Maugham, *Summing Up.*
[If] I hadn't. . . . William Saroyan, in Strickland, ed., *On Being a Writer.*
The professional writer. . . . V. S. Pritchett, *Midnight Oil.*
I find working. . . . Barry Hannah, in Conroy, ed., *Eleventh Draft.*
We are not. . . . Brian Moore, in Boylan, ed., *Agony and the Ego.*
Writing is life. . . . Terry Brooks, *Sometimes the Magic Works.*
I'm egocentric. . . . Isaac Asimov, in Polak, ed., *Writer As Celebrity.*
Many people hear. . . . Meg Chittenden, www.nt.Armstrong.edu (1999).
For a person. . . . Stephen Koch, *Writer's Workshop.*
Among all the. . . . Marc McCutcheon, *Damn! Why Didn't I Write That?*
Most writers enjoy. . . . J. B. Priestley, in Mitgang, ed., *Words Still Count with Me.*
Writing is not. . . . Georges Simenon, in *Writers at Work*, 1st series.
I think aspiring. . . . Gerald Howard, in Winokur, ed., *Advice to Writers.*
I believe that. . . . Anne Tyler, in Sternburg, ed., *Writer on Her Work.*
There is suffering. . . . Ann Patchett, in Blythe, ed., *Why I Write.*
Writing, like other. . . . Judith Barrington, *Writing the Memoir.*
If you're working. . . . Rita Mae Brown, *Starting from Scratch.*
To write is. . . . Joyce Carol Oates, in Darnton, ed., *Writers on Writing.*
I think writing. . . . Paul Theroux, in Polak, ed., *Writer As Celebrity.*
Writers when they're. . . . Joy Williams, in Blythe, ed., *Why I Write.*
Genius did not. . . . John Cheever, in Donaldson, *John Cheever.*
I don't think. . . . Joseph Heller, in *Writers at Work*, 5th series.
My theory is. . . . James Charlton, *Fighting Words.*
When you write. . . . Rebecca McClanahan, *Write Your Heart Out.*
Every time a writer. . . . Jack London, in Walker, ed., *Jack London.*
Writers don't have. . . . William Styron, in Plimpton, ed., *Truman Capote.*
I am against. . . . Georges Simenon, in Mitgang, ed., *Words Still Count with Me.*
Your battle is. . . . J. P. Donleavy, in Polak, ed., *Writer As Celebrity.*
[W]riters, in. . . . Leonard S. Bernstein, *Getting Published.*
[E]nvy is a natural. . . . Dennis Palumbo, *Writing from the Inside Out.*
It used to be. . . . Bonnie Friedman, *Writing Past Dark.*
[Y]ou are probably. . . . Anne Lamott, *Bird by Bird.*
Better to think. . . . Lorrie Moore, in Boylan, ed., *Agony and the Ego.*
I still have. . . . Agatha Christie, *Agatha Christie.*
The frightening fact. . . . Janet Fitch, in Waldman, ed., *Spirit of Writing.*
[Writing is] such. . . . Richard Ford, in Sternburg, ed., *Writer on Her Work.*
Writing is a. . . . Paul Johnson, *Pick of Paul Johnson.*
The seat of my. . . . H. L. Mencken, in Fecher, ed., *Diary of H. L. Mencken.*
The only thing. . . . Rod Serling, in Engel, *Rod Serling.*
There are several. . . . Kingsley Amis, in Dembo, ed., *Interviews with Contemporary Writers.*
Writers are most. . . . Margaret Culkin Banning, in Hull and Drury, eds., *Writer's Roundtable.*
A writer's life. . . . Stephen Koch, *Writer's Workshop.*
I happen to. . . . Ernest Hemingway, in Baker, ed., *Ernest Hemingway: Selected Letters, 1917–1961.*

Most business and. . . . John Cheever, in Donaldson, *John Cheever.*

Writing is the. . . . Hillary Waugh, *Hillary Waugh's Guide to Mysteries and Mystery Writing.*

[W]riting novels is. . . . J. K. Rowling, www.januarymagazine.com (2003).

Male writers have. . . . Ellen Moers, *Literary Women.*

My ideal of. . . . Sylvia Plath, in A. S. Plath, ed., *Letters Home.*

Women are different. . . . Barbara Pym, in Holt, *Lot to Ask.*

Writing at its. . . . Ernest Hemingway, in Hotchner, *Papa Hemingway.*

To write, you. . . . Tobias Wolff, *Writers Harvest 3.*

Life is short. . . . Stephen Jay Gould, interviewed by Doug Brown, www.powells.com (October 2003).

On the whole. . . . Duncan McLean, in Robertson, ed., *Mortification.*

Chapter Eighteen. Getting Started

I didn't begin. . . . Nadine Gordimer, in Wachtel, ed., *Writers and Company.*

I think I was. . . . Anne Tyler, in Sternburg, ed., *Writer on Her Work.*

When I first. . . . John Barth, *Further Fridays.*

I wanted to write. . . . James Patterson, in Abbe, ed., *Writer's Handbook, 2002.*

In the winter of. . . . Lauren Grodstein, *Writers under Influence,* www.amazon.com (2004).

Early in my. . . . Sue Grafton, in Abbe, ed., *Writer's Handbook, 2002.*

When I first began. . . . Erica Jong, in Strickland, ed., *On Being a Writer.*

When I read women's. . . . Toni Morrison, in Plimpton, ed., *Women Writers at Work.*

Writers need *both.* . . . Stephen Koch, *Writer's Workshop.*

[Writing] mentors are. . . . Ann Patchett, in Blythe, ed., *Why I Write.*

From the beginning. . . . Arthur Miller, *Timebends.*

[A]nyone can *become.* . . . Harlan Ellison, in Strickland, ed., *On Being a Writer.*

At some time. . . . Alexander Steele, *Gotham Writers' Workshop.*

Most writers, whether. . . . David Lodge, *Practice of Writing.*

There are people. . . . Elizabeth Berg, *Escaping into the Open.*

When we start out. . . . Phyllis A. Whitney, *Guide to Fiction Writing.*

Pick a subject. . . . John R. Trimble, *Writing with Style.*

I read the essays. . . . Tony Hillerman, *Seldom Disappointed.*

I remember very distinctly. . . . Richard Matheson, in Winter, ed., *Faces of Fear.*

When I began. . . . W. Somerset Maugham, *Summing Up.*

The most difficult. . . . Irving Wallace, in Burack, ed., *Writer's Handbook, 1988.*

A writing career. . . . Ian Jackman, *Writer's Mentor.*

In England, a. . . . Wallace Stegner, *On Teaching and Writing Fiction.*

This is how. . . . Natalie Goldberg, *Wild Mind.*

Chapter Nineteen. Workshops, Creative Writing Classes, and Writers' Conferences

As late as. . . . Alexander Steele, *Gotham Writers' Workshop.*

Unfortunately, the most. . . . Ralph Keyes, *Writer's Book of Hope.*

But you can't. . . . Anne Lamott, *Bird by Bird.*

How can anyone. . . . Wallace Stegner, *On Teaching and Writing Fiction.*

Some well-known. . . . Peter Rubie, *Elements of Storytelling.*

Talent cannot be. . . . David Madden, *Revising Fiction.*

I think that. . . . Paula Fox, in *Paris Review* (summer 2004).

Unfortunately, all too. . . . Stephen Koch, *Writer's Workshop.*

I think one. . . . Mary McCarthy, in Gelderman, ed., *Conversations with Mary McCarthy.*

Creative-writing teachers. . . . William H. Gass, in *Writers at Work*, 5th series.

Most writers who. . . . James Hynes, www.bookslut.com (June 2004).

When I went. . . . Bonnie Friedman, *Writing Past Dark*.

Go to the. . . . John Barth, *Further Fridays*.

Ideally, a college. . . . Martin Russ, *Showdown Semester*.

If I had. . . . Elizabeth Berg, *Escaping into the Open*.

One of the. . . . John Gardner, *On Becoming a Novelist*.

Anyone who will. . . . Ian Jackman, *Writer's Mentor*.

One of the. . . . C. J. Hribal, www.bookslut.com (July 2004).

If there is one. . . . Norman Mailer, *Spooky Art*.

Writers string together. . . . Leonard S. Bernstein, *Getting Published*.

I can think of. . . . Dorothea Brande, *Becoming a Writer*.

Writers are endlessly. . . . William Zinsser, *On Writing Well*.

It's often said. . . . George V. Higgins, in Murray, ed., *Their Word Is Law*.

Creative writing courses. . . . David Lodge, *Practice of Writing*.

In the practice. . . . Frederick Busch, *Dangerous Profession*.

Sometimes . . . [writing] instructors. . . . Jan Burke, in Sue Grafton et al., *Writing Mysteries*.

Recently, I've learned. . . . Stanley Elkin, in Dembo, ed., *Interviews with Contemporary Writers*.

Don't be too. . . . Martin Russ, *Showdown Semester*.

On the first day. . . . T. C. Boyle, in Bowling, ed., *Novel and Short Story Writer's Market, 2002*.

I want my students . . . . David Huddle, in Pack and Parini, ed., *Writers on Writing*.

You can talk to. . . . A. M. Holmes, interviewed by Dave Weich, www.powells.com (24 May 1999).

[T]he first value. . . . John Gardner, *On Becoming a Novelist*.

[Workshops are] . . . dangerous. . . . Terry McMillan, in Leder and Heffron, eds., *Complete Handbook of Novel Writing*.

It's quite true. . . . Martin Russ, *Showdown Semester*.

[Workshop-influenced]. . . . Chris Altacuise, in Olsen, *Rebel Yell*.

Workshops taught me. . . . Judy Budnitz, in *Writer's Digest* (December 1999).

I think for. . . . John W. Rowell, in *Writer's Digest* (July 2003).

When I look. . . . Geoffrey Wolff, in Conroy, ed., *Eleventh Draft*.

Creative writing classes. . . . Anne Lamott, *Bird by Bird*.

I've come to . . . . Lawrence Block, *Write for Your Life*

A [writers'] conference. . . . Kevin James Kage, in *Writer's Digest* (May 2000).

I'm always embarrassed. . . . Steven James in *Writer's Digest* (October 1999).

Chapter Twenty. Rejection

I once decorated. . . . John Jerome, *Writing Trade*.

Rejection slips are. . . . Leonard S. Bernstein, *Getting Published*.

Over and over again. . . . Elizabeth Berg, *Escaping into the Open*.

There is a. . . . Andre Bernard, in Henderson and Bernard, eds., *Rotten Reviews and Rejections*.

Pearl Buck received. . . . Dennis E. Hensley, in Abbe, ed., *Writer's Handbook, 2002*.

I have collected. . . . Ann Petry, in Hull, ed., *Writer's Book*.

What writer doesn't. . . . Janet Fitch, in Waldman, ed., *Spirit of Writing*.

Learning to. . . . Travis Adkins, in Brogan, ed., *Writer's Market, 2003*.

What I clearly. . . . Sophy Burnham, *For Writers Only*.

[W]hen you get. . . . Colson Whitehead, www.writenet.org (2000).

[R]ejections don't distress. . . . Delmore Schwartz, in Phillips, ed., *Letters of Delmore Schwartz.*

My favorite rejection. . . . Lisa Scottoline, www.authorlink.com (June 2004).

An editor rejected. . . . William G. Tapply, *Elements of Mystery Fiction.*

Some degree of. . . . William Maxwell, *Outermost Dream.*

[A] rejection . . . may. . . . Judith Appelbaum, *How to Get Happily Published.*

Rejection is part. . . . Cork Millner, in Henry, ed., *Writer's Market, 1987.*

Rejection follows. . . . John Steinbeck, in Parini, *John Steinbeck.*

One thing about. . . . Alice Sebold, in *Writer's Digest* (December 2002).

A rejection of. . . . Isaac Asimov, in S. Asimov, ed., *Yours, Isaac Asimov.*

The worst job. . . . Alan Landsburg, in Engel, *Rod Serling.*

Next to come. . . . Tony Hillerman, *Seldom Disappointed.*

The world of. . . . Jeff Herman, *Writer's Guide to Book Editors, Publishers, and Literary Agents, 2000–2001.*

Virtually all magazines. . . . C. Michael Curtis, in Eiben and Gannon, eds., *Practical Writer.*

In those days. . . . Renata Adler, *Gone.*

I was trying. . . . Louis L'Amour, *Education of a Wandering Man.*

Rejection slips are. . . . Will Allison, in Bowling, ed., *Novel and Short Story Writer's Market, 2002.*

Don't take rejection. . . . Frank O'Connor, in *Writers at Work*, 1st series.

I have had. . . . Katherine Anne Porter, in Givner, *Katherine Anne Porter.*

My career was . . . . Stephen King, in Underwood and Miller, eds., *Bare Bones.*

In some cases. . . . Robin Hemley, in Henry, ed., *Fiction Writer's Market, 1987.*

If you wrap. . . . Scott Sanders, in Henry, ed., *Fiction Writer's Market, 1987.*

In almost every. . . . in Dennis Palumbo, *Writing from the Inside Out.*

I live in. . . . Bonnie Friedman, *Writing Past Dark.*

Chapter Twenty-one. Work Habits, Rituals, and Daily Word Quotas

The actor works. . . . Daphne du Maurier, in Abbe, ed., *Writer's Handbook, 2002.*

I know very. . . . Alec Waugh, in Brown, ed., *Opinions and Perspectives from the "New York Times Book Review."*

If writing. . . . Jonathan Franzen, in Abbe, ed., *Writer's Handbook, 2003.*

[R]eports of. . . . Dorothea Brande, *Becoming a Writer.*

I have just spent. . . . Gustave Flaubert, in Allen, ed., *Writers on Writing.*

I work almost. . . . Joseph Heller, in Fredette, ed., *Fiction Writer's Market, 1985.*

I'm always quite. . . . Truman Capote, in Grobel, ed., *Conversations with Capote.*

After I get. . . . James Jones, in Plimpton, ed., *Writer's Chapbook.*

In actuality. . . . Rebecca McClanahan, *Write Your Heart Out.*

Making writing a. . . . Julia Cameron, *Writer's Life.*

It's very easy. . . . A. D. Hudler, in *Writer's Journal* (September/October 2004).

Men writers who. . . . Phyllis A. Whitney, *Guide to Fiction Writing.*

A novel is. . . . John Irving, in *Writers at Work*, 8th series.

If one wants. . . . Graham Greene, in Allain, ed., *Conversations with Graham Greene.*

There are tricks. . . . Ramsey Campbell, in Winter, ed., *Faces of Fear.*

I spend most. . . . Clive Barker, in Epel, ed., *Writers Dreaming.*

Most writers work. . . . Ralph Keyes, *Courage to Write.*

I write on. . . . Linda Fairstein, in Murphy, ed., *Their Word Is Law.*

Once I start. . . . Stephen King, in *Writer's Digest* (21 April 2001).

My only ritual. . . . Isaac Asimov, in Murray, ed., *Shoptalk.*

I am a completely. . . . Truman Capote, in Plimpton, ed., *Truman Capote.*

As for me. . . . Delmore Schwartz, in Phillips, ed., *Letters of Delmore Schwartz.*
I write in. . . . Forrest McDonald, in Lamb, ed., *Booknotes.*
When I'm working. . . . Allan Gurganus, in Epel, ed., *Writers Dreaming.*
I prefer to work. . . . John O'Hara, in Farr, *O'Hara.*
I write when. . . . Raymond Chandler, in Gardiner and Walker, eds., *Raymond Chandler Speaking.*
I like to. . . . Ernest Hemingway, in Hotchner, *Papa Hemingway.*
I work on a. . . . David McCullough, in Lamb, ed., *Booknotes.*
[C]onsider the pen. . . . Natalie Goldberg, *Writing down the Bones.*
I work on one. . . . John Barth, in Polak, ed., *Writer As Celebrity.*
I myself cannot. . . . John Gardner, *On Becoming a Novelist.*
I've always worked. . . . Shelby Foote, in Lamb, ed., *Booknotes.*
When it's time. . . . Janette Oke, in *Writer's Digest* (September 1998).
[T]each yourself. . . . Richard Bausch, in Busch, ed., *Letters to a Fiction Writer.*
What the writer. . . . Catherine Drinker Bowen, in Murray, ed., *Shoptalk.*
I write a lot. . . . Donald Barthelme, in McCullough, ed., *People, Books, and Book People.*
What I do. . . . Jack Kerouac, in *Writers at Work,* 4th series.
I keep to. . . . Isaac Asimov, in Daigh, *Maybe You Should Write a Book.*
I get up. . . . Sylvia Townsend Warner, in Steinman, ed., *Element of Lavishness.*
I write every. . . . Erica Jong, in Strickland, ed., *On Being a Writer.*
I usually. . . . Stuart Woods, in *New York Noose* (summer/fall 2005).
When I'm in. . . . Ann Rule, www.writersreview.com (2002).
I write at night. . . . Taylor Caldwell, in Daigh, *Maybe You Should Write a Book.*
I write from. . . . Ed McBain, www.bookreporter.com (21 January 2000).
On a good. . . . James A. Michener, *James A. Michener's Writer's Handbook.*
When I'm. . . . Haruki Murakami, in *Paris Review* (summer 2004).
[I]n my 20's. . . . Donald Westlake, www.bookreporter.com (21 April 2000).
I don't structure. . . . Lawrence Block, in Fredette, ed., *Handbook of Short Story Writing.*

Chapter Twenty-two. Money, the Day Job, and the Economic Realities of Writing

Being a writer. . . . Rob Long, *Conversations with My Agent.*
My generation was . . . . John Updike, in *Writer's Digest* (January 2002).
I didn't want. . . . Sophy Burnham, *For Writers Only.*
There are only. . . . Merle Miller, in Hull and Drury, eds., *Writer's Roundtable.*
For every writer. . . . Isaac Asimov, in S. Asimov, ed., *Yours, Isaac Asimov.*
There's a difference. . . . Margaret Atwood, in Dembo, ed., *Interviews with Contemporary Writers.*
I hate to hear. . . . Andrew Ferguson, in Lamb, ed., *Booknotes.*
More likely, the. . . . John Gardner, *On Becoming a Novelist.*
Almost nobody makes. . . . Rebecca Tope, in *3rd Degree* (December 2002).
When people ask. . . . Rebecca McClanahan, *Write Your Heart Out.*
You would-be. . . . Larry L. King, *None but a Blockhead.*
[Economic] security is. . . . Tennessee Williams, in Burnett and Burnett, eds., *Modern Short Story in the Making.*
[S]ome writers find. . . . Dr. Alice W. Flaherty, *Midnight Disease.*
I'd advise a. . . . Bernard Malamud, in Lasher, ed., *Conversations with Bernard Malamud.*
Perhaps the worst. . . . Donald Maass, *Career Novelist.*

My advice is. . . . R. Barrie Flowers, www.writersreview.com (2001).
The truth is. . . . Julia Cameron, in *Writer's Digest* (March 2003).
I think there is. . . . Nancy Peacock, in *Writer's Digest* (July 2003).
I am sacrificing. . . . Sylvia Plath, in A. S. Plath, ed., *Letters Home.*
I've been trying. . . . Delmore Schwartz, in Phillips, ed., *Letters of Delmore Schwartz.*
Teaching is entirely. . . . Robert Lowell, in Parkinson, ed., *Robert Lowell.*
I've always worried. . . . Christian Bauman, in *Writer's Digest* (July 2003).
The bookstore. . . . Larry McMurtry, in McCullough, ed., *People, Books, and Book People.*
Occasionally, a. . . . Edward Uhlan, *Rogue of Publishers' Row.*
I admire honest. . . . Robert Graves, in Brown, ed., *Opinions and Perspectives from the "New York Times Book Review."*
I never found. . . . Louis L'Amour, *Education of a Wandering Man.*
I believe . . . that. . . . John O'Hara, in Farr, *O'Hara.*
New fiction writers. . . . Donald Maass, *Career Novelist.*
Writing a best-seller. . . . Norman Mailer, *Spooky Art.*
We writers are. . . . Gore Vidal, in Stanton and Vidal, eds., *Views from a Window.*
It is easy. . . . W. Somerset Maugham, *Summing Up.*
[I]f I didn't. . . . Vance Bourjaily, in Duggan et al., eds., *Conversations with Writers.*
Being a professional. . . . Steven Connor, in Waldman, ed., *Spirit of Writing.*
It is a very. . . . Julia Cameron, *Writer's Life.*

Chapter Twenty-three. Productivity

If you apply. . . . Ayn Rand, in Rand and Mayhew, eds., *Art of Nonfiction.*
Evaluate how. . . . Elizabeth George, in Leder and Heffron, eds., *Complete Handbook of Novel Writing.*
To be productive. . . . Sue Grafton, in Burack, ed., *Writer's Handbook, 1998.*
[D]uring the past. . . . H. L. Mencken, in Fecher, ed., *Diary of H. L. Mencken.*
I've written about. . . . Ray Bradbury, in Strickland, ed., *On Being a Writer.*
I don't feel. . . . John Updike, in Abbe, ed., *Writer's Handbook, 2002.*
I wish I had. . . . Cynthia Ozick, in Wachtel, ed., *Writers and Company.*
Productivity is the. . . . Stephen Koch, *Writer's Workshop.*
I can go. . . . David Markson, www.centerforbookculture.org (March 1999).
A mystery writer. . . . Richard Lockridge, in Hull, ed., *Writer's Book.*
It looks as. . . . Jay Pearsal, *Mystery and Crime.*
I've slowed down. . . . Sue Grafton, www.writerswrite.com (October 1999).
I like my. . . . Isaac Asimov, in S. Asimov, ed., *Yours, Isaac Asimov.*
If a full-time. . . . Annie Dillard, *Writing Life.*
If I work two. . . . James A. Michener, *James A. Michener's Writer's Handbook.*
As for my. . . . Graham Greene, in Allain, ed., *Conversations with Graham Greene.*
[M]any writers who. . . . Dr. Alice W. Flaherty, *Midnight Disease.*
Most writers write. . . . Richard Ford, in Darnton, ed., *Writers on Writing.*
I've been. . . . Anthony Burgess, in *Writers at Work,* 4th series.
I would work. . . . Thomas Wolfe, in Tobin, ed., *Golden Age.*
If [novelists] keep. . . . Larry McMurtry, *Walter Benjamin at the Dairy Queen.*
I think there's. . . . William Faulkner, in Meriwether and Millgate, eds., *Lion in the Garden.*
When writers get. . . . Jay Parini, in Pack and Parini, eds., *Writers on Writing.*
[T]here is a. . . . Joan Acocella, in *New Yorker* (14 and 21 June 2004).
I think I do. . . . Truman Capote, in Clarke, *Capote.*
I am twenty-eight. . . . John Steinbeck, in Parini, *John Steinbeck.*

There are several. . . . Jonathan Yardley, *Misfit.*
They [young writers]. . . . W. Somerset Maugham, *Summing Up.*
[T]hose few who. . . . George V. Higgins, *On Writing.*
No one is waiting. . . . Jeffrey Eugenides, in *New Yorker* (14 and 21 June 2004).
[T]here is the. . . . Dorothea Brande, *Becoming a Writer.*
One of the. . . . Edward Uhlan, *Rogue of Publishers' Row.*
A man can. . . . Anthony Burgess, in *Writers at Work,* 4th series.
The thing about. . . . Sylvia Plath, in A. S. Plath, ed., *Letters Home.*
The far greater. . . . Gish Gen, in Leder and Heffron, eds., *Complete Handbook of Novel Writing.*
I wonder if. . . . Alec Waugh, in Brown, ed., *Opinions and Perspectives from the "New York Times Book Review."*
Always I have. . . . John Steinbeck, in Demott, ed., *Working Days.*
A bad novel. . . . Paul Johnson, *Pick of Paul Johnson.*

Chapter Twenty-four. Reviews
I have a. . . . John Irving, in Plimpton, ed., *Writer's Chapbook.*
Criticism and. . . . Dorothea Brande, *Becoming a Writer.*
Is it not. . . . Delmore Schwartz, in Phillips, ed., *Letters of Delmore Schwartz.*
I am never. . . . H. L. Mencken, in Fecher, ed., *Diary of H. L. Mencken.*
People who aren't. . . . Aaron Elkins, in *Mystery Writers Annual, 2004.*
I can get. . . . John O'Hara, in MacShane, ed., *Life of John O'Hara.*
I get. . . . Anthony Burgess, in *Writers at Work,* 4th series.
A recent review. . . . Robert Coover, in Steinberg, ed., *Writing for Your Life.*
I am not. . . . Ann Beattie, in Casey, ed., *Unholy Ghost.*
A lady who. . . . Carolyn See, *Making a Literary Life.*
I'd never dream. . . . Norman Mailer, in Lennon, ed., *Conversations with Norman Mailer.*
Very often. . . . Dorothy Salisbury Davis, in Winks, ed., *Colloquium on Crime.*
It's discouraging. . . . James Lee Burke, interviewed by Dave Weich, www.powells.com (4 August 2000).
It isn't. . . . Joyce Carol Oates, in Johnson, *Invisible Writer.*
The critics don't. . . . Aldous Huxley, in *Writers at Work,* 2d series.
You're always looking. . . . Mary McCarthy, in Gelderman, ed., *Conversations with Mary McCarthy.*
Rotten reviews. . . . Isaac Asimov, in S. Asimov, ed., *Yours, Isaac Asimov.*
Never demean. . . . Truman Capote, in *Writers at Work,* 1st series.
My favorite *Kirkus.* . . . Charles Knief, www.mysteryinkonline.com (29 August 2001).
I am often. . . . Pat Conroy, in Blythe, ed., *Why I Write.*
I quit writing. . . . Luke Walton, in Henderson and Bernard, eds., *Rotten Reviews and Rejections.*
I've known. . . . James Dickey, in Plimpton, ed., *Writer's Chapbook.*
Books are savaged. . . . Warren Murphy, in *Mystery Writers Annual, 2001.*
[G]ood reviews . . . . Thomas Tryon, in Duggan et al., eds., *Conversations with Writers.*
As a writer. . . . Rita Mae Brown, *Starting from Scratch.*
The writer is. . . . William Boyd, in Robertson, ed., *Mortification.*
In general. . . . Jacques Barzun, in Hull, ed., *Writer's Book.*
If you ever. . . . Diane Johnson, in Winokur, ed., *Advice to Writers.*

Chapter Twenty-five. Readers
As you are. . . . Peter Elbow, *Writing without Teachers.*
We in the. . . . Robert Fulford, *Triumph of Narrative.*

I suppose most. . . . W. Somerset Maugham, *Points of View*.

The chief difference. . . . James J. Kilpatrick, *Writer's Art*.

[A] writer. . . . Wallace Stegner, *On Teaching and Writing Fiction*.

Never forget. . . . Elwood Maren, *Characters Make Your Story*.

[A]s long as. . . . John Barth, in Dembo, ed., *Interviews with Contemporary Writers*.

I want my. . . . Allan Gurganus, in Steinberg, ed., *Writing for Your Life*.

My own view. . . . Susan Sontag, in Murray, ed., *Shoptalk*.

I made the. . . . Anita Shreve, in Abbe, ed., *Writer's Handbook, 2003*.

The natural. . . . Wallace Stegner, *On Teaching and Writing Fiction*.

I write for. . . . Edward Albee, in Murray, ed., *Shoptalk*.

I don't write. . . . Robert A. Heinlein, in Stover, *Robert A. Heinlein*.

[R]eaders will be. . . . Judith Appelbaum, *How to Get Happily Published*.

The writer and. . . . John D. MacDonald, in Burack, ed., *Writer's Handbook, 1998*.

[A] writer owes. . . . Louis L'Amour, *Education of a Wandering Man*.

The only catty. . . . James Thurber, in Fensch, ed., *Conversations with James Thurber*.

The country is. . . . H. L. Mencken, in Fecher, ed., *Diary of H. L. Mencken*.

I received. . . . Thomas Wolfe, in Haverstick, ed., *Saturday Review Treasury*.

[T]he most intense. . . . Sean French, *Faber Book of Writers on Writers*.

It is important. . . . John Hawkes, www.centerforbookculture.org (25, 26, and 27 June 1979).

Most of us. . . . Thomas Mallon, *In Fact*.

People *are* deeply. . . . Michael Faber, interviewed by C. P. Farley, www.powells.com.

I will be. . . . Isaac Asimov, in S. Asimov, ed., *Yours, Isaac Asimov*.

I think I. . . . Stanley Elkin, www.centerforbookculture.org (fall 1992).

If you can't. . . . Kingsley Amis, in Mallon, *In Fact*.

The ideal reader. . . . Anthony Burgess, in Plimpton, ed., *Writer's Chapbook*.

I know that. . . . Margaret Atwood, in Dembo, ed., *Interviews with Contemporary Writers*.

I wrote for. . . . Donna Jo Napoli, in Martin, ed., *Writer's Guide to Fantasy and Literature*.

Too many. . . . Jacqueline Susann, in Seaman, *Lovely Me*.

A good novel. . . . Ford Madox Ford, in Allen, ed., *Writers on Writing*.

In my view. . . . James B. Stewart, *Follow the Story*.

People need books. . . . Günter Grass, in McCullough, ed., *People, Books, and Book People*.

Men and women. . . . Henry Seidel Canby, in Tobin, ed., *Golden Age*.

Most science-fiction. . . . Harlan Ellison, in McCullough, ed., *People, Books, and Book People*.

I think detective novel. . . . Peter Dickinson, in Winn, ed., *Murderess Ink*.

Mystery readers. . . . Lucy Freeman, in Winn, ed., *Murderess Ink*.

I can think. . . . Alijandra Mogilner, *Children's Writer's Word Book*.

I have never. . . . W. Somerset Maugham, *Summing Up*.

I think personal. . . . Amy Hempel, in Wachtel, ed., *Writers and Company*.

The decline in. . . . Dana Gioia, www.nea.gov (9 July 2004).

When I despair. . . . William Maxwell, in Steinman, ed., *Element of Lavishness*.

Every writer. . . . Anita Shreve, in Abbe, ed., *Writer's Handbook, 2003*.

A reader, I. . . . Anthony Doerr, *Writers under Influence*, www.amazon.com (2004).

After reading those. . . . David Amsden, *Writers under Influence*, www.amazon.com (2004).

Alice in. . . . Joyce Carol Oates, in Abbe, ed., *Writer's Handbook, 2003*.

On the bookshelves. . . . Margot Livesey, in Conroy, ed., *Eleventh Draft*.

At the library. . . . Thom Jones, in Blythe, ed., *Why I Write*.

As a high. . . . Haruki Murakami, in *Paris Review* (summer 2004).

Most writers. . . . Robert Coover, in Shwartz, ed., *For the Love of Books*.

I have heard. . . . Susan Hill, in Boylan, ed., *Agony and the Ego*.

When I was. . . . Madison Smartt Bell, in Shwartz, ed., *For the Love of Books*.

Robert Penn. . . . Rick Bragg, in Abbe, ed., *Writer's Handbook, 2004*.

I think my. . . . John Steinbeck, *Acts of King Arthur and His Noble Knights*.

What should I. . . . Larry McMurtry, *Walter Benjamin at the Dairy Queen*.

I get the. . . . Lois Lowry, in Abbe, ed., *Writer's Handbook, 2004*.

Chapter Twenty-six. Literary Awards

Any author. . . . John O'Hara, in MacShane, ed., *Life of John O'Hara*.

A would-be. . . . Harland Manchester, in Editors of the *Saturday Review*, eds., *Saturday Review Gallery*.

The Nobel Prize. . . . John Cheever, in B. Cheever, ed., *Letters of John Cheever*.

I do something. . . . Truman Capote, in Clarke, *Capote*.

While the giving. . . . William Styron, *Darkness Visible*.

The Nobel Prize. . . . Truman Capote, in Grobel, ed., *Conversations with Capote*.

Just in case. . . . John Cheever, in B. Cheever, ed., *Letters of John Cheever*.

Winning the National. . . . Ron Chernow, in Winokur, ed., *Advice to Writers*.

The two most. . . . Edward Wyatt, in *New York Times* (27 January 2005).

I should be. . . . John Steinbeck, in *Writers at Work*, 4th series.

Prizes, awards. . . . Erica Jong, in Sternburg, ed., *Writer on Her Work*.

My definition of. . . . John Barth, in Polak, ed., *Writer As Celebrity*.

[W]hile it's. . . . Orson Scott Card, *How to Write Science Fiction and Fantasy*.

[Sinclair] Lewis. . . . H. L. Mencken, in Fecher, ed., *Diary of H. L. Mencken*.

[Literary] prize. . . . B. R. Myers, *Reader's Manifesto*.

The awards are. . . . John O'Hara, in Farr, *O'Hara*.

People tend to. . . . Kage Baker, www.bookslut.com (June 2004).

I told people. . . . Erik Larson, www.sarahweinman.blogspot.com (2004).

The only possible. . . . John Hartley Williams, in Robertson, ed., *Mortification*.

England [as of 1971]. . . . H. E. Bates, *Modern Short Story*.

Chapter Twenty-seven. Despair

Despite depression's. . . . William Styron, *Darkness Visible*.

Every writer. . . . Dorothea Brande, *Becoming a Writer*.

Summer is a. . . . Ernest Hemingway, in Bruccoli, *Fitzgerald and Hemingway*.

Like most. . . . Ralph Keyes, *Courage to Write*.

To be a. . . . John Jerome, *Writing Trade*.

[U]nless the author. . . . Larry L. King, *Night Hank Williams Died*.

Sometimes I. . . . Sylvia Plath, in A. S. Plath, ed., *Letters Home*.

At the age. . . . Thomas Wolfe, in Nowell, *Thomas Wolfe*.

I write a. . . . Raymond Chandler, in MacShane, ed., *Selected Letters of Raymond Chandler*.

[F]or the last. . . . William Thackeray, *Works of William Makepeace Thackeray*.

I've been working. . . . Truman Capote, in Plimpton, ed., *Truman Capote*.

I get moments. . . . Barbara Pym, in Holt, *Lot to Ask*.

Frankly, I. . . . Hunter S. Thompson, in Brinkley, ed., *Hunter S. Thompson*.

If you are. . . . Donald Maass, *Career Novelist*.

Some writers. . . . Terry Brooks, in *Writer's Digest* (June 1999).

My latest tendency. . . . F. Scott Fitzgerald, in Bruccoli, *Fitzgerald and Hemingway*.

American writers. . . . Irwin Shaw, in *Writers at Work*, 5th series.

[O]ne *does* get. . . . Philip Larkin, in Holt, *Lot to Ask.*
Nothing more. . . . Jayne Anne Phillips, in Conroy, ed., *Eleventh Draft.*
Many people ask. . . . Abe Kobo, in Dembo, ed., *Interviews with Contemporary Writers.*
At this moment. . . . Delmore Schwartz, in Atlas, *Delmore Schwartz.*
Because in fact. . . . James Gould Cozzens, in Bruccoli, *James Gould Cozzens.*
And there was. . . . Raymond Chandler, in Gardiner and Walker, eds., *Raymond Chandler Speaking.*
We've always. . . . James Dickey, in Polak, ed., *Writer As Celebrity.*
I spent a. . . . Ernest Hemingway, in Hotchner, *Papa Hemingway.*
The first. . . . John Steinbeck, in *Writers at Work,* 4th series.
I slipped. . . . Graham Greene, *Sort of Life.*
I often thought. . . . Paula Fox, in *Paris Review* (summer 2004).
[Albert] Camus. . . . William Styron, *Darkness Visible.*
I see a world. . . . John Cheever, in S. Cheever, *Home before Dark.*
Life seems. . . . Beatrice Webb, *My Apprenticeship.*
[Anne] Sexton. . . . Diane Wood Middlebrook, in Wachtel, ed., *Writers and Company.*
Virginia [Woolf]'s. . . . Jane Dunn, in Wachtel, ed., *Writers and Company.*
It turned out. . . . William Styron, *Darkness Visible.*
[T]he writings of. . . . Patrick Earnest, www.lib.uchicago.edu (2001).

Chapter Twenty-eight. Booze

Of the seven. . . . Tom Dardis, *Thirsty Muse.*
Boozing does not. . . . James Jones, in Winokur, ed., *Advice to Writers.*
Writers have. . . . Betsy Lerner, *Forest for the Trees.*
[T]he writer's life. . . . Isaac Asimov, *I Asimov.*
Many writers use. . . . Joan Acocella, in *New Yorker* (14 and 21 June 2004).
I used alcohol. . . . William Styron, *Darkness Visible.*
In 1978. . . . Julia Cameron, in Brogan, ed., *Writer's Market, 2004.*
It's unfortunate. . . . Barry Hannah, in *Paris Review* (winter 2004).
Faulkner drank. . . . Philip Roth, in *Guardian* (11 September 2004).
Raymond Chandler. . . . A. B. Guthrie, Jr., *Field Guide to Writing Fiction.*
I've gone on. . . . Irwin Shaw, in *Writers at Work,* 5th series.
I can go. . . . Truman Capote, in Clarke, *Capote.*
I was . . . addicted. . . . Thom Jones, in Blythe, ed., *Why I Write.*
I used to. . . . Pete Dexter, in Steinberg, ed., *Writing for Your Life.*
Not working is. . . . John Cheever, in B. Cheever, ed., *Letters of John Cheever.*
Although none of. . . . Susan Cheever, *Home before Dark.*
You usually. . . . James M. Cain, in Hoopes, *Cain.*
The town. . . . H. L. Mencken, in Fecher, ed., *Diary of H. L. Mencken.*
I haven't. . . . Fred Exley, in Yardley, *Misfit.*
I didn't join. . . . Pete Hamill, *Drinking Life.*
I often wonder. . . . Natalie Goldberg, *Writing down the Bones.*
It was a. . . . Stephen King, in Underwood and Miller, eds., *Bare Bones.*
I was released. . . . Larry L. King, in Holland, ed., *Larry L. King.*

Chapter Twenty-nine. Hollywood

A friend just. . . . E. B. White, *Second Tree from the Corner.*
If you write. . . . William Goldman, *Adventures in the Screen Trade.*
"Writers are a. . . ." Donald Rawley, *View from Babylon.*
The big fear. . . . Richard Russo, in *Writer's Digest* (February 2003).
I knew her name. . . . Ben Hecht, *Child of the Century.*

In the picture. . . . Joseph Hansen, in Henderson and Bernard, eds., *Rotten Reviews and Rejections.*
In the thirties. . . . Stewart Bronfeld, *Writing for Film and Television.*
Because there's. . . . Linda Buzzell, *How to Make It in Hollywood.*
I realized . . . that. . . . Isaac Asimov, *I Asimov.*
If you are. . . . Norman Mailer, *Spooky Art.*
[A]s an older. . . . D. B. Gilles, www.writersstore.com (2003).
What happens when. . . . Art Linson, *What Just Happened?*
Like most managers. . . . Larry Brody, www.writersstore.com (2003).
Celebrities focus on. . . . Andrew Breibart and Mark Ebner, *Hollywood, Interrupted.*
I just despise. . . . Truman Capote, in Grobel, ed., *Conversations with Capote.*
I went to. . . . John Cheever, in *Writers at Work,* 5th series.
Hollywood is the. . . . Raymond Chandler, in MacShane, ed., *Selected Letters of Raymond Chandler.*
I once lucked. . . . Mark Jacobson, in Blythe, ed., *Why I Write.*
If Hollywood. . . . Thomas Wolfe, in Nowell, *Thomas Wolfe.*
Films help. . . . Anthony Burgess, in *Writers at Work,* 4th series.
My own belief. . . . James M. Cain, in Hoopes, *Cain.*
It's said in. . . . Stanley J. Corwin, *Creative Writer's Companion.*
Producers of. . . . Tony Hillerman, *Seldom Disappointed.*
I'm not interested. . . . Norman Mailer, in Lennon, ed., *Conversations with Norman Mailer.*
I'm not a. . . . Barry Hannah, in *Paris Review* (winter 2004).
The screenwriter. . . . Chuck Palachniuk, *Stranger Than Fiction.*
[W]hen you. . . . Larry L. King, in Holland, ed., *Larry L. King.*
I simply don't. . . . Raymond Chandler, in MacShane, ed., *Selected Letters of Raymond Chandler.*
This attitude. . . . Pete Dexter, in Steinberg, ed., *Writing for Your Life.*
The chaotic. . . . Rob Long, *Conversations with My Agent.*
In Hollywood. . . . Dennis Palumbo, *Writing from the Inside Out.*
Hollywood is a. . . . David Baldacci, www.writersreview.com (2000).
The course of. . . . Lynda Obst, *Hello, He Lied.*
I was offered. . . . William Price Fox, in Duggan et al., eds., *Conversations with Writers.*
Why do Hollywood. . . . Andrew Breitbart and Mark Ebner, *Hollywood, Interrupted.*

Chapter Thirty. Fame
Most people. . . . Truman Capote, in Grobel, ed., *Conversations with Capote.*
My idea of. . . . T. C. Boyle, in Miller, ed., *Salon.Com Reader's Guide to Contemporary Authors.*
For a writer. . . . André Maurois, *Memoirs.*
I find myself. . . . Hunter S. Thompson, in Brinkley, ed., *Hunter S. Thompson.*
A very large. . . . Arthur Miller, *Timebends.*
Fame is a worthless. . . . Philip Roth, in *Guardian* (11 September 2004).
[I]t's nice. . . . John Steinbeck, in *Writers at Work,* 4th series.
Fame is a kind. . . . Anne Morrow Lindbergh, *Hour of Gold, Hour of Lead.*
One dreams of. . . . Peter de Vries, in *Guardian* (11 September 2004).
I was famous. . . . Truman Capote, in Clarke, *Capote.*
Learn to spot. . . . Florence King, in *Writer's Digest* (July 1990).
People say. . . . Jerzy Kosinski, in Polak, ed., *Writer As Celebrity.*
Unless he. . . . Wallace Stegner, *On Teaching and Writing Fiction.*

Every time. . . . Norman Mailer, *Spooky Art.*

One bull's-eye. . . . Tom Stoppard, in Plimpton, ed., *Writer's Chapbook.*

I never cease. . . . Malcolm Cowley, in McCullough, ed., *People, Books, and Book People.*

I have a. . . . Dennis Etchison, in Winter, ed., *Faces of Fear.*

I have come. . . . Herman Melville, in Davis and Gilman, eds., *Letters of Herman Melville.*

A writer is. . . . Herman Wouk, in Uhlan, *Rogue of Publishers' Row.*

Of all the. . . . Stephen King, in Underwood and Miller, eds., *Bare Bones.*

The fame thing. . . . J. K. Rowling, BBC News (19 June 2003).

Whatever fame. . . . Jonathan Kellerman, in Gee, ed., *Novel and Short Story Writer's Market, 1995.*

[Literary fame]. . . . Augusten Burroughs, www. bookslut.com (October 2003).

Authors lead. . . . W. Somerset Maugham, *Points of View.*

Yeah, I think. . . . Jacqueline Susann, in Seaman, *Lovely Me.*

You write one. . . . Sue Grafton, www.writerswrite.com (October 1999).

You get the. . . . Thomas Tryon, in Duggan et al., eds., *Conversations with Writers.*

The best thing. . . . George Will, in Lamb, ed., *Booknotes.*

Journalists are. . . . Nora Ephron, *Scribble Scribble.*

When you're. . . . Richard Steel, in Zinsser, ed., *Extraordinary Lives.*

There is. . . . Ben Hecht, *Child of the Century.*

The Devil comes. . . . Margaret Atwood, *Negotiating with the Dead.*

Bibliography

Abbe, Elfrieda, ed. *The Writer's Handbook, 2002.* Waukesha, Wis.: Writer, 2001.

———. *The Writer's Handbook, 2003.* Waukesha, Wis.: Writer, 2002.

———. *The Writer's Handbook, 2004.* Waukesha, Wis.: Writer, 2003.

Adler, Renata. *Gone: The Last Days of the New Yorker.* New York: Simon and Schuster, 1999.

Algren, Nelson. *Nonconformity: Writing on Writing.* New York: Seven Stories, 1998.

Allain, Marie-Françoise, ed. *Conversations with Graham Greene.* New York: Penguin, 1991.

Allen, Walter, ed. *Writers on Writing.* Boston: Writer, 1948.

Altick, Richard D. *Lives and Letters.* New York: Knopf, 1965.

Anderson, Richard. *Powerful Writing Skills.* New York: Barnes and Noble, 2001.

Appelbaum, Judith. *How to Get Happily Published,* 3d ed. New York: Plume, 1989.

Arthur, Anthony. *Literary Feuds: A Century of Celebrated Quarrels—From Mark Twain to Tom Wolfe.* New York: St. Martin's, 2002.

Asimov, Isaac. *I Asimov: A Memoir.* New York: Bantam, 1995.

Asimov, Stanley, ed. *Yours, Isaac Asimov: A Lifetime of Letters.* New York: Doubleday, 1995.

Atlas, James. *Delmore Schwartz: The Life of an American Poet.* New York: Farrar, Straus, and Giroux, 1977.

Atwood, Margaret. *Negotiating with the Dead: A Writer on Writing.* Cambridge: Cambridge University Press, 2002.

Baker, Carlos. *Ernest Hemingway: Selected Letters, 1917–1961.* New York: Scribner's, 1981.

Baker, Donna. *Writing a Romantic Novel.* London: Hodder, 1997.

Barrington, Judith. *Writing the Memoir.* Portland, Ore.: Eighth Mountain, 2002.

Barth, John. *Further Fridays: Essays, Lectures, and Other Nonfiction, 1984–1994.* Boston: Back Bay, 1996.

Barzun, Jacques. *Jacques Barzun on Writing, Editing, and Publishing,* 2d ed. Chicago: University of Chicago Press, 1986.

Bates, H. E. *The Modern Short Story.* Boston: Writer, 1972.

Baty, Chris. *No Plot? No Problem! A Low-Stress, High-Velocity Guide to Writing a Novel in 30 Days.* New York: Chronicle, 2004.

Bell, Anne Oliver, and Andrew McNeillie, eds. *The Diary of Virginia Woolf.* Boston: Harcourt Brace Jovanovich, 1977.

Bendel, Stephanie Kay. *Making Crime Pay.* Englewood Cliffs, N.J.: Prentice Hall, 1983.

Berg, A. Scott. *Max Perkins.* New York: Dutton, 1978.

Berg, Elizabeth. *Escaping into the Open: The Art of Writing True.* New York: HarperCollins, 1999.

Bernstein, Leonard S. *Getting Published: The Writer in the Combat Zone.* New York: Quill, 1986.

Bickham, Jack M. *Setting.* Cincinnati: Writer's Digest Books, 1994.

Block, Lawrence. *Write for Your Life: The Book about the Seminar.* Self-published, 1986.

Blotner, Joseph. *Faulkner: A Biography.* Volume 1. New York: Random House, 1974.

Blundell, William E. *The Art and Craft: Feature Writing.* New York: Plume, 1988.

Bly, Carol. *Beyond the Writer's Workshop: New Ways to Write Creative Nonfiction.* New York: Bantam Doubleday Dell, 2001.

Blythe, Will, ed. *Why I Write: Thoughts on the Craft of Fiction.* Boston: Little, Brown, 1998.

221

Bova, Ben. *Notes to a Science Fiction Writer.* New York: Scribner's, 1975.

Bowling, Anne, ed. *Novel and Short Story Writer's Market, 2002.* Cincinnati: Writer's Digest Books, 2001.

Boylan, Clare, ed. *The Agony and the Ego: The Art and Strategy of Fiction.* New York: Penguin, 1994.

Brande, Dorothea. *Becoming a Writer.* New York: Harcourt Brace, 1934; reprint, New York: Tarcher/Putnam, 1981.

Brandeis, Gayle. *Fruitflesh: Seeds of Inspiration for Women Who Write.* San Francisco: HarperSanFrancisco, 2002.

Branden, Nathaniel. *Judgment Day: My Years with Ayn Rand.* Boston: Houghton Mifflin, 1989

Breibart, Andrew, and Mark Ebner. *Hollywood, Interrupted: Insanity Chic in Babylon—The Case against Celebrity.* New York: Wiley, 2004.

Brinkley, Douglas, ed. *Hunter S. Thompson: The Gonzo Letters.* Volume 2, 1968–1976. New York: Touchstone, 2000.

Brod, Max. *Franz Kafka: A Biography*, translated by Breon Mitchell. New York: Schocken, 1963.

Brogan, Kathryn S., ed. *Writer's Market, 2003.* Cincinnati: Writer's Digest Books, 2002.

———. *Writer's Market, 2004.* Cincinnati: Writer's Digest Books, 2003.

Brooks, Terry. *Sometimes the Magic Works: Lessons from a Writing Life.* New York: Del Ray, 2003.

Bronfeld, Stewart. *Writing for Film and Television.* New York: Touchstone, 1981.

Brown, Dee. *When the Century Was Young.* New York: August House, 1993.

Brown, Francis, ed. *Opinions and Perspectives from the "New York Times Book Review."* Boston: Houghton Mifflin, 1964.

Brown, Rita Mae. *Starting from Scratch: A Different Kind of Writer's Manual.* New York: Bantam, 198

Browne, Renni. *Self-Editing for Fiction Writers.* New York: HarperCollins, 2004.

Bruccoli, Matthew J. *Fitzgerald and Hemingway: A Dangerous Friendship.* New York: Carroll and Graf, 1994.

———. *James Gould Cozzens: A Life Apart.* San Diego: Harcourt Brace Jovanovich, 1983.

Burack, Sylvia K., ed. *The Writer's Handbook, 1988.* Boston: Writer, 1987.

———. *The Writer's Handbook, 1998.* Boston: Writer, 1997.

Burnett, Whit, and Hallie Burnett, eds. *The Modern Short Story in the Making.* New York: Hawthorn, 1964.

Burnham, Sophy. *For Writers Only.* New York: Ballantine, 1994.

Burroway, Janet, *Writing Fiction: A Guide to Narrative Craft*, 2d ed. Boston: Little, Brown, 1987.

Busch, Frederick, *A Dangerous Profession: A Book about the Writing Life.* New York: Broadway, 1999.

———, ed. *Letters to a Fiction Writer.* New York: Norton, 1999.

Buzzell, Linda. *How to Make It in Hollywood*, 2d ed. New York: Perennial, 1996.

Cameron, Julia. *The Right to Write: An Invitation and Initiation into the Writing Life.* New York: Tarcher/Putnam, 1998.

———. *The Writer's Life: Insights from the Right to Write.* New York: Tarcher/Putnam, 2001.

Capote, Truman. *In Cold Blood.* New York: Random House, 1965).

Card, Orson Scott. *How to Write Science Fiction and Fantasy.* Cincinnati: Writer's Digest Books, 1990.

Casey, Nell, ed. *Unholy Ghost: Writers on Depression.* New York: Morrow, 2001.

Charlton, James, ed. *Fighting Words: Writers Lambaste Other Writers—From Aristotle to Anne Rice.* New York: Algonquin, 1994.

Cheever, Benjamin, ed. *The Letters of John Cheever.* New York: Simon and Schuster, 1988.

Cheever, Susan. *Home before Dark.* Boston: Houghton Mifflin, 1984.

Chiarella, Tom. *Writing Dialogue.* Cincinnati: Story Press, 1998.

Christie, Agatha. *Agatha Christie: An Autobiography.* New York: Dodd, Mead, 1977.

Clark, Tom, ed. *Handbook of Novel Writing.* Cincinnati: Writer's Digest Books, 1992.

Clarke, Gerald. *Capote: A Biography.* New York: Simon and Schuster, 1988.

Cleaver, Jerry. *Immediate Fiction: A Complete Writing Course.* New York: St. Martin's, 2002.

Collier, Oscar, with Frances Spatz Leighton. *How to Write and Sell Your First Novel.* Cincinnati: Writer's Digest Books, 1986.

Collins, Brandilyn. *Getting into Character: Seven Secrets a Novelist Can Learn from Actors.* New York: Wiley, 2002.

Conroy, Frank, ed. *The Eleventh Draft: Craft and the Writing Life from the Iowa Writers' Workshop.* New York: HarperCollins, 1999.

Corwin, Stanley J. *The Creative Writer's Companion.* New York: St. Martin's, 2001.

Curtis, Richard. *Beyond the Bestseller.* New York: New American Library, 1989.

Daigh, Ralph. *Maybe You Should Write a Book.* Englewood Cliffs, N.J.: Prentice Hall, 1977.

Dardis, Tom. *The Thirsty Muse: Alcohol and the American Writer.* New York: Houghton Mifflin, 1989.

Darnton, John, ed. *Writers on Writing: Collected Essays from the "New York Times."* New York: Holt, 2001.

Davis, J. Madison. *The Novelist's Essential Guide to Creating Plot.* Cincinnati: Writer's Digest Books, 2000.

Davis, Merrill R., and William H. Gilman, eds. *The Letters of Herman Melville.* New Haven, Conn.: Yale University Press, 1960.

DeMaria, Robert. *The College Handbook of Creative Writing.* San Diego: Harcourt Brace Jovanovich, 1991.

Dembo, L. S., ed. *Interviews with Contemporary Writers, 1972–1982,* 2d series. Madison: University of Wisconsin Press, 1983.

Demott, Robert, ed. *Working Days: The Journals of "The Grapes of Wrath," 1938–1941.* New York: Viking, 1989.

Dibell, Ansen. *Plot.* Cincinnati: Writer's Digest Books, 1988.

Dickson, Frank A., and Sandra Smythe, eds. *Handbook of Short Story Writing.* Cincinnati: Writer's Digest Books, 1981.

Dillard, Annie. *Living by Fiction.* New York: Perennial, 1988.

———. *The Writing Life.* New York: Harper and Row, 1989.

Donaldson, Scott. *John Cheever: A Biography.* New York: Random House, 1988.

Dufresne, John. *The Lie That Tells a Truth.* New York: Norton, 2003.

———. *Love Warps the Mind a Little.* New York: Plume, 1998.

Duggan, Margaret M., Glenda G. Feducci, and Cara L. White, eds. *Conversations with Writers.* Detroit: Gale, 1977.

Edelstein, Scott. *The No-Experience-Necessary Writer's Course.* London: Scarborough House, 1990.

Editors of the Saturday Review, eds. *The Saturday Review Gallery.* New York: Simon and Schuster, 1959.

Egri, Lajos. *The Art of Creative Writing.* New York: Citadel, 1993.

Eiben, Therese, and Mary Gannon, eds. *The Practical Writer: From Inspiration to Publication.* New York: Penguin, 2004.

Elbow, Peter. *Writing without Teachers.* 25th anniversary edition. Oxford: Oxford University Press, 1988.

Elledge, Scott. *E. B. White.* New York: Norton, 1984.

Engel, Joel. *Rod Serling: The Dreams and Nightmares of Life in the Twilight Zone.* Chicago: Contemporary, 1989.

Epel, Naomi, ed. *Writers Dreaming.* New York: Carol Southern, 1993.

Ephron, Nora. *Scribble Scribble: Notes on the Media.* New York: Knopf, 1978.

Farr, Finis. *O'Hara: A Biography.* Boston: Little, Brown, 1973.

Fecher, Charles A., ed. *The Diary of H. L. Mencken.* New York: Knopf, 1989.

Fensch, Thomas, ed. *Conversations with James Thurber.* Jackson: University Press of Mississippi, 1989.

Fenson, Harry, and Hildreth Kritzer. *Writing about Short Stories.* New York: Free Press, 1966.

Flaherty, Dr. Alice W. *The Midnight Disease: The Drive to Write, Writer's Block, and the Creative Brain.* Boston: Houghton Mifflin, 2004.

Flesch, Rudolph. *The Art of Readable Writing.* New York: Harper and Brothers, 1949.

Fredette, Jean M., ed. *Fiction Writer's Market, 1985.* Cincinnati: Writer's Digest Books, 1984.

French, Sean, ed. *The Faber Book of Writers on Writers.* London: Faber and Faber, 1999.

Frey, James N. *How to Write a Damn Good Novel, II: Advanced Techniques for Dramatic Storytelling.* New York: St. Martin's, 1994.

Friedman, Bonnie. *Writing Past Dark: Envy, Fear, Distraction, and Other Dilemmas in the Writer's Life.* New York: HarperPerennial, 1994.

Fulford, Robert. *The Triumph of Narrative: Storytelling in the Age of Mass Culture.* New York: Broadway, 2000.

Gardiner, Dorothy, and Katherine Sorley Walker, eds. *Raymond Chandler Speaking.* Boston: Houghton Mifflin, 1962.

Gardner, John. *On Becoming a Novelist.* New York: HarperColophon, 1983.

Garner, Bryan A. *The Elements of Legal Style.* New York: Oxford University Press, 2002.

Gee, Robin, ed. *Novel and Short Story Writer's Market, 1994.* Cincinnati: Writer's Digest Books, 1994.

———. *Novel and Short Story Writer's Market, 1995.* Cincinnati: Writer's Digest Books, 1995.

Gelderman, Carol, ed. *Conversations with Mary McCarthy.* Jackson: University Press of Mississippi, 1991.

George, Elizabeth. *Write Away: One Novelist's Approach to Fiction and the Writing Life.* New York: HarperCollins, 2004.

Givner, Joan. *Katherine Anne Porter: A Life.* London: Cape, 1983.

Goldberg, Bonni. *Beyond the Words: The Three Untapped Sources of Creative Fulfillment for Writers.* New York: Tarcher/Putnam, 2002.

Goldberg, Natalie. *Wild Mind: Living the Writer's Life.* New York: Bantam, 1990.

———. *Writing down the Bones: Freeing the Writer Within.* Boston: Shambhala, 1986.

Goldman, William. *Adventures in the Screen Trade.* New York: Warner, 1983.

Grafton, Sue, with Jan Burke and Barry Zeman. *Writing Mysteries,* 2d ed. Cincinnati: Writer's Digest Books, 2002.

Grant-Adamson, Lesley. *Writing Crime and Suspense Fiction.* London: Hodder and Stoughton, 1996.

Greene, Graham. *A Sort of Life.* New York: Simon and Schuster, 1971.

Grimes, Tom, ed. *The Workshop: Seven Decades of Iowa Writer's Workshop.* New York: Hyperion, 2000.

Grobel, Lawrence, ed. *Conversations with Capote.* New York: New American Library, 1985.

Guthrie, A. B., Jr. *A Field Guide to Writing Fiction.* New York: HarperCollins, 1991.

Hamill, Pete. *A Drinking Life: A Memoir.* Boston: Little, Brown, 1994.

Haverstick, John, ed. *The Saturday Review Treasury.* New York: Simon and Schuster, 1957.

Hecht, Ben. *A Child of the Century.* 1954; reprint, New York: Fine, 1985.

Hemingway, Ernest. *The Short Stories of Ernest Hemingway.* New York: Scribner's, 1968.

Henderson, Bill, and Andre Bernard, eds. *Rotten Reviews and Rejections.* Wainscott, N.Y.: Pushcart, 1998

Henry, Laurie, ed. *Fiction Writer's Market, 1987.* Cincinnati: Writer's Digest Books, 1986.

———. *The Novelist's Notebook.* Cincinnati: Story Press, 1999.

Herman, Jeff. *Writer's Guide to Book Editors, Publishers, and Literary Agents, 2000–2001.* New York: Prima, 1999.

Hershman, Dr. Jablow, and Julian Lieb. *Manic Depression and Creativity.* New York: Prometheus, 1998.

Higgins, George V. *On Writing: Advice for Those Who Write to Publish.* New York: Holt, 1990.

Highsmith, Patricia. *Plotting and Writing Suspense Fiction.* Revised edition. New York: St. Martin's, 2001.

Hillerman, Tony. *Seldom Disappointed: A Memoir.* New York: HarperCollins, 2001.

Holland, Richard A., ed. *Larry L. King: A Writer's Life in Letters, or, Reflections in a Bloodshot Eye.* Fort Worth: Texas Christian University Press, 1999.

Holt, Hazel. *A Lot to Ask: A Life of Barbara Pym.* New York: Dutton, 1991.

Hood, Ann. *Creating Character Emotions.* Cincinnati: Story Press, 1998.

hooks, bell. *Remembered Rapture.* New York: Holt, 1999.

Hoopes, Roy. *Cain: The Biography of James M. Cain.* New York: Holt, Rinehart, and Winston, 1982.

Hotchner, A. E. *Papa Hemingway: A Personal Memoir.* New York: Random House, 1966.

Hull, Helen, ed. *The Writer's Book.* New York: Harper and Brothers, 1950.

Hull, Helen, and Michael Drury, eds. *Writer's Roundtable.* New York: Harper and Brothers, 1959.

Ivers, Mitchell. *The Random House Guide to Good Writing.* New York: Random House, 1991.

Jackman, Ian, ed. *The Writer's Mentor: Secrets of Success from the World's Great Writers.* New York: Random House, 2004.

Jacobs, Hayes B. *Complete Guide to Writing and Selling Nonfiction.* Cincinnati: Writer's Digest Books, 1981.

Jamison, Kay Redfield. *Touched with Fire: Manic-Depressive Illness and the Artistic Temperament.* 1993; reprint, New York: Free Press, 1996.

Jerome, John. *The Writing Trade: A Year in the Life.* New York: Viking, 1992.

Johnson, Greg. *Invisible Writer: A Biography of Joyce Carol Oates.* New York: Plume, 1999.

Johnson, Paul. *The Pick of Paul Johnson: An Anthology.* London: Harrap, 1985.

Jones, Ernest. *The Life and Work of Sigmund Freud.* New York: Basic Books, 1953.

Kaplan, David Michael. *Revision: A Creative Approach to Writing and Rewriting Fiction.* Cincinnati: Story Press, 1997.

Kernen, Robert. *Building Better Plots.* Cincinnati: Writer's Digest Books, 1999.

Keyes, Ralph. *The Courage to Write: How Writers Transcend Fear.* New York: Holt, 1995.

———. *The Writer's Book of Hope: Encouragement and Advice from an Expert.* New York: Holt, 2003.

Kilpatrick, James J. *The Writer's Art.* Kansas City, Mo.: Andrews, McMeel, and Parker, 1984.

King, Larry L. *The Night Hank Williams Died.* Dallas: Southern Methodist University Press, 1989.

————. *None but a Blockhead: On Being a Writer.* New York: Viking, 1986.

King, Stephen. *On Writing: A Memoir of the Craft.* New York: Scribner's, 2000.

Koch, Stephen. *Writer's Workshop: A Guide to the Craft of Fiction.* New York: Modern Library, 2003.

Lamb, Brian, ed. *Booknotes: America's Finest Authors on Reading, Writing, and the Power of Ideas.* New York: Times Books, 1998.

Lamott, Anne. *Bird by Bird: Some Instructions on Writing and Life.* New York: Anchor, 1995.

L'Amour, Louis. *Education of a Wandering Man.* New York: Bantam, 1989.

Lasher, Lawrence, ed. *Conversations with Bernard Malamud.* Jackson: University of Mississippi Press, 1991.

Layman, Richard. *Shadow Man: The Life of Dashiell Hammett.* New York: Harcourt Brace Jovanovich, 1981.

Leder, Meg, and Jack Heffron, eds. *The Complete Handbook of Novel Writing: Everything You Need to Know about Creating and Selling Your Work.* Cincinnati: Writer's Digest Books, 2002.

Lennon, J. Michael, ed. *Conversations with Norman Mailer.* Jackson: University Press of Mississippi, 1988.

Lerner, Betsy. *The Forest for the Trees: An Editor's Advice to Writers.* Reprint, New York: Riverhead, 2001.

Levasseur, Jennifer, and Kevin Rabalais, eds. *Novel Voices: 17 Award-Winning Novelists on How to Write, Edit, and Get Published.* Cincinnati: Writer's Digest Books, 2003.

Levin, Martin P. *Be Your Own Literary Agent: The Ultimate Insider's Guide to Getting Published.* Berkeley, Calif.: Ten Speed, 1995.

Lindbergh, Anne Morrow. *Hour of Gold, Hour of Lead: Diaries and Letters, 1929–1932.* New York: Harcourt Brace Jovanovich, 1973.

————. *Locked Rooms and Open Doors: Diaries and Letters, 1933–1935.* New York: Harcourt Brace Jovanovich, 1974.

Linson, Art. *What Just Happened? Bitter Hollywood Tales from the Front Line.* New York: Bloomsbury, 2002.

Lodge, David. *The Practice of Writing.* New York: Penguin, 1996.

Long, Rob. *Conversations with My Agent.* New York: Plume, 1998.

Lubbock, Percy. *The Craft of Fiction.* New York: Viking, 1957.

Ludwig, Arnold M. *The Price of Greatness: Resolving the Creativity and Madness Controversy.* New York: Guilford, 1995.

Lukeman, Noah. *The First Five Pages: A Writer's Guide to Staying out of the Rejection Pile.* New York: Fireside, 2000.

————. *The Plot Thickens: 8 Ways to Bring Fiction to Life.* New York: St. Martin's, 2002.

Maass, Donald. *The Career Novelist: A Literary Agent Offers Strategies for Success.* Portsmouth, N.H.: Heinemann, 1986.

————. *Writing the Breakout Novel.* Cincinnati: Writer's Digest Books, 2001.

MacShane, Frank, ed. *Collected Stories of John O'Hara.* New York: Vintage, 1984.

————. *The Life of John O'Hara.* New York: Dutton, 1980.

————, ed. *Selected Letters of Raymond Chandler.* New York: Columbia University Press, 1981.

Madden, David. *Revising Fiction: A Handbook for Writers.* New York: Barnes and Noble, 1988.

Mailer, Norman. *The Spooky Art: Some Thoughts on Writing.* New York: Random House, 2003.

Malarkey, Stoddard, ed. *Style: Diagnoses and Prescriptions.* New York: Harcourt Brace Jovanovich, 1972.

Mallon, Thomas. *In Fact: Essays on Writers and Writing.* New York: Pantheon, 2001.

Maren, Elwood. *Characters Make Your Story:* Boston: Writer, 1942.

Marnham, Patrick. *The Man Who Wasn't Maigret: A Portrait of Georges Simenon.* New York: Harcourt Brace Jovanovich, 1994.

Marston, Doris Picker. *A Guide to Writing History.* Cincinnati: Writer's Digest Books, 1976.

Martin, Philip, ed. *The Writer's Guide to Fantasy Literature.* Waukesa, Watson-Guptill, 2002.

Martin, Rhona. *Writing Historical Fiction.* New York: St. Martin's, 1988.

Maugham, W. Somerset. *Points of View.* New York: Bantam, 1961.

———. *The Summing Up.* New York: Doubleday, Doran, 1938.

———. *A Writer's Notebook.* New York: Doubleday, 1949.

Maurois, André. *Memoirs: 1885–1967.* New York: Harper and Row, 1970.

Maxwell, William. *The Outermost Dream: Essays and Reviews.* New York: Knopf, 1989.

McCarthy, Mary. *The Writings on the Wall and Other Literary Essays.* San Diego: Harcourt Brace Jovanovich, 1970.

McClanahan, Rebecca. *Word Painting: A Guide to Writing More Descriptively.* Cincinnati: Writer's Digest Books, 1999.

———. *Write Your Heart Out.* Cincinnati: Writer's Digest Books, 2001.

McCollister, John. *Writing for Dollars.* New York: Barnes and Noble, 1995.

McCormack, Thomas, ed. *Afterwords: Novelists on Their Novels.* New York: St. Martin's, 1988.

McCullough, David W., ed. *People, Books, and Book People.* New York: Harmony, 1981.

McCutcheon, Marc. *Damn! Why Didn't I Write That: How Ordinary People Are Raking in $100,000.00 . . . or More Writing Nonfiction Books and How You Can Too!* New York: Quill Driver, 2001.

McMurtry, Larry. *Walter Benjamin at the Dairy Queen: Reflections at Sixty and Beyond.* New York: Simon and Schuster, 1999.

Mencken, H. L., and S. T. Joshi, eds. *H. L. Mencken on American Literature.* Athens: Ohio University Press, 2002.

Meredith, Robert C., and John D. Fitzgerald. *Structuring Your Novel: From Basic Idea to Finished Manuscript.* New York: Barnes and Noble, 1972.

Meriwether, James B., and Michael Millgate, eds. *Lion in the Garden: Interviews with William Faulkner, 1926–1962.* New York: Random House, 1968.

Mettee, Stephen Blake, ed. *The Portable Writers' Conference: Your Guide to Getting and Staying Published.* New York: Quill Driver, 1997.

Metzger, Deena. *Writing for Your Life: A Guide and Companion to the Inner Worlds.* San Francisco: HarperSanFrancisco, 1992.

Michener, James A. *James A. Michener's Writer's Handbook: Explorations in Writing and Publishing.* New York: Random House, 1992.

Miller, Arthur. *Timebends: A Life.* New York: Penguin, 1995.

Miller, Laura, ed. *The Salon.Com Reader's Guide to Contemporary Authors.* New York: Penguin, 2000.

Mitgang, Herbert, ed. *Words Still Count with Me: A Chronicle of Literary Conversations.* New York: Norton, 1995.

Moers, Ellen. *Literary Women: The Great Writers.* New York: Oxford University Press, 1985.

Mogilner, Alijandra. *Children's Writers World Book.* Cincinnati: Writer's Digest Books, 1999.

Moore, Thomas H., ed. *Henry Miller on Writing.* New York: New Directions, 1964.

Morrell, David. *Lessons from a Lifetime of Writing: A Novelist Looks at His Craft.* Cincinnati: Writer's Digest Books, 2002.

Murphy, Stephen M., ed. *Their Word Is Law: Bestselling Lawyer-Novelists Talk about Their Craft.* New York: Berkeley, 2002.

Murray, Albert, and John F. Callahan, eds. *Trading Twelves: The Selected Letters of Ralph Ellison and Albert Murray.* New York: Vintage, 2000.

Murray, Donald M., ed. *Shoptalk: Learning to Write with Writers.* Portsmouth, N.H.: Boynton/Cook, 1990.

Muscatine, Charles, and Marlene Griffith, eds. *The Borzoi College Reader,* 6th ed. New York: Knopf, 1988.

Myers, B. R. *A Reader's Manifesto: An Attack on the Growing Pretentiousness in American Literary Prose.* Hoboken, N.J.: Melville House, 2002.

Nelson, Victoria. *On Writer's Block.* New York: Houghton Mifflin, 1993.

Newman, Edwin. *Literary Trivia: Fun and Games for Book Lovers.* New York: Vintage, 1994.

Noble, William. *Conflict, Action and Suspense.* Cincinnati: Writer's Digest Books, 1999.

———. *Writing Dramatic Nonfiction.* Forest Dale, Vt.: Eriksson, 2000.

Novakovich, Josip. *Fiction Writer's Workshop.* Cincinnati: Story Press, 1995.

Nowell, Elizabeth. *Thomas Wolfe: A Biography.* Garden City, NY: Doubleday, 1960.

Oates, Joyce Carol. *Where I've Been, and Where I'm Going: Essays, Reviews and Prose.* New York: Plume, 1999.

Obst, Lynda. *Hello, He Lied and Other Truths from the Hollywood Trenches.* Reprint, New York: Broadway, 1997.

O'Conner, Patricia T. *Words Fail Me: What Everyone Who Writes Should Know about Writing.* New York: Harcourt Brace Jovanovich, 1999.

Olsen, Lance. *Rebel Yell: A Short Guide to Fiction Writing.* San Jose, Calif.: Cambrian, 1998.

Orr, Alice. *No More Rejections: 50 Secrets to Writing a Manuscript That Sells.* Cincinnati: Writer's Digest Books, 2004.

Orwell, George. *The Collected Essays, Journalism, and Letters of George Orwell.* New York: Harcourt Brace, 1968.

Pack, Robert, and Jay Parini, eds. *Writers on Writing: A Bread Loaf Anthology.* Hanover, N.H.: Middlebury College Press, 1991.

Palachniuk, Chuck. *Stranger Than Fiction.* New York: Doubleday, 2004.

Palumbo, Dennis. *Writing from the Inside Out: Transforming Your Psychological Blocks to Release the Writer Within.* New York: Wiley, 2000.

Parini, Jay. *John Steinbeck: A Biography.* New York: Holt, 1995.

Parkinson, Thomas, ed. *Robert Lowell: A Collection of Critical Essays.* Englewood Cliffs, N.J.: Prentice Hall, 1968.

Pearsal, Jay. *Mystery and Crime: The New York Public Library Book of Answers.* New York: Fireside, 1995.

Peck, Dale. *Hatchet Job: Cutting through Contemporary Literature.* New York: New Press, 2004.

Phillips, Larry W., ed. *Letters of Delmore Schwartz.* Princeton, N.J.: Ontario Review Press, 1984.

Plath, Aurelia Schober, ed. *Letters Home: By Sylvia Plath.* New York: HarperPerennial, 1975.

Plimpton, George, ed. *Truman Capote.* New York: Doubleday, 1997.

———, ed. *Women Writers at Work: The Paris Review Interviews.* New York: Viking, 1989.

———, ed. *The Writer's Chapbook: A Compendium of Fact, Opinion, Wit, and Advice from the 20th Century's Preeminent Writers.* New York: Viking, 1989.

Polak, Maralyn Lois, ed. *The Writer As Celebrity: Intimate Interviews.* New York: Evans, 1986.

Polito, Robert. *Savage Art: A Biography of Jim Thompson*. New York: Vintage, 1995.

Prescott, Peter S. *Never in Doubt: Critical Essays on American Books, 1972–1985*. New York: Arbor House, 1986.

Pritchett, V. S. *Midnight Oil*. New York: Random House, 1972.

Rand, Ayn, and Robert Mayhew, eds. *The Art of Nonfiction: A Guide for Writers*. New York: Plume, 2001.

Rawley, Donald. *The View from Babylon*. New York: Warner, 1999.

Rees Cheney, Theodore A. *Getting the Words Right: How to Rewrite, Edit and Revise*. Cincinnati: Writer's Digest Books, 1990.

Reynolds, Barbara, ed. *The Letters of Dorothy L. Sayers, 1899 to 1936*. New York: St. Martin's, 1995.

Robertson, Robin, ed. *Mortification: Writers' Stories of Their Public Shame*. New York: Fourth Estate, 2004.

Rozelle, Ron. *Description and Setting*. Cincinnati: Writer's Digest Books, 2005.

Rubie, Peter. *The Elements of Storytelling*. New York: Wiley, 1995.

Russ, Martin. *Showdown Semester: Advice from a Writing Professor*. New York: Crown, 1980.

Scura, Dorothy, ed. *Conversations with Tom Wolfe*. Jackson: University Press of Mississippi, 1990.

Seaman, Barbara. *Lovely Me: The Life of Jacqueline Susann*. New York: Morrow, 1987.

See, Carolyn. *Making a Literary Life: Advice for Writers and Other Dreamers*. New York: Random House, 2002 .

Seger, Linda. *Creating Unforgettable Characters*. New York: Holt, 1990.

Seidman, Michael. *The Complete Guide to Editing Your Fiction*. Cincinnati: Writer's Digest Books, 2000.

Shaughnessy, Susan. *Walking on Alligators*. San Francisco: HarperSan Francisco, 1993.

Sheean, Vincent. *Dorothy and Red*. Boston: Houghton Mifflin, 1963.

Shwartz, Ronald B., ed. *For the Love of Books: 115 Celebrated Writers on the Books They Love Most*. New York: Berkeley, 2000.

Silverberg, Robert, ed. *New Dimensions II*. Garden City, N.Y.: Doubleday, 1972.

Sims, Norman, and Mark Kramer, eds. *Literary Journalism*. New York: Ballantine, 1995.

Staff of the *New York Times*, eds. *Writers on Writing: Collected Essays from the "New York Times."* New York: Times Books, 2001.

Stanek, Lou W. *Story Starters*. New York: HarperResource, 1998.

Stanton, Robert J., and Gore Vidal, eds. *Views from a Window: Conversations with Gore Vidal*. Secaucus, N.J.: Lyle Stuart, 1980.

Steele, Alexander, ed. *Gotham Writers' Workshop: Writing Fiction*. New York: Bloomsbury, 2003.

Stegner, Wallace. *On Teaching and Writing Fiction*. New York: Penguin, 2002.

Stein, Sol. *Stein on Writing*. New York: St. Martin's, 1995.

Steinbeck, John. *The Acts of King Arthur and His Noble Knights*. New York: Farrar, Straus, and Giroux, 1976.

Steinberg, Sybil. *Writing for Your Life*. New York: Pushcart, 1992.

Steinman, Michael, ed. *The Element of Lavishness: Letters of Sylvia Townsend Warner and William Maxwell, 1938–1978*. Washington, D.C.: Counterpoint, 2001.

Sternburg, Janet, ed. *The Writer on Her Work*. New York: Norton, 1981.

Stewart, James B. *Follow the Story: How to Write Successful Nonfiction*. New York: Touchstone, 1998.

Stover, Leon. *Robert A. Heinlein*. Boston: Twayne, 1987.

Strickland, Bill, ed. *On Being a Writer*. Cincinnati: Writer's Digest Books, 1989.

Strunk, William, Jr., and E. B. White. *The Elements of Style*, 3d ed. New York: Macmillan, 1979.

Stuhlmann, Gunther, ed. *The Diary of Anaïs Nin, 1934–1939.* New York: Harcourt, Brace, and World, 1967.

Styron, William. *Darkness Visible: A Memoir of Madness.* New York: Vintage, 1992.

Szeman, Sherri. *Mastering Point of View: How to Control Point of View to Create Conflict, Depth and Suspense.* Cincinnati: Writer's Digest Books, 2001.

Tapply, William G. *The Elements of Mystery Fiction: Writing a Modern Whodunit.* Boston: Writer, 1995.

Thackeray, William Makepeace. *The Works of William Makepeace Thackeray.* London: Smith, Elder, 1879.

Thurston, Jarvis A., ed. *Reading Modern Short Stories.* Chicago: Scott, Foresman, 1955.

Tobin, Richard L., ed. *The Golden Age: The Saturday Review 50th Anniversary Reader.* New York: Bantam, 1974.

Trimble, John R. *Writing with Style: Conversations on the Art of Writing,* 2d ed. Upper Saddle River, N.J.: Prentice Hall, 2000.

Ueland, Brenda. *If You Want to Write: A Book about Art, Independence, and Spirit.* St. Paul, Minn.: Graywolf, 1987.

Uhlan, Edward. *The Rogue of Publishers' Row.* New York: Exposition, 1956.

Underwood, Tim, and Chuck Miller, eds. *Bare Bones: Conversations with Stephen King.* New York: McGraw-Hill, 1988.

Unkefer, Duane. *Basic Fiction: The New Writer's Handbook for Creating Fiction That Sells.* Moorpark, Calif.: Charters West, 1991.

Wachtel, Eleanor, ed. *Writers and Company.* San Diego: Harcourt Brace Jovanovich, 1993.

Waldman, Mark Robert, ed. *The Spirit of Writing: Classic and Contemporary Essays Celebrating the Writing Life.* New York: Tarcher/Putnam, 2001.

Walker, Dale L., ed. *Jack London: No Mentor but Myself.* Port Washington, N.Y.: Kennikat, 1979.

Waugh, Hillary. *Hillary Waugh's Guide to Mysteries and Mystery Writing.* Cincinnati: Writer's Digest Books, 1991.

Weidman, Jerome. *Praying for Rain.* New York: Harper and Row, 1986.

Welty, Eudora. *One Writer's Beginnings.* Cambridge: Harvard University Press, 1984.

Wharton, Edith. *The Writing of Fiction.* Reprint, New York: Scribner's, 1997.

White, E. B. *The Second Tree from the Corner.* New York: Harper and Brothers, 1954.

Whitney, Phyllis A. *Guide to Fiction Writing.* Boston: Writer, 1982.

Winks, Robin W., ed. *Colloquium on Crime: Eleven Famous Writers Offer Intriguing Insights into How and Why They Write As They Do.* New York: Scribner's, 1986.

Winn, Dilys, ed. *Murderess Ink: The Better Half of the Mystery.* New York: Workman, 1979.

Winokur, Jon, ed. *Advice to Writers: A Compendium of Quotes, Anecdotes, and Writerly Wisdom from a Dazzling Array of Literary Lights.* New York: Random House, 1999.

Winter, Douglas E., ed. *Faces of Fear: Encounters with the Creators of Modern Horror.* New York: Berkeley, 1985.

Wolff, Tobias, ed. *Writers Harvest 3: A Collection of New Fiction.* New York: Delta, 2000.

Wood, Monica. *Description.* Cincinnati: Writer's Digest Books, 1999.

Writers at Work: The "Paris Review" Interviews
1st series, edited by Malcolm Cowley. New York: Viking, 1958.
2d series, edited by George Plimpton and Van Wyck Brooks. New York: Viking, 1963.
3d series, edited by George Plimpton and Alfred Kazin. New York: Viking, 1967.
4th series, edited by George Plimpton. New York: Viking, 1976.
5th series, edited by George Plimpton. New York: Viking, 1981.
8th series, edited by George Plimpton. New York: Viking, 1988.

Wyatt, Will. *The Man Who Was Traven*. London: Cape, 1980.

Yardley, Jonathan. *Misfit: The Strange Life of Frederick Exley*. New York: Random House, 1997.

Zinsser, William, ed. *Extraordinary Lives: The Art and Craft of American Biography*. New York: American Heritage, 1986.

———. *Inventing the Truth: The Art and Craft of Memoir*. Boston: Houghton Mifflin, 1998.

Index

About the Editor

A graduate of Westminster College (Pennsylvania) and Vanderbilt University Law School, Jim Fisher, a former professor at Edinboro University of Pennsylvania, has published five narrative nonfiction books, two of which were nominated for Edgar Allan Poe awards. In *Ten Percent of Nothing* (2004), Fisher exposed a bogus literary agent who had victimized hundreds of aspiring writers. You can visit his website at *http:// piper.edinboro.edu/cwis/polisci/jimfisher/forensics/general.html.*